INDIAN WARS
OF THE
GREAT PLAINS

INDIAN WARS
OF THE
GREAT PLAINS

*"Westward the course of empire
takes its way"*
—Bishop Berkeley, 1795

STEPHEN LONGSTREET

Indian Head Books
New York

TO THE MEMORY OF
Charles Catlin
AND
Will Rodgers

One talked to me of Indians—and the other drew images.
Both excited me to write this book.

Originally published as *War Cries on Horseback*

This edition published by Indian Head Books,
a division of Barnes & Noble, Inc.,
by arrangement with Doubleday,
a division of Bantam, Doubleday, Dell.

1993 Indian Head Books

ISBN 1-56619-297-X

Printed and bound in the United States of America

M 9 8 7 6 5 4 3 2 1

Contents

Book III   Uprising in Minnesota

Book IV   Blue Soldiers and Redmen

Book V   The Enigma of George Armstrong Custer

Book VI   The Great March of the Nez Percés

Book VII Cheyenne Sunset and Apache Fury

Epilogue

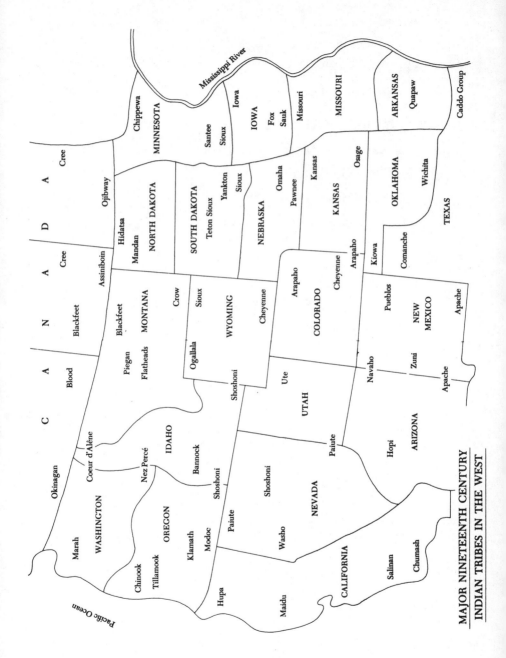

MAJOR NINETEENTH CENTURY INDIAN TRIBES IN THE WEST

On the American Indian: In the savage the organs of generation are small and feeble. He has no hair, no beard, no ardor for the female. Though nimbler than the European because more accustomed to running, his strength is not so great. His sensations are less acute, and yet he is more cowardly and timid. He has no vivacity, no activity of mind. It is easy to discover the cause of the scattered life of savages, and of their estrangement from society. They have been refused the most precious spark of nature's fire . . . their heart is frozen, their society cold . . .

—COMTE DE BUFFON, *Histoire Naturelle*

People were always telling the Indian what was wrong with him. Truth was, the poor fella thought paper was as valuable as gold. He kept signing all those treaty papers in good faith, when any galoot could have told him the white man had no more moral sense of obligation to what he wrote down as promises, to the Indian, than the dead fish they wrapped in the newspaper announcing they had just again saved the redman's dignity and britches. By stealing his birthright for his own good.

If the Indian had only known he was starving, being shotgunned off his hunting-grounds and having his squaw debauched for his own good, he'd have tried harder to be like his white brothers looting the treasury . . .

—WILL ROGERS, *in conversation*

Some observations with regard to the animals, vulgarly called Indians . . . What use do these ringed, streaked, spotted and speckled cattle make of the soil? Do they till it? Revelation said to man "Thou shalt till the ground." This alone is human life.

—HUGH HENRY BRECKENRIDGE, *1790*

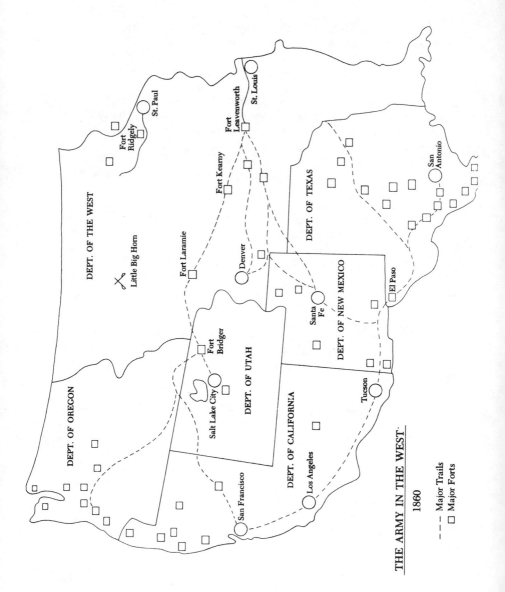

THE ARMY IN THE WEST
1860

- - - Major Trails
□ Major Forts

DEPT. OF THE WEST

DEPT. OF TEXAS

DEPT. OF NEW MEXICO

DEPT. OF UTAH

DEPT. OF OREGON

DEPT. OF CALIFORNIA

St. Paul

Fort Ridgely

Fort Leavenworth

St. Louis

San Antonio

Fort Kearny

Fort Laramie

Little Big Horn

Denver

Santa Fe

El Paso

Fort Bridger

Salt Lake City

Tucson

Los Angeles

San Francisco

On Writing a History of the Western Indian Wars

This is not a history of the Indians—but a narrative of the white men and Indian wars of the Great Plains. There are for the specialist and the student many fine individual studies of tribes, customs, rites, and much research into the nuances of Indian lore and cultures. You will find some of it here—but in the main the aim is the history of a warfare, long drawn out, desperate and brave.

With newer research and more actual documents and journals turning up, and with state historical societies indexing their collections, there is a need for a history that would cover the seventy years of Indian wars on the Western American frontier. This book is an attempt to fill such a need for the general public, to outline the physical images of savage warfare—on both sides.

I began to read Indian and Western history at the age of eight; much of this early knowledge was slanted, outmoded and faultily researched, overromantic and blood-stirringly exciting, but often not after the facts that are now available.

One begins with the piling up in my research bins of early volumes, photocopies of original diaries, journals, newspapers, reports by all kinds of Commissions, Committees, Hearings—Federal and by states—works by dedicated scholars, also a great deal of Indian material reinterpreted in the light of modern values and our new attitudes toward both the Indian tribes of the West and the Indian, himself: his visions, dreams, the primitive but intricate dogma and theology he lived by and took to war with him. One sensed, too, today's historian mellowing toward a more truthful search of the atmosphere in which he once saw, fought, and vanquished a vast Indian culture in its native state.

Today it is a far journey from the early prejudices by which one might be amused by quoting: "The Pilgrims landed on Plymouth Rock, fell on their knees to give thanks to God and then fell on the Indians . . ." A more moral sensibility now re-records history at times.

Never fully valid was the old picture of the noble redskin, silent, dignified, nature's nobleman, placid in his splendid native culture, nor the image of the brave pioneer and his family—not always bearing proud Anglo-Saxon genes—determined to prove themselves in a new world. Neither are the comic mountain men, nor the banjo-plucking pioneers.

Charles Russell, the cowboy painter, was close to the real Indian. As Russell puts it in some letters he wrote about the fate of the Indian:

"Once nature gave him everything he wanted, now the agent gives him bib overalls, hooks his hands around plow handles and tells him it's a good thing, push it along. Maybe it is, but they're having a hell of a time proving it. I remember one day we were looking at buffalo carcus and you said, 'Russ, I wish I was a Sioux Injun a hundred years ago,' and I said, me to Ted: 'There's a pair of us.' I have often made that wish since, an' if the buffalo would come back tomorrow, I wouldn't be slow shedding to a britch clout and you'd trade that three-deuce ranch for a buffalo hoss and a pair of earrings . . ."

There is in this book no invented dialogue, incident, or scene. Wherever several versions of an event are recorded, I have selected or merged together what seemed most reliable and possible. As for dialogue, when the official report reads that scouts hunting a trail had one of them cry out: "By thunder, there is the road!" I prefer a soldier's letter which sets down their words as, "Christ, there's the damn road!" Often we know little of some Indian or white soldier beyond his name and his last moments—no more.

I have tried to check all facts and dates for error; where there is a difference of opinion, I have said so. In the matter of those long and noble speeches made by Indian leaders at conferences and meetings, we have usually only the translation by an official interpreter writing it up in a dramatic Lord Byron prose that no Arapaho, Cheyenne, or Arivaipa Apache could ever have mastered

or wanted to. So, in the main, I have avoided these grand out-
bursts of rhetoric, for this is a history of warfare, not the whole
Indian culture.

Yet one can now and then find in the strangest places a small
polished gem that suggests the dignity of these often gabby chiefs.
Here, from the Congressional Reports of 1852, is a Congressman
defending an Indian:

> I have often admired that lofty expression of the great Tecumseh
> —for he was great, though a savage; he was one of Nature's
> great men, made in God's own image, he spoke God's own language
> —the voice of Nature—who, when General Harrison . . . was ne-
> gotiating a treaty with him . . . (and) ordered his interpreter
> to set the great chief a chair, and to tell him that his father
> desired him to take a seat . . . drew himself up, only as he
> can who feels the dignity of a man, and replied: 'My father!
> the Great Spirit is *my* father, the earth is my mother and upon
> her bosom will I repose.' And he stretched himself upon the
> bosom of our common mother.

At the end of this volume I have listed some of the places
where sources of much of this book were found, and some, a
small percentage, of the vast mountain of the major texts I
burrowed in. Those I found most helpful and which the general
reader might turn to to widen his knowledge of the field. To my
three friends, experts in western history, who read the manuscript,
J.R., B.J., and H.W., much thanks for advice and corrections.

Nothing is as educational as direct contact with original sources,
so I shall always treasure those noon lunch-periods at a film
studio with Will Rogers (part Cherokee) when he was in a drawl-
ing, talking mood on the subject of what he called "My relatives on
my good side . . . Why, any surviving Indian should be thankful
the moving pictures have done so much to show him how good
he looked in feathers and how much he used to holler and get
carried away when he had a head of steam on—that's if he can
ever raise the price of admission to see himself on the screen . . ."

STEPHEN LONGSTREET

Miradero Road, California

Prologue

THE FIRST PEOPLE

Where did they come from? Who were these bronze-colored people called the American Indian who had numbered a million in this vast nearly untouched wilderness when first the white man rimmed in iron and clothed in velvet came in contact with them? What are the historic sources of this people? scattered tribal barbarians with carefully selected rituals and habits, taboos, fetishes, prides, skills who began a long, long war—in the end, a futile struggle against an enemy skilled in machines, in the making of complex weapons, driven by a vast urge to move west in wheeled objects (no Indian had ever even dreamed of inventing the wheel), pulled by gelded oxen who could transport loads no Indian pony could carry—ponies descended from the horses of the first Spaniards, steeds crossed with runaway stock that had managed to get across mountains and rivers from north or east, perhaps?

The first explorers called America The New World, but it was already an old world and Dawn Age man, the forefathers of the Indian, had been here for thousands of years. Yet, compared to the rest of the globe, human life had come late to the vast forests, the great grass Plains where at one time twenty million buffalo grazed. Men came to valleys lush and green where no one planted crops but much that was eatable grew wild, and amazing flocks of birds darkened the skies. There were bear and wild turkey and deer and elk. The coyotes and wolves, the rattlesnake and the Gila monster, had no contact with man.

But long before that the last Ice Age and its mile-high glaciers retreated, so scientists tell us: about 20,000–30,000 years ago. There was then a land bridge, 10,000 years ago, to what is now called Asia in what is now Siberia. This bridge was in what is Bering

Strait—fifty-six miles of rocky road covered with snow and ice most of the time. Dawn Man, hunters, came this way over this road to the American continent, following the hairy mammoth, the musk-ox, the giant elk, and a form of small horse. They all died out except for the early hunter, his family, his fire, his wolf-bred dog —survivors of glacial epochs, the four major Pleistocene glaciations.

It must have been warmer then in places and the Siberian immigrant and his family found hunting and living better on the coastal fringe down to warmer climate. There were herds of reindeer, small game easy to snare, salmon in the streams. The Ice Age wasn't fully gone: glaciers came and went, opening up roads at times toward warmer places, better grass, more tasty game. The Siberian stone-age hunters disappeared in Asia—but the new world hunters increased, pushing always onward and south. Some few stayed behind and were driven by stronger bands to the Arctic to become in time what we call Eskimos. But the main bands went south slowly over thousands of years, and the lack of fossil remains of anthropoid apes shows man came here as an immigrant.

Were they Mongoloids, those dusky *homo sapiens*? Most likely there were heavy strains of all peoples that finally produced China, Korea, Mongolia, Japan. They were true travelers and came originally from a starting point of the Altai Mountains in the Great Circle Route, then across to Alaska and down to the Mackenzie River Valley. Not in one lump of a tribal migration, most likely, but in little groups as game vanished or floods came or an icecap moved too close or the witch doctor, tribal priest produced some omen; a vision, and the will of the spirits ordered them to go elsewhere. So the Yukon, Mackenzie, Lizard, and Peace rivers were sowed with man. Man, who penetrated the ice of the Great Basin, who roamed down the eastern side of the Cordillera, down to those Great Plains they were to love and die for; to make such savage wars against those who came later. A Zumi chant tells us "The fogs of creation are mist fertile with growing . . ."

The Great Plains spread from the Rocky Mountains east to mighty rivers, and forest and the Plains became one of the trans-mission belts pumping tribal man into the wilderness, the eastern shores, the Big Lakes regions, past the Mississippi, south to Florida and the roads to Mexico, South America, until man—in some way—

was in residence on both North and South America; to the tip of the Horn. His chewed-up sloth bones, flints, ivory tools are scattered from pole to pole, almost, as artifacts and fossils.

The experts say that 9000 years ago the land bridge to Asia went down. The climate changed. The Siberian side grew cold, thickets of taiga and stunted firs clogged the icy land. On the Alaska side, the giant prehistoric animals died out. Man, the Dawn-Age Adam, was here to stay. At first rains fell for hundreds of years and for man, cave-dwelling, hunting in the wet for a miserable existence, took over. But the climate changed again as an ice age withdrew—there was warmth and man could move about. Inventors appeared (we know this to be so because the flints, tools were a native product).

The hunters learned how to drive and lure buffalo over cliffs to mass suicide. Village life began to become possible with good hunting. They were never large groups—no royal houses nor kings appeared. Mound Builders, Copper Cultures, Pottery Eras came and went. The tribal and family chiefs stuck to the game trails, to the seasonal movements of the animals they existed on—pelts that clothed them, built their lodges, bones they used as weapons and fishhooks. Tanned hides they decorated with totem and fetish signs, with a love of primitive décor.

Such were the beginnings of the American Indians of the Great Plains. They changed little: no great inventors of machines appeared, no vast lands were put under cultivation, no bridge or highway systems, for they traveled at first on foot and then on Castilian-descended ponies. They pulled, by dog or horse, their belongings, lashed to poles dragging on the earth. There were a million Indians when the white man came, but they rarely existed as units of more than a hundred or two hundred, except when banded together in some war plan and then only for a short time. The women grew the squash, beans, gourds, maize, tobacco, picked berries, and jerked (dried) meat.

There were, some anthropologists think, new recruits from Asia. The Huns with their war bows did drive some forest-dwellers to the Siberian shore where they looked across at Alaska for safety. The Aleutian Chain were steppingstones and a favorite current was there; boats could come across—most likely between 1200–500

B.C. when the horse-nomads of the Huns warred on the steppes and against the luxury-filled Chinese river towns.

So the newcomers came with the secrets of the spliced bow of Asia, better dogs, basket making, cord nets, tree-trunk canoes, harpoons, designs for body and lodge decorating, ritual body tattooing.

To the south were the Mayan, Aztec, Inca cultures that approached a true civilization, but the Plains people moved in a hard, punitive life. Hunger was common; starvation, and most likely, cannibalism, for—as an old mountain-man accused of eating a partner during a hard winter, answered—"meat's meat."

They were not, however, a miserable people, easily cowed by nature. They were fighters, bold travelers, raiders, as savage as the animals they fought. But they were man—seeing, in some Great Spirit, some vigorous life-force, a pattern of their existence dominated by dreams and spirits beyond their daily rounds of war, torture, hunt, rape, mating, feeding, dying. They saw a relationship to the sun, the wind, the water, the sky, the great animals, and the small game whose names and special virtues or skills they put into their clans or family groups. Anthropologists point out these carved signs on bones and stones.

They had begun in time to divide into various dialects—some experts claim 9000 different dialects resulted. Whatever language Indians had once had, newer forms and meanings were invented and added. In their own ways, they called themselves *Tinde, Tinneh, Dine, N'de*—all of which add up to meaning almost the same thing: *The People*. On the Great Plains they found a way of life that was pleasant and often easy. By the time white men came, they claimed as their own the land from the Black Hills to the Sierra Madre. The whites called the Plains Indians *Vaqueros, Escanjaques, Faraons,* and *Padoucas* (an early French name for what the Spanish were to call the Apache). Columbus preferred the name *Indian* in the blind belief that he must be some place near India. That name was the one that identified the native hunters of America.

The Plains saw trouble first when the Chippewas were being pressed westward by the advancing coon-capped white hunters with their Kentuck' rifles, forcing the Sioux in turn to move West to seize the Great Plains as a hunting ground. From the West came other eager, hungry tribes, out of the Rockies, called the Shoshones.

It meant war. War it was. The Shoshones had to give ground and go back into the safety of the mountains. All but a branch that was wiser, crueler, more crafty; these were the Comanches.

So this was the pattern of Tribes attracted to the Plains as if by a dowsing rod. The Sioux pushed the Comanches southward; the Comanches, in turn, pushed on the original *Tinde* people, into the sterile, dreadful deserts of the Southwest, to the smoke tree, the cactus, fringe-toed lizard, alkali sinks, salt bush, sidewinder, the desert tortoise, and dunes.

But the desert was a Spartan testing ground of the *Tinde* people. The sun, the barren waste, the great lofting spaces, the cruel struggle to exist, made them the most cruel of all Western Indians. They became known as the *Apache,* meaning *Enemy.* And they were the enemy of mankind, of the wild animal, of the tribes of the Pueblos, the Pimpas, the Diggers who huddled away from the Apache in the nooks and corners, cliffs and arroyos of the desert, living with the pinion jays and shrike and eagles.

The Chippewa had named the Sioux *Nadoweisiv*—the Adder Snake—and from this, in some strange way, the French-Canadians make a contraction called *Sioux.*

In the wars against the whites, the greatest of all adversaries were the two Indian nations called the Sioux and Apache. But one must not overlook the lesser tribes, the Cheyennes, the Nez Percés, Modocs, Pueblos, Comanches, Kiowas, Arapahos.

With the arrival and taming of the horse—1750 to 1800—the Plains Indian became one of the best riders in the world, and military men called him "the finest light cavalry in the world." The origin of the Indian horse is fuzzy, but in 1680 there had been a great Indian revolt against the Spanish cruelty and the Jesuit missions in the Southwest; when they left the territory, they turned loose great herds of horses. These soon went wild and spread all over the Plains. The Indians at first called them *elk-dogs* and used them for food. But soon the Plains Indian saw the horses' merits as riding animals, and so tribal wealth in time was judged by the size of the Indian's horse-herd. With the aid of *travois* poles, a horse could carry two hundred pounds, including squaw and children, even puppies. The Plains Indians became a horse culture, as we, today, are an auto culture.

Buffalo hunting from horseback brought Indian prosperity, made war an even better game. Journeys on horseback of five hundred to eight hundred miles in good weather were like picnics. Migrations of buffalo could be followed and there was grass for everybody in those days before the white man came to bring the plow and whisky.

Before that, wars for horses and women were made great Indian games; scalps and horses were social status (the way modern art collecting is for us today).

We are today far enough away from the historic events of the Indian wars to view them without the passions they once engendered or to accept the self-righteousness of the actions taken. Moral obligations are crowded out in a struggle for survival and the Indian never understood the expediencies of the wider world or the white man's stubbornly rationalistic temperament. The Indian had self-reliance, but no long-range steadfastness; he at first believed in the obscene farce of politics that ordered his life from Washington. So the failure of the treaties to be upheld did permanent psychological damage to the Indians' relationship with even those few whites who treated him with honor and faith. Humane disciplines, the whites felt, do not make new frontiers in a hurry. And they *were* in a hurry.

They did not see the Indians' personal identity with the Plains, that the hunting-grounds were their sacred holy earth, the buffalo migrations their dogma and creed, sent down to them by their visions and dreams. The Indian character was essentially rigid and closed, yet in marvelous effective balance with nature. It also meant the Sioux, the Apache, the other tribes had firm limits to any infinite receptiveness of their intelligence.

It was a war between the predicaments of savage magic, set against the unyielding logical materialism of the whites. The antagonism of nomads against plowmen and planters tied to their land, a people who claimed a remorseless insistence of their superiority over savages. The pioneer, the frontiersman, had an arbitrary skepticism; to him, the Indians were not fully human.

The cruelty of seventy years of war on both sides resulted because of their different visions of life. For the Indian, myth and simplification resulted in an exaltation of power through cruel, brave war, yet hampered by the failure of the unification of loosely coordinated tribes into lasting military power. The Calvinist theology of the whites ("live by the sweat of your brows") in their appetites for expansion and their version of a God-blessed civilization led to an irascible assault on whatever stood in the way of an intractable drive West. Both sides felt war, and war to extermination was the only answer.

VISIONS AND OMENS

What made the Indian such a splendid warrior?

The first educated eighteenth-century travelers who saw the Indian mistook him for Rousseau's Simple or Happy Savage: a myth in itself, as the world was to discover. For the savage every place—back to the stone-age—was beset by fears, fetishes, taboos, bad omens, spirits, and supernatural legends.

The American Indians had their own version of how it all began. The Bureau of American Ethnology gives one Indian legend of creation:

"Awonawilona—the Maker and Container of all, the All-father Father—solely had being. There was nothing else whatsoever throughout the great space, everywhere black darkness, everywhere void desolation.

"In the beginning, the new-made Awonawilona conceived within himself and thought outward in space; mists of increase, steams potent of growth, were evolved and uplifted. With his substance of flesh drawn from the surface of his person, the Sun-father formed the seed-stuff of twin worlds, impregnating the great waters, and in the heat of his light the waters of the sea grew green, scums rose upon them, waxing wide and weighty until they became Awitelin Tsita, the fourfold containing Mother-earth and Apoyan Tachu, the all-covering Father-sky."

This is so close in some ways to the Japanese version of creation that one wonders if some trans-Pacific travel did not take place.

As with the Japanese text—it begins with a great mating:

"From the lying together of these two upon the great world waters, vitalizing, terrestrial life was conceived; began all beings of earth, men and the creatures, in the four-fold womb of the world.

"Thereupon the Earth-mother repulsed the Sky-father, growing big and sinking deep into the embrace of the waters below, separating from the Sky-father in the embrace of the waters. A woman forebodes evil for her first-born ere born, even so did the Earth-mother forebode, long withholding from birth her myriad progeny and meantime seeking counsel with the Sky-father. 'How,' said they to one another, 'shall our children, when brought forth, know one place from another?'"

The Indians of the Great Plains were surrounded by visions, dreams, and potents of magic. Spirits controlled their destinies, and, like the Greek Gods, could help or do harm to earthly beings, ward off evil, predict the future. It was best to have a guardian spirit on one's side—a ghost pal, a close friend.

The life of the Plains depended on the migrations of the buffalo for food, clothing, warmth, and gear. So the *Great Unseen Buffalo* in the sky surely controlled the movement of the vast herds of bison. The Teton-Dakota tribes placed their bets on him.

As for protections from the evils of this earth, of death in battle, the use of sacred objects of strong power were best. Holy medals of saints—as in St. Christopher—are our versions of this. Or, as in the use of Christian relics, the Indian had faith in the medicine bundle he carried always, even if it were only grains of corn, a special feather, a stone pipe, the skin of some animal, the ear or finger of an enemy, a tobacco pouch made of a human scrotum.

Fasting helped; both Jews and Christians fasted to atone—and to torture the flesh (nuns and monks did it), mortifying the body by punishing it to draw blood, to feel the agony of deep pain. It was the white men that called this Indian belief in sacred bundles and odd rituals "medicine." There was *good* medicine and *bad* medicine. One protected, the other brought trouble, disasters—big or small.

The Indian medicine bundle was a personal grab bag of magic objects, a do-it-yourself package assembled as dictated by visions, dreams, thoughts, unexplainable events. If one could afford it one could buy good medicine bundles for a horse or two—the horse was the customary currency of the Indians until the whites put a value on furs.

Tribes had a mutual public or community medicine bundle—

a sort of group insurance plan. Not all tribes had the same faith in what was holy and magic.

As an Indian named Two Leggings explained it:

"When we receive a medicine our sacred helper gives us certain instructions. Sometimes we must not do certain things—like eating certain foods. If we disobey we may have bad luck or sickness or suffer a wound in battle. If we keep disobeying our sacred helper, he will grow angry and place the life of his child as a stake against some powerful opponent who always wins. The souls of people who die this way are of a lower kind, but they are allowed to enter the Other Side Camp. However, the souls of suicides and murderers must roam the earth as ghosts."

The Arapaho had a sacred tribal pipe kept in cloth wrappers with its own temple tepee, guarded by its keeper who saw that it never touched the earth—that would bring on calamity. The guard was the narrator of the holy pipe's history and it took three nights to tell. "The pipe soon after the world began was given to the first Arapaho after being brought to the earth from under the Great Water by the Great Turtle. He gave it to the Great Duck who presented it to the Arapaho with an ear of corn." So came corn, and all the corn of the earth came from the seeds of that one ear.

The medicine man accepted gifts and offers to the sacred pipe and saw it was held in the proper ritual manner to get the best happy results.

Purification rituals were used by most tribes: by sitting in steam caused by dashing water on heated stones in a closed hut. In steam and sweat, repeated several times, a man could purify his being to welcome a vision or ask a godly favor. Rolling in snow or dropping into a cold stream between hot stone rituals was the accepted custom.

Just as early saints prayed for visions as a sign, so the Plains Indians ordered most of their lives by visions. Fasting was the best road; no water, no food and a high hill, a lonely lake shore, all aided the solitary vision-seeker asking for an answer.

What did he see? The spirit of some great animal or bird, or a version of nature—lightning, wind, fire—all often in human form and voice. They would speak to him, offer to share their secrets, instruct him as to how to stuff his medicine bag. He saw colors, designs for his war gear, heard battle chants, magic words to cure his ills.

If an Indian was a slow vision-seeker, or failed to stir up a mighty spirit, he could buy the visions of others, but it was costly—only for those who were horse-herd rich. Anyone who had more visions than he could use up in a lifetime could usually find a buyer for the surplus (as in the western world one could pile up prayers and indulgences, novenas, and masses for the next world). Religions were often a kind of spiritual banking system, where one was able to put away salvation, to draw heavenly interest in the next life.

Good medicine was great protection unless the Indian broke a taboo, then confession and purification had to begin again often by a dance. The dance if prolonged brought visions—and if bad he had to begin to seek new visions, create or buy a new medicine bundle.

Mass tribal worship and ceremony led to the Sun Dance of the Plains Indians. Actually, it was of Sioux origin at first, as the Sun-Gazing Dance. Buffalo time, corn-harvest, a tribal protest or end of winter—almost any Indian event could end in dance.

It was replaced at the end of the nineteenth century by the more mournful Ghost Dance—a mass religious hysteria of the Plains Indians. A dance was a military gathering, courting time, game season, renewing of old friendships—and a great deal of eating with a bottle of white trader's "pizon" whisky if on hand.

The War Dance was to make fervid patriots of the warriors, to insight, then to battle; the survivors—if lucky—to have a Victory Dance.

The female was often more deadly than the male in camp, having their own war dance and stepping off wild gestures while displaying fresh cut scalps on long poles. They were deadly torturers of prisoners.

Medical services were in the hands of the tribe's *shaman* or medicine man, who cured, as the middleman in direct contact with the spirits; to chant and bang and dance and rattle health into a patient. He dispensed spirit powders "direct from the spirits" and, if he lost a patient, he could always claim the loss was the result of the patient "offending the spirit world."

The *shamans* did sleight-of-hand vaudeville magic and some

dispensed cures for snake-bite, bone-healing, arrow-, lance-, and bullet-wounds. From a stubborn case, the *shaman* could be seen— or so it seemed—removing pebbles, bugs, bits of bone, other objects from a patient's head or body—one way of beating out the Indian version of the devil in possession.

It was faith in visions, the unseen, that made the Indian brave— he was the Great Spirit's Chosen One.

Many Indians were sure they were immune to white men's bullets; all harm was turned away from them in battle. As such an Indian lay dying with a stomachful of lead, he often admitted he had broken or violated a ritual, some sacred taboo, and the magic had been withdrawn. Some Plains Indians chewed chunks of cactus called peyote during the time of the Ghost Dance and amassed new visions from its drug content.

Taken as a whole, Indian religion was like most faiths—very satisfactory for the believer's needs. It made him a member of belief in a supernatural world, in most cases little different from other great faiths that have dominated man's history. He was not alone; he was part of a special whole, and would have abhorred the existentialism of Sartre, which claims man is merely a savage marooned alone in an indifferent universe with no answers. In rejecting such ideas, some claim the Indian was one with the Pope and all dogma and theology that did not accept—except for cash offerings—the mere material world. Like the Chinese, the Indian was aware of his ancestors and, like most of the world, he was sure that as spirits, they waited for him to join them.

It was a powerful faith for a splendid savage who had only war, loot, hunting, sex, and horses to pass the time. Manual work, clothes-making and breaking camp, was for women. Great Buffalo, Great Spirit, Rain God, or Chief Thunder were for man.

> Now I walk with Talking God . . .
> With Goodness and Beauty
> In all things around me
>   I go . . .
> With Goodness and Beauty
> I follow immortality
> Thus being I, I go . . .
>   *Indian Song*

INDIAN CLOSEUPS

He who speaks of symbols enters an area where reflection, synthesis and contemplation are more important than investigation, analysis and science. One cannot apprehend a symbol unless one is able to awaken, in one's own being, the spiritual resonances which respond to the symbol not only as *sign* but as "sacrament" and "presence" . . .

—THOMAS MERTON

The first explorers, settlers, and soldiers of the West who came in contact with the Indians felt the natives' style and gear, their colors and patterns of dress and clothing were all alike. As they got to know the Indians better they began to read details, colors, and costume as different identifying signs by which tribal markings could be separated and even clothing and paint distinguished as used in war, ceremony, or everyday dress.

It is worth taking space here to point out some special differences in costumes, signs, and marks of a few tribes, so that we can come closer to the Indians as human beings rather than accept generalizations of a people called *redskins* and *hostiles*.

The Sioux were divided into many branches, from a group called the Eastern Dakotas to the river Osage. Like most Plains Indians, for everyday attire they wore merely a breechclout and moccasins. In the chill of autumn, the frost of winter, they added leggings and a buffalo or wolf robe. There was no ornamentation—all that was saved for war or ceremonial clothing. Males (but not women) were permitted to decorate their ceremonial shirts with painted figures that boasted of personal brave deeds, and certain markings were magic omens to protect the wearer. Shields had magic symbols on them, and to the Indians these signs—of sacrament and presence—were protection, as much as the heavy leather shield made from the tough neck hide of the buffalo.

In war the bonnet with its feathers was not merely millinery—*each* feather denoted a coup touch (an enemy tapped in battle by a coup stick).

Sioux war shirts or dance shirts were heavy with beads and

colored quills, painted with images of war, buffalo, or guns, Indian figures, sun and moon symbols, arrows in flight. Quills would be dyed yellow, red, or black, and the beaded edges of the garment in white, scarlet, and blue. Fringes, long or short, completed the shirt. The final touch were seams of long strands of hair, and while this could be from scalps taken in battle or raids, often the hair came as offerings from the women of the tribe. The leggings of the Sioux fitted tightly. Long fringes on the outer seams were rich with quill work.

The Siksika, Bloods, and Piegan making up the Blackfeet nation were a handsome race, their women in such demand by trappers and hunters, and the men often over six feet tall. Their war shirts were of deer or antelope, as near white as they could get them, the sleeve loose and hung at times with rows of whole white weasel pelts. Their leggings were dyed yellow and decorated with quills and small feathers.

They were a people who delighted in the splendid English-made Hudson's Bay Company blankets for use as leggings. Red was a favorite color. To this was added a broad strip of green felt worked over with multicolored beads, usually in a geometric pattern. Above the knees of the leggings it was common to add the design of a horse's head. As with most Plains Indians, in winter a furred robe served to keep them warm, and in summer a tanned skin on which was painted the wearer's heroic life's work in battle, his bravery, his coups. The Blackfeet wore an odd headdress, usually in battle. It was a sort of tall pot made of feathers resting and set on a red band. Weasel, ermine, and feathers hung over the ears of the wearer.

Most of the tribe wore a single feather rather than a bonnet. This feather could stand up straight in the back, or hang from one braid. The red stripes painted on a feather added up to all the wounds the warrior had received. The Blackfeet had special societies of warriors; men's clubs, and one could identify these by their headdresses. The *Horn* group wore a buckskin cap done up with ermine pelts and in front one buffalo horn pointed back, colored red, and with streamers of strips of fur at the end. There was also a trailing band of feathers tied on behind. The face colors called for, by this headdress, were a yellow face with a red stripe across the eyes and one more across the mouth.

The *Buffalo Bull* society had an ermine-covered cap with two horns wrapped in red cloth. The left side of the headdress was colored yellow, the right side red. The face color matched these, the dividing line between the two tones being the nose ridge.

The Apache of the desert and mountain country were divided into three main groups: the White Mountain, the San Carlos, and the Chiricahua, with many subdivisions among these. Some Apache went to war wearing a poncho made of a tanned skin with a hole cut out for the head, and the sides formed wide sleeves, with fringes across the chest and down the sleeves. The poncho was dyed yellow and there were painted symbols of people, animals, and nature marked out on it.

Often the Apache wore a round little buckskin cap covered with painted patterns and a bunch of feathers set on top. The poncho and cap, if of sacrament magic quality, had the power of making the wearer undefeatable.

Apache moccasins were like no others. They were actually boots tied up under the knee and then folded over, the toe extending beyond the foot and turned up like a Turkish slipper.

Dance costumes for ritual affairs were unique. For the Puberty Rites of Apache girls, the Mountain Spirit Dance, the Indian painted his body, put on a skin kilt, hung a fan-shaped headdress on the back of his head. Some ceremonies called for a skin skull cap with two bumps or ears, like a cut-down version of a Mickey Mouse mask, which was tied under the chin. Usually the Apache wore a wide band around his head, of skin or cloth, almost like a turban. He is usually portrayed in this manner.

The Chiricahua Apache wore a cap with a pair of pronged antelope horns coming out of the sides with strands of hair around the back and sides. Beads were used every place, on leggings, belts, arrow cases, shoulder straps. The pattern often followed the signs of the four winds or the four points of the horizon.

As raids on settlers brought in much loot in the form of cloth, the Indians of the Plains began to make their garments of it rather than of hide, except for ritual garments. They made the cloth shirt very long, copied the white man's vest but with much ornamentation. The turban gave way to the silk or calico kerchief knotted to hold the long loose hair in place. They also used thin metal strips and made tinkling clashing objects almost like small bells to hang on their clothing.

One thing the Indian would not wear were the white man's pants. Trousers that crowded his crotch and hips seemed foolish. If he stole or stripped a dead settler of his pants, he made leggings out of the garment, by pulling them on and having his squaw tie them tight with buckskin thongs. The seams were then opened and sewed back tighter, with colored cloth and ribbons added and a few scalp locks if on hand.

The Pueblo Indian lived in towns in houses called *Pueblos* from the Spanish word for *town*. These Indians wore headbands, long hair done up into braids and tied with cords. The Hopi often cut their hair into Prince Valiant bobs or the just-gone hippie style. Cotton shirts were heavy with embroidery. This was one culture where the men did the sewing. Loose white trousers or high leggings of flannel were popular. Breechclouts were also often of flannel, with ends long enough to reach the ground.

Moccasins were bright red or turquoise blue. Rabbit skin robes were good for cold weather. The women wore a woolen *manta* or blanket bunched under the right arm and across the right shoulder, together with a wide belt looped around the waist a couple of times. Unmarried girls wore moccasins with spiral puttees reaching to the knees, covered with white pipe clay. Married squaws wore white boots, very loose at the ankle. On all other attire buttons, rings, earrings, necklaces, bracelets were widely used.

Some tribes painted their bodies and faces in great detail. Vermilion face color was popular and at one time both forehead and cheek tattooing was done in colors. Some smeared clay on their backs before going into battle and, as it dried, figures and symbols were painted on it. Special Indian societies such as the *Midewiwin* painted their faces to depict four classes of their membership. The first degree warrior put a green line across his forehead and a red line under the eyes and across the nose. The second degree man called for a green line across the eyes and a red line below and one above. The third degree buck merely covered his face with red and black dots. Low man on the totem smeared his face with vermilion and added two green bands across the brow.

The Navaho made some of their costumes out of grass and yucca fibers woven with strips of rabbit fur. Their moccasins were the nearest likeness to our shoes, for the flaps were wrapped around the ankle and closed by three silver buttons. These were weaver Indians, skilled on their looms, unlike other tribes who had to capture their cloth. Like later trouser styles in a sharp modern period, the sides of the trousers were slit a foot or so at the lower seams and a row of silver buttons added. The men wore their hair tied up in a figure eight knot on the nape of the neck in a style called *chinga* knot of hair. The Navaho also was the first among the Indians to take to the broad brimmed black Western hat, only they never creased the crown or tilted it to one side but wore it straight, flat on the head, with perhaps some silver ornament in the band.

The Crows wore a bib on their shirts with horizontal beadings of quills. Many tribes wore quills in horizontal bands as a form of armor. The Crows liked loose hair, and were given to high pompadours, usually stiffened with animal grease or tallow.

Although Indians rode bareback at times, or on skins, they did use saddles built on wooden hulls under leather forms, with elk horns often added high in front and back and bead pendants. The stirrups when used also had bead work and below them a panel of fringes and more beads. A buffalo pelt served as saddle pad and over this a saddle blanket of tanned skin with bead bands, and behind were two saddlebags, again decorated.

Squaws on horseback called for bands of bead work around the horse's neck and a square of decoration resting on the chest. Even the steed's forelock was hung with a rosette of beads and dyed horse hair, and a pendant that bounced between the horse's eyes. We sense in all this a human desire for splendor.

Warriors often stamped their ponies' flanks with their own hand dipped in paint.

During the Indian wars no one paid much attention to the very artistic nature of the Indian—his "savage frou frou"—and only the twentieth century was to make a cult of primitive art and patterns, without truly understanding the Indian's ritual meanings or nuances in his hunt for presence in his forms.

> In a sacred way I live
> To the skies I look
> My ponies are many.

Me the buffalo me the buffalo
Start the buffalo moving
I am the buffalos' relative.

Sioux prayers

INDIAN SOCIETY

The moo of a buffalo cow in parturition, the snort of a bull, all were welcome sounds. The horse and the ownership of horse herds made Indians mobile, made them more warlike, created hunting habits on horseback that changed their old way of life . . . The buffalo-hide tepee was an innovation when it became easier to kill bison in great numbers. The short bow, the drag *travois* for travel also aided their nomadic habits. So, facing the white invader was a more dangerous mounted Indian, and daringly mobile. A great war chief could become a minor Clausewitz on horseback.

The Indian still retained his ancestorial aura of magic and derived excitement and ritual from it, but the rifle and gunpowder made him a splendid savage, and within his limits a skilled professional warmaker. He saw himself as being biologically unique —dominating, but related to *all* animal life; existing by instinct, impulse, an uncomplex phenomenon of visionary elements.

To the whites he was a "varmint." "Drunken cadger, dirty trash, mean-eyed critter, lousy blanket scalawag" were other pet names. The white man never understood him—just as the Indian was never able to contemplate his own ruin by his own actions, his reaction to alcohol, bribes, gifts.

The simplicity of Indian material life consisted of a wealth of horses, scalps, or wounds upon his body which showed his courage. He slept on the earth or on buffalo robes; he cooked and warmed himself by a fire in the center of his lodge. He ate with relish whatever he could find—meat, mostly, and in various states of decay if he had to. Indian cooking was—by any standards— dismal; food was usually unseasoned, but for wild onion or garlic- like plants. Yet buffalo hump and gut, beaver tail, fish baked in clay, berries pounded into dried meat and suet had their gourmet following among the whites, also. Jerked or smoked or sun-dried meat helped carry them on a journey or through a winter.

The Plains Indians never learned to distill alcohol from their corn crops and, just as they never created a wheel, almost any simple process of most bronze-age, iron-age cultures passed them by. This was not due to inferior brainpower; it was their pride in tradition that kept them from new advances into a higher culture.

The Indian had no flair for hypocrisy, but only for spendthrift action. He avoided the sly justification of the white man's civilization, and he survived by the colossal vitality of his illusions, the ferocious traumas of his rituals.

To the white, he was "a red sonofabitch, a no-good, futzing varmint, better off dead." Yet, he had a dignity lacking in the dusty desolation of frontier towns. The lodges or tepees were each often personal temples or churches; for the patterns and art that were painted on the outside of the lodge were the owner's dreams, visions that could trigger or direct his reactions. Often a frieze of buffalos symbolized the Indian and his wife, areas dotted white were the night stars, a band of red meant the earth. These symbols were often mistaken by the whites as mere graffiti—savage scribbles. Skin tepees were used for travel or summer camps. Semipermanent dwellings were earth, log, grass, and bark lodges—home for up to fifty people at a time, not counting colts and dogs and small animal pets. Rawhide thongs or "wangs" held the lodges together rather than nails, and the white frontiersman soon learned to "wang" off a rawhide thong to repair anything from a rifle stock to a wagon spoke. Many early settlers and freighters were called "the rawhiders" from this use of strips of hide. An important corner in any lodge was the area reserved for prayers and a sort of pole altar for the medicine bundle, which must never touch the ground.

The Indian at home was not the feathered dandy of popular films. Feathers were not mere décor, but, rather like modern military jacket service bars, spelled out a great deal. The Sioux used eagle feathers to show a warrior's standing. One feather, untrimmed, meant one enemy dead; another notched or flat-trimmed feather indicated he had cut an enemy's throat. Other and different shapings could tell that he had been among the first to touch or strike the enemy and a split feather signaled

that he had been wounded in battle. A hand painted upon a shirt told that he had done in a foe in hand-to-hand fighting.

Feathered war bonnets were not just for any day but were kept for ritual ceremonial duty. Riding into battle, the chiefs in their flowing, trailing yards of long feathered bonnets were stirring sights, and also easy targets for a buzzard-eyed scout.

Hair was a fetish among the male Indians. Dressed in buffalo fat, tied off in ribbons, braided, protected in skins of small animals or the feathers of small birds, the hair was to the Indian a sign of his vital strength—much as Samson's in the Old Testament. The Indian had an extravagant relish for the grotesque and a flair for setting the fashion among the male peacocks of the tribe.

Hairdressers or hair stylists didn't merely improvise: hair, too, was for tribal or clan identification. Pawnees shaved the head, leaving one strip of hair from brow to the nape of the neck. The Crows greased up a tall pompadour until it was gamey, shiny, and proud. The Omahas were great braiders of locks using feathers. Hair was also a sign of personal victory and most Plains Indians scalped their victims, some of whom were not dead and who recovered to live a life of bald scar tissue.

Indians did not hamper themselves with too much clothing a great deal of the time. A breechcloth or hidestrip was usually enough. A sport would add a doeskin shirt or tunic, often, also, made of trade-goods' flannel or calico. Buffalo robes worn around the shoulders served as coats. Children under ten years of age rarely wore clothes.

But ceremonial clothes were quite splendid with decorations— shirts, leggings, headdresses, and gear were all full of magic symbols and dream visions. Some symbols were to prevent wounds; some to make the wearer bulletproof. Elaborately worked by the squaws with beads, quills, bear claws, elk, and wolf teeth, strips of human scalp locks, hung with British, French, and American medals, a man went to ceremony or battle like a Dark Ages' knight in mail or plate armor with etched patterns, lance, sword, dagger, and a helmet; as much a work of art as a war chief's feather bonnet (it might be added, equally proud, ignorant of reality and the higher culture—war machines on horseback full of the apocalyptic rhetoric of their godheads).

Only two teeth from any one elk could be used for a shirt. The hunter's wife who incorporated three hundred elk teeth in a

garment was certainly married to a mighty striker-down of elk. Porcupine quills or fake elk teeth of buffalo bone did for the inferior hunter's shirt.

The Indian moccasin was amazingly practical. They were made by folding properly a piece of leather. A peace pipe or calumet was worthy to own and each Indian had a coup stick with which to touch the enemy on contact—a touch being held as desirable a victory as killing. Coup-touching was a game to show courage—the way two modern hot-rodders play "chicken" when approaching each other head-on on a highway at great speed.

In a way, the Plains Indian was more democratic than the whites. No chief truly had supreme power; his men listened to his advice or plan and then had a council or *pow wow* to decide on what to do. Age, wisdom, battle records, and skill in debate counted. Murder inside a tribe was rare. Exile was the usual punishment, and the Crows made murder poor pay by requiring the killer to give gear and horses to the victim's wife and family. Women were brutally treated by our standards, and adultery was punished by some tribes by cutting the heel tendons of the offending woman so she could not walk upright for the rest of her life but had to crawl. The male sinner could have his nostrils slit or be killed by the husband, or just slip away and ride for it.

The whites never fully understood the rigid poetical or vision-dominated life of the Indian. His hymns of lamentation were, to settlers, merely animal howlings. And the Indians' deficiencies of technical ingenuity was mistaken for an inferior brain. But the Indian was soon aware that white covenants and promises were irrelevant cant and that, deceived, cheated, debauched, his only desperate course was to fight the white man—kill, torture, and destroy with all the fury and skill at his command. And making war was an Indian tradition, to which the Indian was profoundly dedicated.

II

War Without Mercy

White man never cared when an Indian was wronged, but always reported bad doings of Indians.

—GERONIMO

AN ACT OF MERCY

Trailed the Indians with dogs, cornered them in a cave and killed about thirty. In the cave were some Indian children. Kingsley could not bear to kill these children with his 56-calibre Spencer rifle. It tore them up so bad! So he did it with his 38-calibre Smith & Wesson revolver.

—*Sacramento Valley Report, 1871*

Chapter 1

LAND OF THE DRY DEATH

The Indian wars of the west were fought mainly on the plains and the deserts, moved at times into the canyons and the valleys of the mountain country, boiled over into the forests of those territories that touched on the Mississippi. But most of the wars were on the great plains and in the dreadful hostile desert country. To set the scene one must imagine (see front endpaper map) the western United States before most of it became states in the Union. Near the middle of the nineteenth century the tribes were, by the map, roving over what they called their hunting grounds; some already had been pushed west by treaties and promises hardly ever kept.

Along the Mississippi lived the Chippewa, Santee Sioux, the Fox, and Sauk. As we study the map, we see that on the northern plains the Sioux, under various subnames such as Ogala, Teton, Yankton, and other titles, and the Shoshone were the most powerful tribes. Farther south were the Cheyenne and Arapaho, often in federation with the Sioux in frontier warfare. In the deserts to the south lurked the savage Apache and Comanche, mixed with Arapaho and Kiowa. Though often at war with each other, they frequently merged for some raid or campaign against the whites.

Along the Pacific coast were other natives who fought and came under American domination. But not the Modocs, who fought to the end in an epic battle in the Lava Beds. Between the coastal tribes and the Plains Indians were the Nez Percé, drifting exiles, who, under an Indian Napoleon, were to make a Great March and defeat four armies sent against them.

The white man's map of the wars in the west looks quite different (see back endpaper map). The west was divided by Washington desk generals into six Departments, each under a commanding general. The Department of the west took much of the area west of the Mississippi from the Gulf to the Canadian border. This was the largest Department with St. Paul and St. Louis as major jumping-off points. The area ran well past Denver. The Department of Texas took in not only Texas but almost all of the states that would one day border it. The major settlements were San Antonio, Austin, and El Paso. The Department of New Mexico contained the old Spanish city of Santa Fe set on the dusty Santa Fe Trail. The Department of Utah contained not only the Salt Lake City of Brigham Young's Mormon Kingdom but also Fort Bridger. The Department of California was made up not only of that state but most of what is now Arizona and Nevada. San Francisco was building itself up from the mining camp shacks of the 49ers. There was Los Angeles still sleepily Spanish and Tucson, a base for greedy and powerfully political Army contractors getting rich on Indian wars. To the northwest the Department of Oregon incorporated the coastal tribes and had little to do with the wars on the plains and in the desert.

By the map we can see how the major trails connected these Departments and also how the major forts were set up to protect the trails and some of the strategic areas.

It is logical to begin the story in the southern desert country, for the Spaniards were the first invaders. The Federal government of the United States was to find itself involved in nearly a half century of savage Indian warfare.

The War with Mexico had spelled trouble for Henry Thoreau of Walden Pond and to the Indians of the Southwest. Thoreau did not approve of the war and, in 1846, he refused to pay a one dollar poll tax in Concord because, as he said, the money would, in time, buy "a man or a musket to shoot with." He was arrested and jailed, but released the next day when Emerson paid his tax.

Thoreau wrote: "There will never be a really free and enlightened State until the State comes to recognize the individual as a higher and independent power . . . and treats him accordingly."

No one paid much attention to this homespun anarchy. They preferred a more striking set of ideas promulgated a year before in the New York *Morning News* by its editor, John L. O'Sullivan: "Our manifest destiny [is] to overspread and possess the whole continent which Providence has given us for the . . . great experiment of liberty."

That was more like it. More like the slogan: *"Fifty-four Forty, or Fight!"* The population demanded that the United States of America extend its borders to the fifty-fourth forty-degree, claiming *all* the western land up to Alaska, including all the Canadian Pacific harbors and the entire western fur trade. England said that meant war. The country settled for the 49th degree, the present American, Canadian borders. The nation turned to the Southwest for a spread of *Manifest Destiny*, in the direction of the great land masses that Mexico still claimed, after losing Texas. With annexation of Texas, it was simple to order General Zachary Taylor—following a cooked-up border incident—to move into the disputed territory and set up military shop on the north bank of the Rio Grande.

The morality of the matter was perfectly in keeping with Christian thought; the Anglo-Saxon and European nations had been expanding as colonizers for centuries all over the world. This was considered good for the native people who needed their guiding hands in making the most of their souls and resources.

The Indian tribes of the desert Southwest were caught between the civilizing forces of this invasion, proclaiming its Destiny and sure that only the white races carried the true culture. The Indians of the desert were different from the Indians of the Plains. Their hardy life, with less food, had made them smaller, made them more raspy-tempered and wiry. Some, with their hooked noses, resembled the Aztecs or Mayans of Mexico rather than the people of the plains.

The desert Indians—the Apache, Pueblo, Navaho, Zumi, Hopi, Comanche, and others, lived in the salt barrens, in the low chaparral growths, in canyons and valleys, among strata of yellow and brown and red rock. Existing among the juniper growing in rock fissures with the company of whiplash lizards, gila monsters, and horned toads. Their food was maize, piñon nut, the sparse animal game that could live in the salt and alkali desert among the cord grass and burro weed and stunted greasewood, and those mountain creatures who had flesh to eat and fur or hide to use. Some of the land was composed of cinders and barren lava where grew a thin wild buckwheat and silver plant. Unlike the prairie, the desert was not desired for some time by the American whites. The Spanish and Mexicans had listlessly mined veins of copper and silver there.

The desert represented a road west, however—a hard, dry one, shared by the coyote, the jackrabbit, the gray and olive sagebrush, all clinging dryly to the surface of some of the most bizarre geology on earth. The rocks were often marked by the scabrous graffiti of long-gone Indian migrations. Even the trees were pre-historic in spots—turned to stone. Jim Bridger, to gullible strangers, talked of seeing "petrified birds, on petrified limbs, singin' petrified songs . . ." The American influence, in force, was moving toward the desert; Mexico was to lose all of that vast spread that held, among other things, the deadly Apache.

The Indians' elder statesman of the Apaches was *Mangus Colorado* (Red Sleeves). He was called Red Sleeves, because as a youth, in 1825, he had robbed the furnishings of white fur hunters on the San Pedro River, and, as part of the booty, had pur-loined a red flannel shirt which he donned and wore. He is variously reported as being six feet seven inches in his heelless legging moccasins. Other reports take off an inch, two, or three. He *was* tall for a desert Indian. As a lifetime horse rider, his legs were bowed and too small for his torso. His head was over life-size, the hawk-curved beak that of an Aztec carving.

Mangus Colorado was a Mimbreno Apache. The term Apache was applied to several related tribes, linguistically allied. They comprised, among others, the Chiricahua, San Carlos, Mescalero, Lipan, Jicarilla (on the frontier, pronounced as Hee-Car-eeya), and Kiowa Apache. (The whites confused this terminology even more by speaking sometimes of the Bronco Apache.) Their stalk-ing ground was both sides of the Mexican border, western Texas, southern Arizona, New Mexico, and eastern Colorado.

Mangus Colorado was the first of the great Apache chiefs, a Machiavellian scoundrel from all reports, a bully and a power-house whom some historians would consider perfectly at home in modern world politics if dressed and educated to protocol. As a statesman, until outraged physically by the whites, he pre-sented a façade of peace, and co-existence with the invaders. Like so many modern men of power he did not seem to have been lovable. He played the game by ear and lacked the integrity of a Chief Joseph or a Sitting Bull.

Compared to fellow Apache chiefs Cochise and Geronimo (pro-nounced in his lifetime as Heronimo), Mangus showed a fuller grasp of political wariness and cunning. Until his humiliation, at the hands of crude and brutal miners, he was, on the surface, pliable and reasonable in his dealings with the whites. He seemed to be as aware of their games as they, perhaps, were of his. He was an amazing figure to find leading a semibarbaric group of tribes in the wild country. He so resembles many of the strong man leaders of the twentieth century, on both sides of the Iron Curtain, that the comparison can be carried much *too* far to make a point and isolate a type.

We must see Mangus Colorado as an Indian chief before we probe his resemblances to other times. In his sly tranquillity, as compared to his outrageous actions, he often appears to be a man on the crest of a manic-depressive cycle. He was a tribal sex symbol, the husband of two pretty Apache women and the owner of a Mexican beauty, captured in a raid.

The tribe frowned on the outsider being treated as the equal and not the slave of his Apache wives. A brother of one of the Apache wives challenged Mangus Colorado to the Apache Duel, where both men strip naked and with only knives as weapons, work on each other until one man is dead. Mangus Colorado leaped into this terrible duel. After much slashing and the flowing of blood, he killed his brother-in-law and no one again took offense of the way he ran his harem nor dared conspire against the forms his sex life took.

In 1837, he was forty years of age—chief and victor of the Apache Duel. The Americans were not yet ready to take over the country the Mexicans claimed, so the Apaches raided and killed. Then the Mexican Junta of Chihuahua set up the *Proyecto de Guerra*—a war plan aimed at the Indians.

Among the features of this plan was an offer of the equivalent of one hundred dollars today for the scalp of every Apache warrior. The price for Apache squaw hair would come to fifty dollars the head; children, twenty-five dollars. This dreadful law (some of the British in both the American Revolution and the War of 1812 also bought scalps—white ones) instilled into the Apache a hatred of white men that carried over to the American occupation of the Southwest and its ocher and dun deserts.

The Indians had little directed hatred before this law was passed. Some horse-stealing, a little fling with trappers' whisky, petty pilfering by young bucks from hunters had been the extent of harassment. But now some whites found the idea of easy money in Indian hair a fine prospect. Such a one was James Johnson, one of the *Pinda Lick-o-yi*—the White Eyes (an Indian term for a white man). Johnson saw nothing wrong in collecting hair (Grant County, Arizona, was to pay two hundred and fifty dollars for every Apache scalp brought in until well past the middle of the nineteenth century).

Johnson got together a batch of querulous Americans and a partner, a man named Gleason, and a group of Missouri hunters under a man called Eames. They moved with letters of commendation from Mexico on to the mines of Santa Rita in New Mexico—there the owners added a promise of a bonus on top of the Mexican offer for Apache scalps. They were in business with a lethargical indifference to the value of human life.

All the Apache—known as the Copper Mine People—were invited to a great feast at the mines in Santa Rita: Men, women, and children came in droves. Mescal was served in unlimited quantities; steers were roasted, on great beds of charcoal with hot sop sauce and *soccoro* mush in pots. Everyone ate until nearly bursting—an old Indian habit: Eat while you see it; it's a long time between plenty.

Behind a screen of burlap and tree branches to one side of the feast site, Johnson lay in ambush with his men. Piles of corn grist was dumped in front of this screen behind which there was placed what has been described as a "howitzer," but what was probably a six-pounder cannon. Whatever it was, it was loaded for Apache with slugs and sections of chain, old nails, and bullets, and set to take in the general target area where the corn grist was heaped up for the taking by an inadequately fed people.

Soon the Indians were drunk.

Crafty as they were, liquor made them careless. So, when the *alcalde* stood up and declared to all that his dear Indian friends should help themselves to the corn grist—a gift from Santa Rita— the squaws and children rushed at the free offering. When there was a goodly group bent over the grist (a group worthy of the gunpowder) Johnson held his glowing *cigarro* to the powder vent of the cannon.

Fired through the camouflage screen, a rushing roar of death cut into the massed Indians. The carnage was fearful. Johnson and his band burst into the open and, aided by soldiers from the *presidio*, went over to the final slaughter. Corpses filled the square. History indicates that four hundred Indians were murdered by the "Johnson Plan." Few Indians who were not lucky and fast of foot escaped. Mangus Colorado lived and he replaced the top chief of the Mimbreno Apache—Juan José—who had overeaten and overdrunk and lost first his senses and then his life in this massacre.

Mangus moved quickly to hold the shattered people together. He appointed a general staff of chiefs to consolidate his orders. They were to become well-known to the whites. They included the celebrated *Victorio, Cuchillo Negro, Delgradito* (Slender One), *Ponce, El Chico, Pedro Azul, Coletto Amarillo* (Yellow Tail).

Mangus Colorado moved his tribe to a region of hot springs, away from the danger of James Johnson's greed. From then on they were known as the Warm Springs Indians. The Apaches, outraged at the massacre, attacked two bands of trappers in their war against the whites. Twenty-two men under Charlie Kemp were wiped out and their weapons confiscated. Ben Wilson and two trappers were captured alive and, oddly enough, Mangus Colorado saved Wilson's life in a kind of life-or-death lottery. But Wilson's two companions were tortured to death while hanging head-down over a very slow fire. Nearly dead, Ben Wilson staggered into Santa Fe. In time he became an Indian agent, a state senator from California, and the first American mayor of Los Angeles. He seems a protean, opulent type, familiar to a later-day Hollywood.

Meanwhile, Mangus Colorado attacked in all directions. He wiped out a *conducto* (pack-train) guarded by soldiers in a mountain pass, gaining rifles, powder and lead, cloth, horses, mules, *soccoro* meal—all destined as supplies to miners. The prisoners were tortured in leisured and dreadful detail—each little group of huddled Apaches working grimly over the remains of a quivering, screaming white man. The Apache was the most cruel of all Western Indians. One cannot bestow a higher quality of horror award for sadism. The agonized death screams must have echoed and re-echoed through the dry and barren canyons. *Homo sapiens,* as Charles Darwin, a best-seller of the time, was to discover, remains a highly unstable creature so far, in his evolution.

At Santa Rosa Rita, the stains of spilled Indian blood were

still visible in the town square, but the main worry was that the *conductas* of supplies from Mexico were no longer coming through the Apache country. The town had lived from *conducta* to *conducta* for fifteen years, since the very opening of the mines. Supplies had never been stockpiled. Now work stopped at the mines. Soon everyone was hungry. The people lined the slopes of Needle Mountain looking southward for the mule trains that never came.

Johnson and his gang must have sensed that something had gone wrong. They picked up and took off west to the Chiricahua Mountains. Here they walked directly into an Apache ambush and were almost all slaughtered. Johnson was one of the few who escaped. His later fate is unknown but he is said to have settled in Texas.

Santa Rosa Rita knew nothing of this. The *alcalde* called the population of Santa Rita together in the plaza and the mayor announced the time had come to send out a party of mounted troopers to see what had happened to the *conductas*. No one wanted to stay in the village with most of the soldiers going away, so it was decided to take along the four hundred men, women, and children of Santa Rita.

It was a mad march into a desert of a prickly austerity of forms—a simplicity of desolation. Unlike Moses' people, they did not have (nor believe they had) supernatural nor divine help. Carts, mules, burros, horses all were loaded—even overloaded—with unnecessary and useless items. Packs were carried by women and children. The exodus took its way south toward nothing. Two days out most of the paltry household treasures, the bulky burdens, were tossed aside. Soon dead mules and broken wheels made a mockery of their hopes. The trail went on in its lonely winding way, and above them, crags held only hawks and wild vegetation. The travelers regretted that they had left their tight little homes, now entirely deserted, behind them in Santa Rosa Rita. Perhaps they now felt some guilt in their dealings with Johnson and his Americans. Actually, Apache scouts had followed every mile of their slow progress and observed their desperate moves to lighten their journey.

We have no worthwhile detailed account of what eventually happened to most of the population of this village. It is surmised they were attacked by massed groups of fierce Apache warriors on the fourth or fifth day of their journey (bones later found cannot be authenticated). The half-dozen survivors who reached the first village to the south, Janos, told confused and hysterical stories of attack, death, horror, and Indian war cries.

Chapter 2

REBELS AGAINST THE *AMERICANOS*

The Apaches were at war with the world and war was their way of life. Under Mangus Colorado, the Mimbrenos Apaches took on as allies other Apache groups and raiding Sonora, Chihuahua, Durango in Mexico became a way of existence. Threat of terror, loot, captives for torture were inspired by a hate for the white man not to be seen in our time until the arrival of the Black Power fanatics.

Mangus Colorado, like some royal king of Europe (when the Divine Right of Kings was absolute) got allies by marrying off his three beautiful daughters, born of his Mexican captive. One went to *Cochise* of the Chiricahua Apache; one to *Hash-kai-la* of the Coyotero Apache, and the last one to *Ku-tu-hala* of the White Mountain Apache. Mangus increased his power by way of these marriage beds (or, rather, deerskin couches) an esoteric doctrine favored by many royal lines.

The United States of America—after annexing the Republic of Texas and pledging not to escalate the war beyond a river boundary—on May 13, 1846, proclaimed that a state of war existed between Mexico and the United States and hot pursuit was to be carried out across the Rio Grande.

Mangus Colorado watched all this from his stronghold free of the Americans. But the Indians of the Taos Pueblo seemed to be in the path of the American Army moving across the plains and through the mountains toward New Mexico.

West of the Pueblo was San Fernando de Taos, where whites and half-breeds, Yankees called *Americanos*, Mexicans, and Spaniards all lived in confusion as to what the war would mean to them. Obligations and betrayals would ripen in the structure of events to come.

Tomasito—as war chief of the Pueblo Indians—had in his lifetime seen the Spanish town of Taos grow as a base for trappers like Kit Carson and Broken-Hand Fitzpatrick, men like Charles Bent and Ceran St. Vrain who came to trade or cavort or set up shop. How would the *Americanos*, "half-hoss, half-alligator" look upon the Indians when they were masters? Progress, their priests hinted, is usually the exchange of one mistake for another.

Loud-mouthed Governor Don Manuel Armijo of New Mexico talked big against the damn *Americanos*, marched an army out, and when he saw the force of Missourians and Tennesseans of General Stephen W. Kearny, the Mexican forces fell away and Don Manuel led all the rest in leaving. On August 19, 1846, General Kearny took over New Mexico for the United States, raised the flag in Santa Fe, with not a thought that the local Indians might object to becoming part of this seizure. The Indians had been there since Dawn-Man—mostly hard-working, liking peace —and had set up seventy-six towns with solid buildings, like sky-scrapers against many cliffs.

Taos Pueblo had structures five stories high. The Taos knew how to use irrigation, designed aqueducts fifty miles long, often chiseling through solid rock for several hundred feet (today many of these old Indian irrigation systems are still in use, but not by the Indians). They were craftsmen, tillers of the soil, hunters. They never produced (because of their isolation) a fierce brand of warriors. The cliff-dwellings were fortresses and could stand long sieges by enemy tribes. In time, they traded with the cliff-dwellers when they could not pogrom them.

Withdrawing their long ladders from their lower windowless stories, the Indians were safe, perhaps too safe to know the dangers and damage the Americans could bring. Spanish rule had been a burden to bear, but the Mexicans were casual and demanded merely nominal returns from the Indians.

Charles Bent was appointed United States Governor of the territory; he was one of the brothers who had built Bent's Fort for trade on the Arkansas. A resident of Taos, he had a Mexican wife and as the armies moved south, he felt sure the natives, Mexican and Indians, as well, had accepted American rule. After all, the natives should be grateful to be under the protection of the flag. This is meant with no ironic nor cynical content, for he was a serious, honest man.

The Mexicans, however, began to plan a liberation from the

Americanos. Diego Archuleta and Tomás Ortiz were perfect conspirators. Their plan was for "you and him fight," to persuade the Taos Indians to revolt against a new set of rulers, and bring back Mexican rule. The priests of the missions entered gleefully into the plan against the Protestant heretics and began to preach hate of the *gringos* to their Indian converts and friends.

The schemers moving in behind the padres held talks with the chiefs, making great promises. The chiefs, with wry and quizzical faces, listened to talk of much booty, much American weaponry, oxen, furnishings. And of the weakness of the *Americanos* who had been left to hold the territory. The chiefs agreed to join the revolt; in what malignant loss of intelligence we don't know.

Records show that the Mexican rebels in the revolt didn't know their job. Plans and dates were changed; things went wrong with organization. The first attack and massacre of the *gringos* was to take place on December 19. The priests would have the church bells clang out the signal for everyone to move to the plaza of Taos and seize the Yankee cannon placed there, turn them on the Americans and kill them all wherever they were found. A Mass for their souls would be said.

Something went wrong and the date of extermination was moved to Christmas Eve. It was known that the heretics—soldiers and civilians—celebrated the Birth of the Son of God by getting as drunk as they could get.

The coup was exposed three days before Christmas by a mulatto girl married to a former Mexican soldier. She went to Colonel Sterling Price, the commander at Santa Fe, with the details of the plot. Orders for arrest went out but Ortiz and Archuleta made a run for it to Mexico, letting others hold the bag. This should have stopped the entire idea of turning out the Americans.

The Indians, however, did not seem to mind losing the Mexican leaders. They felt strong enough to carry out the plot themselves with whatever Mexican aid there was on hand. Much of their planning is in doubt, but when they went into action the records were accurate and give us solid facts.

Three Taos Indians were in jail on the charge of stealing. On January 19, 1847, a mob of Indians appeared in front of the jailhouse demanding the Indians be set free.

Sheriff Stephen Lee (unlike his cinema counterparts later) decided if they wanted the Indians, why, they could sure have them. A Mexican citizen and a careless soul named Virgil faced the sheriff and the mob. He insisted on "law and order" and loudly told the sheriff to hold his prisoners. He also added a few low, racial insults that the Indians resented. They knocked Virgil down and cut him to bits with their hunting knives, while he was still alive, and calling upon the saints for aid. This lasted until a merciful Indian plunged a knife into Virgil's throat. A mob records show is often more brutal and evil than an individual within it.

The sheriff tried to run for it. After the Indians set free their jailed friends, they searched out the sheriff. He was hiding on his rooftop and they shot him down. The Territory Circuit Attorney (one James Leal) was then spotted by the mob of Indians (and by now, some Mexicans had joined in), was scalped alive and dragged screaming through the streets until their spears had ended his outcries. Many Americans—young and old alike—were killed.

Governor Bent became the prime objective of Indian and Mexican hatred. He was at home when the mob sounds reached him. His wife came into the bedroom, hysterical, carrying his pistol: If he or all of them had to die, she wanted him to take a few Indians with them.

The governor appears to have been a singularly calm man. His plan was to give himself up to the Indians on the condition they spare the rest of the people in his house. Bent said to his wife: "At present, my death is all these people want."

This speech, as recorded, may sound stilted but that is how it was set down as a part of the whole record. It contains the implication—if not the actual words—of a man facing an incurably deranged mob and sacrificing himself.

Meanwhile, the Mexicans had joined the Indians in greater numbers and were chopping a hole in the roof of the Bent house. They dropped into the bedroom, Chief Tomasito in the lead, and Governor Bent appealed to them to listen to reason, always an odd request to make of a group showing the lowest common denominator of debased humanity.

Bent reminded them he had been a most fair governor and had endeavored to take care of their interests. The mob broke into hoots of nihilistic laughter. Three arrows were driven into

Bent's body. As he fell he was shot through the body. Chief Tomasito moved to stand over the fallen man, shattered his head with a pistol shot. As Bent twitched in his death agony he was scalped. His wet scalp was nailed to a flat board with brass tacks while war cries, hoots, and dancing announced the death of a brave man to his wife and family. The mob went off carrying the scalp on the board, as though it were a flag. Mrs. Bent and her family were, in the end, spared death.

The Indian wars of the desert against the Americans had begun —priest-inspired, Mexican-plotted. This is one of the few times that it can be said that the fault was *not* with the Americans. The Taos Indians had been under the rule of the Spaniards for centuries. The United States was there to grab as much territory as possible, while the taking was good, from a weaker neighbor. The Indians were *not* part of the immediate United States plan. The hasty token trophy of Charles Bent's scalp would lead to a whole series of Desert Wars.

Of the priests who had other faults—some local freethinker wrote: *"Post coitum omne animal triste—Praeter asinum et sacerdotum."* ("All animals are sad after fornication—except the ass and the priest.")

Chapter 3

THE SIEGE OF TURLEY'S MILL

The revolt was messianic, sybaritic, and an excuse for drinking. The Taos Lightning was a potent whisky distilled from the local grains, and famous among the transient crews of trappers, freighters, traders, and any Indians who could afford it.

On the Arroyo Hondo, in New Mexico, one Simon Turley had settled in with a Mexican wife and prospered with a grist mill and whisky distillery. He was a well-to-do *ranchero*-owner, with land, outbuildings, the mill, the distillery. One day he was entertaining friends—old trapper-buddies—when a dusty rider, shouting information, came by. He cried out that the Taos Indians had risen and were *massacring* Americans in Taos with the help of the Mexicans! Killing all *Americanos* and that Governor Bent was done for—his hair lifted! Turley's guest trappers, about a half-dozen of them, felt the situation was dangerous.

It was suggested the host should bar the gates to his mill and his collection of ranch buildings. The men began to inspect rifles and whet Bowie knives. Turley assured them that some of his best friends were the Taos Indians but he closed and barred the gates. His overlong drinking intimacy with the Indians might fail him.

None too soon were the bars in place, for the mob came, crying out its hate, waving guns, bows, lances, and some fresh, damp scalps. Pueblo Indians had gotten into the whisky barrels and Mexicans were ready to lynch every gringo and White-Eye they could catch. A flag of truce was petulantly put forward by the miller.

"Have you anybody with you, Señor Turley—besides yourself?"

"Eight Americanos."

"As a friend of the Indians and of the *Nuevo Mexicanos*, we don't want to shed *your* blood, but all other Americanos in the valley must die. Give up the men and you'll be spared."

"I'll never surrender my house nor my men. You want them, you come and get them!"

From the brush, from the piñon pines, from the boulders around the mill, the Indians began to fire their guns into the rancho. That familiar, chilling metallic timbre of whining bullets filled the air. The strong, steady fire from the buildings answered. From behind grain sacks and logs of firewood packed against the windows the trappers' rifles did deadly work among the attackers. It was a day-long fight, with howls from the mob and rifle fire from the mill windows of the Turley Rancho.

The heightened consciousness of death increased among the trappers as the day progressed, even if they still had their hair. The Indians and Mexicans began to carry off their dead and wounded. When night came, the defenders were still without casualties. They set up night guards and began to melt lead for bullets, cut linen patches for ramming atop ball-and-powder. They were strained by anxiety and didn't hold out too much hope that the attack wouldn't begin again at dawn. They didn't care to figure out just what their chances of survival were. They were all seared old timers, hard-shell mountain men. They didn't plan too much ahead in hazardous times.

They had the fantods, were riled up, as the saying was. By morning the five hundred members of the mob had increased and eight attacking Indians had got as far as a shed by the Rancho's stables. But, failing to break in, they began to run back to safety, only to meet the deadly rifle aim of the trappers.

A chief fell. An Indian came forward to perform the good deed of getting the body away. He was shot dead, and so was a second Indian. Again, a lone attempt to recover the dead chief was made and a new death resulted. There was a rush by three Pueblo Indians as a group. They grabbed up the body and began to move away with it, but well-placed shots called all the pallbearers to the Great Beyond.

The Indians now began to fire heavier and heavier volleys, hitting two hunters. One with a bullet in his hip was in great pain. Both men soon died. Bullets and powder were running low in the mill. Their luck seemed that of a catfish snagged on a trotline.

All afternoon the fight raged on. The mill was set afire but Turley and his friends managed to keep the flames away from the main buildings. The outbuildings were lost to the attackers and everything past the corral was captured. The mob had a fine time reasonlessly killing off the sheep, pigs, and other livestock. As the fire spread—with the help of fire arrows—the ranch buildings began to burn in earnest. It was time to talk things over inside the mill. The caucus decided that, when dark fell, it would be "every man for himself"—each to make his way out past the attacking mob on his own. When the night came, the trapped men charged out of the mill with a rush and a cry, weapons firing, hoping to break free by the surprise of their action. Two trappers moved out of the postern gate, firing, then, their ammunition gone, fighting with rifle butts.

One trapper was knocked down. The other, a man named John Albert, hid under a fence while his companion was beaten and knifed to death; his screams no tranquilizer for the calming of Albert's nerves. Near dawn, Albert managed to creep off, unseen, and started walking toward the mountains. He met friendly hunters near what is now Pueblo, Colorado. Two other trappers made it safely through the mob.

So did Simon Turley. He hid out in the mountains. There, he found a Mexican friend of long standing whom he felt he could trust. Turley offered him his watch in trade for the other's horse. The Mexican said he would ride for help. Instead he set out for the mill which was still being looted. Here he informed the Indians where Turley could be found. Turley was run down and killed in a brutal fashion.

If this account seems unusually detailed it is because the trapper, Albert, told his story to an Englishman who was traveling in those parts, one George Frederick Ruxton, who included it in his book: *Wild Life in the Rocky Mountains*. Later it was proved that Ruxton had been a British spy sent over to see what "those Americans were up to." His two books on the early American West (his other one is called: *Adventures in Mexico and the Rocky Mountains*) give us the best picture we have of Americans in these areas during that period. Ruxton records for us the dialects and conversation patterns of the trappers and hunters: Some of them are rare examples of how the people actually talked and sounded. Other versions of Western speech in the books of the day are often stilted and far too literary.

The attacks on Turley's Mill and Rancho had cost several lives and left many wounded among the Indians. The Mexicans began to withdraw as Indian allies. Sterling Price receiving news of the massacre and uprising began to amass troops in Santa Fe and he shortly started his march to Taos. A second force departed from Las Vegas but ran into trouble and lost its commander, Captain Isaac Hendly.

Price's expedition was a good one with a group of howitzers capable of throwing twelve-pound shells. There were over three hundred and fifty soldiers and, while his sixty-five riders, called "The Avengers" (under Ceram St. Vrain) couldn't be considered cavalry, they would do. Most were friends of the murdered Americans. Trappers and ranchers had been murdered wherever they were discovered on the Rio Colorado, at Mora. It was a spotty revolt, but while it lasted, it was mean and cruel.

On January 24, 1847, Price's forces met the Mexicans in battle at La Canada and, outnumbered three-to-one, Price brought up his cannon and drove the Mexicans from the field. A few days later he fattened his forces, being joined by Captain Burgwin and a company of U. S. Army Dragoons. At the village of Embuedo (which was set in a canyon) nearly seven hundred armed Mexicans held firmly to both sides of a deep ravine. The dragoons went along one bluff; the Avengers along the other, and the Mexican forces took to their heels. Pablo Chavez, one of the uprising's firebrands, died in this engagement.

There were now no longer any Mexicans in the field. The Pueblo Indians of Taos faced the white soldiers alone. The Taos Pueblo still exists and consists of two large buildings—a series of stories, one atop the other. On one side a church stands and on the other, there are stables and storage space. Taos Creek ran between the two buildings. The enclave was protected by a high adobe wall. The church was loopholed for defense firing and the lower floors of the main pueblo had no windows (it was possible to withdraw all the entrance ladders inside the buildings).

On February 2, Price's forces were ready to attack this strange-but-strong fortress: The howitzers were put into position and Lieutenant Dyer in charge of the battery, piled shells into the building. The heavy church walls merely engulfed the cannon balls and showed no damage. Price saw it was best to pull his forces back as night fell. The Indians (thinking he was retreating for good) began to howl with contempt at his efforts. Dancing or squatting on their haunches, they mocked the Americans.

Next morning, the Americans were back. Now Price was ready for an all-out assault. The dragoons and two howitzers were stationed west of the pueblo. The Avengers, mounted, went to the east to keep the Indians from making a run for the hills. The infantry took up a position north of the structures with two cannon. The plan needed no amplification or clarification.

For two hours the guns fired. Smoke and noise filled the air. Adobe fragments went flying, bricks falling. At the stroke of eleven in the morning the call to charge was given in proper military order. Price was a stickler for that: Ranks in line, officers with swords at proper slant, even drums and fifes setting a tempo for the troop to "March!" They stepped out and the assault on the walls began. The misery of war still had a sense of style in those days.

Soldiers and dragoons advanced at once into deadly Indian fire. Every loophole seemed to spout flames. The best place for the soldiers seemed to be under the high walls by the church, where the rifle fire could not reach them. Axes and picks began to dig into the heavy wall. Hastily made ladders carried some soldiers to the roof of the church where a fire was set. Through holes at last cut into the walls, hand-lit canisters of explosives were tossed into the interior where the smoldering fuses set them off to burst, scattering shards of steel in every direction and meeting flesh and bones.

Captain Burgwin decided to break in the doors of the church which was being used as fortress. He and his men went over the adobe wall and began to batter at the heavy oaken door with whatever was at hand. Some dragoons joined in to aid them.

Indians in the pueblo soon had them all under fire. The captain and five soldiers were shot down. Carrying their wounded, the Americans went back to the shelter of the wall. Price had his guns up close. At sixty-yard range, they began to enlarge the holes the axes and picks had made. Through one huge breach, the soldiers rushed into an interior filled with smoke and fire from the burning roof. Coughing and choking, they moved in to find the Indians had pulled out ahead of them. Some hostiles tried for the pueblos; others walked into the weapons of the awaiting Avengers, who, shouting the rallying cry of the mountain men, put spurs to horse and attacked the Indians, who were running on foot.

Jesús Tafoya, wearing the coat and shirt of the murdered Bent, was pistolled down by St. Vrain. Dismounting to observe the Indian prone on the ground, St. Vrain discovered the corpse was still alive and ready to fight. A trapper brained him with a tomahawk. Almost all of the Indians who fled from the church—there were over fifty—were killed.

With darkness, the fighting stopped. The Americans garrisoned the church and waited to carry on the fight in the morning. Of the six hundred and fifty people in the pueblos, a hundred and fifty were now dead and there were many more wounded. Morning saw the Indians, men and women, coming forward, carrying white flags and holy images and crucifixes. They knelt in submission.

Price accepted their surrender, but held Chief Tomasito and the other ringleaders for trial as the murderers of Charles Bent. The trial was held by Judge Beaubein, whose son had been senselessly murdered in the uprising. Testifying against the Indians were witnesses to the murder of Bent—the widow of Bent, and Kit Carson's wife.

Found guilty, Chief Tomasito was sentenced to hang but, instead, was shot by his guards while "attempting escape." (One juror had cried out "Hang 'em all! They may not be guilty now—but they soon will be!") Six Indians found guilty by a jury carefully picked for a quick verdict were hanged in Taos, all on the same mass gallows, with the Army and the populace standing by to witness their punishment.

The Pueblo Indians had been duped and misled by the Mexicans who fled from any real fighting. Grandiose gestures and bold words win no rebellions.

Mangus Colorado also reacted to the American takeover, but he led no hasty attack. His was a baroque mind. The talk that he heard from hotheads was to the effect the Americans (the White Eyes) were moving to attack the Apache.

Mangus had respect for the *Americanos*. They were tough fighters. His scouts hung on the flanks of General Kearny's columns in New Mexico but made no hostile gestures. Kearny was interested in getting to California to help take that place over—not in fighting Indians. He met with Mangus Colorado and some other chiefs near San Lucia Springs. One chief said: "You have taken New Mexico; you will take California. Go, then! Take Chihuahua, Durango, Sonora—we will help you."

Kearny, who had other orders, merely bought mules and horses and moved on. One war at a time for him. (Early in the twentieth century, William Randolph Hearst was supposed to have suggested the same idea of taking over part of Mexico for mining interests and landowners.)

In 1848, something big was in the air. Wrote J. P. Dunn in his history: "The discovery of gold in California on February 9, 1848 was fraught with greater evil for them [the Indians] than any other single event in the history of America, except the discovery of America itself."

The California Gold Rush was on as soon as news of it got around. Moving westward in great mobs—reckless, overheated miners-to-be went wild. Indians were murdered as they were met. The Indians stood in the way of the greedy migration where it was every man for himself, and every man was addicted with the gold fever. Nothing could stop the mad rush—not even Indian wars, or fantastic prices: 25 cents for a nail; boots, $50 a pair; pick-and-shovel, $15 each.

The hostiles began to attack the wagon trains, the loners, any invader of their lands they came across. Here is one closeup of such an event. Nineteen Tonto Apaches attacked the Catman family crossing the Gila River. The parents, two girls and a son were killed; one son was left for dead. The Apaches carried off two surviving Catman girls—Olive and Mary Ann. The son, Lorenzo, survived, being rescued by Pima tribesmen. He spent five years hunting for his captive sisters. Mary Ann had died of her experiences, but he did rescue Olive who—her face tattooed with Indian designs—went on the lecture platform to talk of her ordeal in the Indians' hands, and her life among "the savages."

At first, Mangus' Mimbreno Apache tribe was not involved in the gold-rush traffic. After the Mexican War, in 1851, a survey party under J. R. Bartlett got to Santa Rita of tragic memory. Here Johnson had collected bounty scalps and from the village had come many who had been massacred.

Chief Cuchillo Negro out hunting ran into a lone white man, Captain John Cremony, the Bartlett party's interpreter. The captain pulled out his weapons and rode right at the chief, pistol out. The chief called for a talk. The captain said he was the head of a large party of whites on the march and, true enough, soon the sun in the distance picked up the rifles of the soldier-escort. The Indians got away quickly. Mangus Colorado visited the camp at Santa Rita and was assured the party was passing through, not settling in.

Mexican traders also appeared with a captive slave-girl they had bought from the Pinal Apaches. They were offering her for sale as a delicious partner for any male. But Bartlett set her free. Slavery in the United States was frowned upon, except for Negroes. Most American forces overlooked the traffic in Mexican concubines.

The name of the girl Bartlett freed was Inez Gonzales. She was fifteen and reports indicate she was very beautiful. She was reunited with her parents in Santa Cruz and became the mistress of Captain Gomez, commander in Sonora, with her parents' approval. On his wife's death, Gomez married Inez and when he died (of natural causes, one hopes) she married the *Alcalde* of Santa Cruz, where her past did not lower her standing in the society of the place.

The Apache also held prisoners, among them, two Mexican boys named Savero and José, ages thirteen and eleven, respectively. They escaped and ran to Bartlett for protection but Mangus Colorado came in person to reclaim his property. A long speech he gave ended with the words: "We believed your talk of friendship . . . Why did you take our captives from us?"

Bartlett offered to buy the boys. He seems to have been a born sucker for the stratagems of slave-dealers. (Today he'd be the patsy of secondhand car dealers.) The chief shook his head. "The brave who owns these captives does not wish to sell. He has had one of these boys six years . . . He is a son of his old age . . . Money cannot buy affection. The heart cannot be sold."

Bartlett was hooked and didn't know it. By the treaty of Guadalupe-Hidalgo, he said, he was under orders to free *all* Mexican slaves. In the end, and after much bickering, the Indians took two hundred dollars worth of trade items for the boys. But the Indians were not happy about it. It all seemed somehow illogical to them, even if they were well-paid for it. The whites could keep black slaves, but the Indian had to give up his Mexican slaves.

The Indians now began to gather; first three hundred of Mangus Colorado's warriors and their families; then, four hundred Navahos who settled in the Gila Valley. Others came. A flare-up took place July 6, when a Mexican working for Bartlett got into a disagreement with an Indian and settled it by shooting him.

The Indians all rode off at the sound of that shot. Bartlett arrested the Mexican for murder and sent word to the Indians that justice would be done in their name, but the Apache demanded not a trial in Santa Fe, but an execution of the man on the spot.

Said Chief Ponce: "The Apaches will not be satisfied to *hear* that the murder has been punished in Santa Fe . . . all the Apaches must *see* him put to death."

The logic of this Old Testament talk of an eye-for-an-eye troubled Bartlett. He offered to make the Mexican work in chains and give the money to the family of the slain Indian.

"No. Money does not satisfy an Apache for the blood of a brave!"

In angry retaliation at this slur on their honor and code, the Indians stole two hundred of the Bartlett party's mules and horses.

Bartlett moved on . . . most of his party were on foot. Mangus Colorado felt that he had run the Americans out of the country. It was a mistake any chief could make. He had the audacity of a guerrilla-fighter; he was to learn in a most humiliating way how little the *Americanos* thought of the pride of native people in their ways of life. The whites, too, had an excessive credulity in thinking *they* knew *Indians,* and classed them all in a mass as a faceless crowd, in which some were adorned with more feathers than others.

Labyrinths of deception and ignorance remained between the two forces, soon to face each other in what would seem an endless battle, malicious treaties, bloody revenge, and the flow of so much arterial blood. The theatre was to be a dry land of black volcanic rock, of sand and sage, ironwood, cactus, tamarask and mesquite under a grilling sun—and always the hunt for water.

And everybody was as "jumpy as a stump-tailed-bull in fly-time!"

Chapter 4

THE WHIPPING OF MANGUS COLORADO

There are times when one doesn't suffer experience—one provokes it. Mangus Colorado was aching for trouble and he was destined to get it. In 1851, gold—that magpie nest of trouble—was found at Pinos Altos, and the gold-rush brought in the wild flock of goldminers. A hundred and fifty of them went to digging, unaware of the dangers of working in wild Apache country.

Mangus Colorado saw it was that damned *ora*—that worthless yellow-butter of a metal—the whites wanted. He told the miners if they followed him, he'd show them more gold than they ever found scratching the ground at Pinos Altos.

We do not know if the chief was telling the truth or setting a trap, but even greedy miners who would kill each other for a buckskin poke of flake-gold did not trust the Indians. Under their lousy shirts, they shared a tenacious love of life.

"We'd druther stay where we are."

Mangus came back and again made the miners his offer. The miners, who had managed to get hold of some whisky, were drunk as a country fiddler and someone suggested they tie up this pesky Injun and give him a hell of a flogging. With screeching, drunken laughter, nearly a dozen men jumped the chief from behind and, no matter how the giant fought, there were too many for him. Prone on the ground, rawhide thongs were tied around his big wrists and he was then spread-eagled against a tree. A heavy-muscled miner took hold of a blacksnake whip used for debates with balky mules. It was a brutal flogging. Mangus Colorado uttered neither cry nor groan as the whip broke again and again the skin of his back, cutting it into fearful ribbons of raw, ripped flesh. He was covered with his own blood and bits of splattered flesh; blood flowed in streams down his legs.

After a time the miners untied the chief, gave him a few kicks in the rump and ran him out of camp. Allowing him to survive was an error. The entire Southwest frontier was to pay for that.

Mangus' rage, bitterness, and shame were enlarged by the fact that, in his own mind, he *had* tried to remain on friendly terms with the White Eyes. Not only his back was damaged; his heart, his pride, had suffered a change as drastic as a crippling disease. He, the Great Chief, had been flogged like a camp cur stealing a bone and jeered at by the scum of the mining camps. Revenge could be sweet and horrible. Consolation and surfeit would never come; always there must be more whites to kill, to torture, for that scarred back.

If his whipping were cruel and uncalled for, his revenge on prisoners was so cruel it is hardly fit for print. One sample from Captain John C. Cremony's *Life Among the Apaches,* who found some of the victims' bodies, will do:

". . . each man was seized, bound to a wheel of a wagon head-downward, about eighteen inches from the ground. A fire was made under him and their brains roasted from their heads . . . The busted heads, the agonized contortions of the facial muscles . . . were horribly depicted . . ."

A Chiricahua Apache, Chief Cochise, has been so distorted by motion picture fiction as a King Arthur of the Desert that it is a surprise to run across a text that honestly identifies him as "the snake-like Chiricahua." He was the partner of the bloody crimes of his close friend and father-in-law, Mangus Colorado. They shared the best grazing lands and, like barbarians raiding Rome, had made wolflike attacks down into Mexico for murder, loot, and women. In council the two chiefs stood together, always, against the others.

A minor incident brought Cochise into war against the whites.

A Mexican girl-captive, who had had a child by an Apache warrior, had been rescued and gone with her son to live with an Irish rancher named Johnny Ward.

In October of 1860, when the girl and her child were alone on the Ward ranch, Apaches raided the place, ran off the cattle and carried off the child. Returning home, Ward rode on to Fort Buchanan a dozen miles away. A fresh West Pointer shavetail lieutenant, George N. Bascom, was put in command of sixty troopers to find the cattle and recover the boy.

A detachment of soldiers started down the stagecoach road that ran through the dark, narrow passage of Apache Pass. Cochise made a little income here by supplying the stagecoach station with firewood. The station agent, a man called Wallace, and the chief were good friends. Cochise's own village at the time was set up a few hundred yards from a stone-and-boulder stagecoach station in Apache Pass.

Lieutenant Bascom commanded his men down the canyon to the station. Wallace said he'd bring the chief to the station for a talk to see what could be done about the cattle and the stolen boy. Bascom, in excessive credulity and arrogance, was sure Cochise had the steers and the child—not that any such evidence existed. But, after all, bluster might get results, the West Pointer figured in what he regarded as his overwhelming position as an officer of the United States Army.

Cochise came to the station with a small group of warriors and had to listen to a direct order he give up the cattle and the boy; if not, there would be a military crack-down, in force. Cochise was surprised at the haughty tone and also puzzled as to why this young whelp of the *Pindu Lick-u-yi* (White Eyes) thought he, the chief, had anything to do with such a paltry raid. The insolence of potty people in power was brand new to him.

The young shavetail began to shout and threaten in even louder tones. In his rage, he ordered the arrest, on no evidence, and while under a flag of truce, of the chief and his warriors. They were to be held as hostages until cattle and boy were returned.

Cochise, amazed at what he heard, saw a split-second for action still remained for him. With a war cry that would chill spines, he made a dash for freedom, breaking through the soldiers' ranks, moving so fast that rifle fire only wounded him. After him trailed his warriors, but five of these were captured. Running quickly, despite his wound, the chief sped toward his camp. The Indians began to mass and gather high above the station and fire down upon it. Soldiers took wounds and a fight raged at the station until darkness set in. The Overland Mail Coach, usually passing in safety through the canyon, was attacked down the pass. One horse was killed; one passenger shot and the driver, with a shattered leg, cut his dead horse out of harness and drove on to the station as a storm came up. The Overland

Mail Coach Service was out of business in Apache Pass for some time.

As usual, in an Indian attack and siege, somebody had to volunteer to carry the news of the trouble to the fort and get a rescue expedition started. A soldier rode out on a mule and got to Fort Buchanan, in the teeth of a snowstorm. An Indian woman, held prisoner at the stage station, was sent out to Cochise to inform him that the Indian prisoners were going to be taken to the fort. Cochise came forward with another flag of truce.

Lieutenant Bascom, with two soldiers, Wallace, and some of the men from the stage station went out to meet the chief. He didn't seem friendly any more. A sentry on the roof of the stage building cried out that the Indians were crowding up in the ravine behind the chief, massing for an attack. Bascom decided it was time to call off the meeting, but it was too late. Warriors jumped out and began to circle the group. Rifles were fired. Some slugs made holes in Bascom's uniform, but did not hit flesh. Wallace and two of his men were carried off by the Apache.

The Indians, prisoners at the stage station, made a break for it but a shot knocked off one in his flight and another was nailed to the ground with a horrible bayonet thrust. The rest of the prisoners were tied up. Bascom and his escort of two soldiers made it to the corral. They were now in a tight spot—having no water—and lived for a time on the melted snow. When that gave out (by the third day) the men and horses were in great agonies of thirst. The nearest spring was six hundred yards away, and directly under Apache eyes. Bascom began to drive part of the horse herd to the spring. The Indians attacked, wounded several soldiers and seized the horses.

Help was coming but was in short supply. The fort sent only fifteen men under a Captain Irwin. They rushed a messenger to the northwest, one hundred miles, to Fort Breckenridge, to ask if they could borrow two troops of cavalry for Apache Pass, as if asking for the loan of a cup of sugar. Captain Irwin's small group ran into Indians herding stolen cattle, took those back and added three Indian prisoners.

Cochise had now sealed off both ends of the pass with his warriors—some were off, raiding, when Irwin came through—and Irwin, riding on next day, came across the remains of a five-wagon train burned out, eight bodies tied to wheels with their brains sautéed in the fashion of the torture popular among Apaches. Three prisoners had been carried off, alive, in that raid.

Cochise took his three wagon-train prisoners up close to the stagecoach station and announced he'd trade, even, for the Indians held prisoner. But no deal was made. Soon the two troops of horse-soldiers from Fort Breckenridge were in sight. Cochise pulled out his entire camp for the high-mountain country.

Marching out of the pass, the soldiers saw a great gathering of vultures. Scouts found them tearing at the bodies of Cochise's friend, Wallace, two of his men, and the three captured wagon drivers, who had been tortured and left for the buzzards.

Captain Irwin in an angry, bellicose mood decided to hang his Indian prisoners, then and there—even if they had nothing to do with the grisly fate of the dead Americans. As he wrote later, piously: ". . . it was I who suggested their summary execution—man for man."

The hangings proceeded with what Captain Irwin calls "merited punishment," including the hanging of the Indian horribly mangled in the stomach by a bayonet. This man walked a mile and a half to the spot picked for the hangings without a word. The Mosaic "eye-for-eye and tooth-for-tooth" system was later called unworthy of the United States as represented by these two officers. Worst of all, it had begun when a foolish young officer did not believe Cochise when he said he knew nothing of the stolen cattle and boy. Both Mangus Colorado and Cochise started the twenty-year war against the whites because of wrong treatment and misjudgment against them. Thousands would die. Impertinent, insolent relationships with Indians never paid off. As for the captured child, he grew up an Apache and, as Mickey Free, was a scout and interpreter in the war against Geronimo.

Meanwhile, John Brown's Raid, Lincoln's election, the firing at Fort Sumter, the Battle of Bull Run (first one) all had their effect on the Indians of the Southwest, for, as the white men's war grew more bloody, most of the soldiers in New Mexico and Arizona left. The land was often deserted and given back to the rattlesnakes and the lizards. Mines were abandoned, villages turned into ghost towns. What remained knew terror. Mangus Colorado, Cochise, and other Apache chiefs led raids, burned ranches, laid waste the work of ranchers and miners. Hostile

Indians were on the outskirts of the only town left, Tucson, which was down to two hundred citizens who feared for the sound of war cries every night. Prophecies of doom were exchanged as greetings in the streets.

The Confederacy began to take over some of the Union forts as the blue soldiers pulled out, fighting their way past the Apaches along the Chihuahua Trail. The Confederacy held Fort Davis on Limpus Creek and some other posts. Fort Davis's officers had mostly deserted the United States and their oaths of loyalty and had gone over to the Confederacy. Those Union troops who objected to this were turned over to the mercy of the "Texas Mounted Rifles," concepts of honor turning to mere impulses in the war. The Mescalero Apache, under Gian-na-tah and the Confederates, fought a little war, bloody and cruel, of their own; scalawags, outlaws took on claims as patriots.

Mangus Colorado fought Americans and Mexicans wherever he could find them. In September of 1861 he sent two hundred warriors against the Pinos Altos mines. But Captain Martin, with some Arizona Guards, had garrisoned the place the night before. The Apaches gave up the fight, turned their attention to a U. S. Army wagon train, put it under attack for fourteen hours and were run off by troops coming to the help of the fighters.

Otherwise, the Indians had it all their way. The Pinos Altos setback annoyed Mangus Colorado, and he formed a plan with Cochise to help take it. Cochise in the mountains needed help himself just then. An expedition was marching against him. Mangus Colorado moved in to help his friend as the dustcloud of the troopers drew near.

These were soldiers who were marching east to fight in the Civil War. While waiting for these soldiers to walk into a trap, Mangus discovered that a party of fourteen miners were coming toward Apache Pass. He attended first to the miners, ambushing them in a gulch and leaving their bodies full of arrows for the buzzards to dine on. This small task out of the way, the two chiefs combined their forces—probably four or five hundred warriors. Moving with steady purpose toward them was the advance guard of the California Volunteers, with Captain Thomas Roberts of the 1st California Infantry up ahead with three companies of men. There was also a troop of horse soldiers, three hundred men in all, with two howitzers—all unaware of Indians. Nobody seemed to be doing anything but cursing the dust and admiring the scenery. No scouts were out; there was no recognition of Apache Pass or its sinister reputation.

The three hundred marched in and two-thirds of the way through they heard the high cry of the Apache war howl and then felt the arrows and rifle fire coming down from both rims of the deep canyon. There was that record of shock, the stare of amazement and then the heated worry for survival. The soldiers were drawn out in moving groups and in no position to fight back with any military precision. After some disorganized firing, Captain Roberts ordered them to retreat the way they had come.

They were in bad shape: They had come a long way—forty miles of that march under the hot sun and the only springs anyone knew of were up in the canyon, out of reach. Dust, heat rash, alkaline-impregnated air made their thirst maddening. All their grievances and sensibilities became magnified.

The only solution at all was to attempt to force their way through the pass, again, and reach the springs. The howitzers were put into position; the infantry—setting itself in battle rank—went once more into the mouth of the canyon.

It was a strongly fought action by both Apache and soldiers. The stage station was captured but the springs with their precious water were still six hundred yards ahead. Thirst brings on a morbid introspective mood at first, then a raging disregard of all reason.

The Indians knew that if they could hold on to the water, they were in a position to win. Indian sharpshooters held the two peaks that flanked and dominated the springs. Behind piled-up strong points they could not be dislodged by the soldiers. They—the soldiers—were tired and bone-dry thirsty from the long march. Captain Roberts brought up his howitzers. The men still did not know too much about managing them. One overturned as it was aimed at the heights.

Men ran relentlessly forward under Indian rifle fire to pull the tumbled howitzer back and reset it into position. Soon the howl and bang of the howitzers in action echoed and re-echoed in the canyon as they threw blasting power against the stonework peaks. They were using exploding shells, not just cannon balls. The Apaches had never seen anything as deadly as the shells that exploded into fragments and scattered death in all directions. Like the knights of old, the Indian always disdained the big wagon guns as unsporting weapons.

The Apaches broke and ran from the deadly shelling and Captain Roberts' men moved up to the life-prolonging water at the springs. That night, the soldiers camped by the springs and wondered what the morning would bring. Captain Roberts sent a detachment back to General J. H. Carleton, commander of all the Californians, who was coming up a day's march behind with the supply train.

Dawn came with the rising sun and inspection of arms, and then the slow, wary move up the canyon. A few shells dropped onto the cliffs where an Indian or two showed himself and kept the hostiles out of range. The soldiers went on through the pass, wondering at lack of Indian pressure—even beyond the howitzer range.

What had happened was that the horse-soldier detachment sent back to warn the general was chased in the night by fifty mounted Indians. A running fight took place. Sergeant Maynard got a shattered arm; two horses were killed, and the dismounted soldiers had to be carried double behind friends. Private Teal's horse was in bad shape and he began to fall behind. His horse was shot down and Teal was alone on foot—facing the Apache band while the small detachment rode on with no hope of helping him.

From behind his dead mount, Teal began to fire on the onrushing yipping warriors with his breech-loading carbine. Its scattering shots kept the hostiles, at first, at respectful distance. They began to systematically circle him, howling, their painted faces grimacing, waving their weapons. Teal, particularly, noticed the leader—a giant heading the attacking group. It was Mangus Colorado himself, but Trooper Teal didn't know that. Still, it was a chief and he was big—damn big—so Teal got him in his sights and pressed the trigger. Down went the chief, shot right out of his saddle.

It had grown very dark and the Indians seemed to have suddenly lost their zest for the fight. Then they were gone—the chief carried off with them. Private Teal knew where General Cremony was supposed to be camped. As a good soldier, careful of government property, he packed the saddle and bridle of the dead horse on his shoulders and walked out of the canyon— and walked and walked—reporting to the camp . . . "assdragin' tired and dusty."

Mangus Colorado was not dead but he had Private Teal's slug in his chest and he was bleeding badly. The Apaches carried the big body away and kept going across the mountain until they were in Mexico with their still-living burden. They passed the fort to the Presidio del Jonos, informing the soldiers to stay out of it, and went on into the town nearby. They seized the place and looked for a doctor known to practice there.

They said to the wide-eyed medical man, staring at their bloody burden, "You make Indian well. He no die. Everybody live. He die. Everybody in Jonos die."

The slug in the big chest was taken out and the wound bound up. The strong constitution of Mangus Colorado did the rest. He recovered from the Mexican surgery and by the time he re- covered—cared for by Indian women—and returned to his old stamping-grounds, the soldiers were gone to a bigger war.

Indian women were a remarkable lot and their part in history is often underestimated. The lowly *squaws* (even the Indian used the word as a degrading one) were the burden bearers of the tribe. The Indian woman made possible the daring long marches, traveled with the warriors in flight, bound up the wounds, and did much to help the braves in time of battle. Captain Richard Carter, that keen observer of Indians who fought them, gives us a picture of the Indian woman as she was—not the Indian maiden of fiction.

He saw her dressed in her best: ". . . Gaudy colored flannels —red, yellow, green, and blue, if she could procure them—were ingeniously made into different articles of feminine apparel and, with the inevitable paint on her face, thickly smeared on and red flannel in her braid of coal-black hair, she was a singular picture of wild, savage, tawdry vanity.

"When a near-relative died or was killed, off went all of her finery; her hair was cut short and gouged in the most shocking manner; she slashed her breasts and body with her knife; black paint—which took the place of red-and-yellow—was smeared on her copper-colored face and she at once became a revolting picture of hideousness, painful to the eye and to every feeling of female beauty or taste.

"She literally grovelled in the dirt and covered herself with sack-cloth and ashes. Any deviation from a correct life, or being unfaithful to her marriage vows, was punished by her losing her nose which was cut off close to her face. The writer saw several of these cases before he thought to inquire the true cause of such an infliction.

"It was a terribly barbarous means of punishment or retribution, being a disfiguration for life and marking her ever afterwards in the village of her tribe as an object of supreme disgust, wretched indifference and neglect.

"On the march when changing camp, which was frequently done, she carried the papoose on her back, tended ponies, brought wood and water and prepared the family meal. In battle, her post was to the rear, bringing up fresh ponies to replace those exhausted, carrying off the wounded, and supplying ammunition, etc.; all the time, keeping up a shrill, piping, high-keyed yell or screech which, with the well-defined whoops of the bucks, made such a discordant noise or Babel of sound as to seem like a veritable pandemonium.

"When cornered she fought with all the strength of her savage nature and the desperation of a tigress, using her bow and arrows and six-shooter with both of which she was an excellent and most effective shot. There were few or none of the 'peace-and-order' loving members of the pussy-footed pacifists of that period, or members of the press, who often times referred to her as the 'poor defenceless (?) squaw' who would have cared to put themselves in her way under any conditions of battle—especially when she screamed in a perfect fury of rage. After the fight she helped scalp and torture the wounded, shooting arrows into their bodies and cutting off fingers and toes; even when they were alive, committing the most horrible and nameless barbarities and atrocities —too revolting for recital . . .

"This is the true reason why she often got killed when our troops got into close contact with hostile Indians. Not a gleam of pity entered her feminine breast . . . She was a cold-blooded, thirsty vulture, only intent upon her prey. As good as the warrior himself; fighting like a fiend with the same deadly weapons and mixing in with the former, it was then rarely the case that more or less squaws were not killed and wounded in our attacks upon their villages.

"There was little or no time for the false sentiment, courtesy or knightly gallantry in the face of a gun in the hands of an infuriated squaw intent on 'getting' somebody. Their attachment or motherly instincts for the children was very strong but no more so than the whites; it partakes, perhaps, and is more suggestive of the savage devotion and instinctive traits of the wild animal. The same animal instinct is seen in the white mother. It was while shielding and trying to convey their children from the village to a place of safety that they were sometimes accidentally killed or wounded."

The last sentence is a cover-up for all the Indian women massacred by the soldiers without mercy.

II

Toward the Sunset

The thermometers of Arizona have but four reading points: blood-heat, boiling, Phoenix and Hell.

Frontier news item

Whatever region was most recently reclaimed from the wilderness, was most characteristically Western. In adjustment of themselves to completely new conditions, the settlers underwent a process of Americanization. Men who had lived under developed institutions were transplanted into the wilderness with the opportunity and the necessity of adapting their old institutions to their new environment, or of creating new ones capable of meeting the changed conditions.

—FREDERICK JACKSON TURNER

Chapter 5

THE CONFEDERATES IN THE WEST

The Civil War, deadly to millions, and the cause of death for hundreds of thousands, took precedence over the battle against the Indians of Arizona and New Mexico. The whites had chosen up sides—Union or Confederate. The South held most of the Southwest. Jefferson Davis appointed Colonel C. John R. Baylor as Governor of Arizona. Baylor—a fire-eating, disquieting windbag, proposed a full policy of extermination of the Indians—for every Apache male—shoot him on sight; for every woman and child—sell them into slavery. There were many slaves and there was money in slaves—at least, if you were a slave dealer.

Jefferson Davis was cold to the Baylor Indian Policy and said No. Baylor gave dates and names of Indian massacres and sent on the long-haired scalp of a Miss Jackson, to be shown to Davis.

He (Baylor) wrote: "The general belief among the people is that extermination of the grown Indians and making slaves of the children is the only remedy. The system has been practiced in New Mexico. There is not a family of wealth in that country but has Indian slaves derived from that source. In fact, so popular is this system of civilizing the Indian that there have been several efforts to pass a law—making all Indians slaves for life."

It is to the credit of Davis that he wrote: "It is an avowal of an infamous crime!"

Arizona Delegate, M. H. McWillie, to the Confederacy tried again. "Captive Indian women and children are reckoned in the same caste as peons . . . This state of servitude, it would naturally seem is indefinitely preferable to . . . having them perish of starvation and exposure . . ."

This humanitarian appeal was also rejected. No one brought up Dean Swift's ironic advice, as to the use of the children of the poor in Ireland—serve them as tasty roasts and tan their skins for gloves. These disquieting disclosures point up a nation's blind animosity toward the Indian.

The Union recaptured some of the forts and it, too, carried on a war against the Apache, burning their villages, *rancherias, jacales,* running off or killing their herds. The Indians did likewise for the settlers. The Union orders were in the same spirit as the South's, in part.

"The men are to be slain wherever and whenever they can be found. The women and children may be taken prisoner, but, of course, they are not to be killed."

However, as Mr. Lincoln was preparing his Emancipation Proclamation freeing the Negro slaves, 1863's vote-catcher, for his running for re-election (few people remember today he went to war to preserve the Union, *not* free the slaves), it was not made part of the American Army's orders.

Mangus Colorado still was alive and to the best accounting he was over seventy years of age, a remarkably ancient age for an Indian. He was still large, still impressive and still held in respect as the chief of much of the allied Apache tribes. Now, as his joints stiffened, his old wounds ached (including the whip-scars on his back), the old man wondered about peace.

General Cremony, who knew him well, had a high regard for Mangus Colorado. "His sagacious counsels partook more of the character of wide and enlarged statesmanship than those of all the other Indians of modern times . . . Take him, all in all, he exercised influence never equaled by any savage of our time." Fulsome praise from a soldier who passes over the brutal and bestial side of the man he still labeled a "savage."

The Union needed gold for its war, so miners were encouraged to go out and find it. Soldiers were sent to protect them. (Karl Marx, already busy in the British Museum on his work, *Das Kapital,* could have seen here an economic base for the frontier warfare that would have perhaps delighted his sedate, boil-plagued life.) Wealth in our society remains the measure of most things and gold is the best example of wealth as power.

Captain Joseph Walker was protecting gold prospectors in central Arizona. He and a Captain Shirland, working with some Californians, decided on a plan to try and capture the Apache chief who was camped nearby. A Mexican carried a message to Mangus Colorado to come on down for a peace-talk meeting with the soldiers. Mangus and fifteen Mimbreno Apache rode out in their best. But on the trail Mangus Colorado sensed troops all around them, and he sent back his escort and said he'd ride in alone. He seems to have been a mixture of a man possessed of some psychic sense of actuality and an Indian fatalism.

When his escort had gone off, Mangus was surrounded by soldiers with weapons on the ready and taken to Captain Walker's camp. Colonel J. B. West at nearby Fort McLean, hearing of this capture, rode over at nightfall in a state of exaltation. A big fire burned, the night was cold and there, by the crackling flames, he saw the gaunt old Indian, stretched his full length in his blanket. West decided there should be a special guard over this special prisoner. Privates Collyer and Mead, with fixed bayonets, were told off to make the security of the chief their special task, their vigilant duty. Colonel West, from all the evidence, appears to have been a predatory, destructive personality.

What he said to the guards is quoted by an eyewitness to the scene (Clark B. Stocking, a soldier from California). Colonel West said, "Men, that old murderer has got away from every soldier-command and has left a trail of blood five hundred miles long on the old stageline. I want him, dead or alive, tomorrow morning; do you understand? I want him *dead!*"

The soldiers looked at one another in wonder as the officer walked away. One soldier stirred up the fire and placed his bayonet into the heart of it among the cherry-red charcoal coals. The chief either continued to sleep (which does not seem likely, for, while he spoke Spanish and had no English, he must have become aware of what was happening). Suddenly the soldier plunged the red-hot bayonet into the chief's leg. (One version is the searing of the soles of his bare feet.)

Perhaps Mangus tried to anticipate the attack and planned to leap up, but his limbs were stiff, he misjudged his timing. As he jumped to his feet, both soldiers fired their rifles directly at him at close range. Colorado fell, a giant crashing down to the earth like a stone falling from a height. The two soldiers bent over their victim and let him have the full contents of their revolvers.

Next day the chief's head was cut off by an Army surgeon who also removed the brain and weighed it. He announced it was even larger than Daniel Webster's. The skull of Mangus

Colorado is now a proud exhibit for visitors at the Smithsonian Institution, Washington, D.C.

In his official report, Colonel West stated the chief was killed in the classic fashion—"while trying to escape." There is no need in this history to detail the murder and exterminations of the Apache that followed the killing of Mangus Colorado. It was not war; it was massacre—a manhunt to wipe out the Apache like a plague of rabid dogs. The official orders were: "Kill every Indian man capable of bearing arms, and capture the women and children." The women and children were not always spared, and the white horror was matched by the red horror as Indians desperately took revenge with no hope of surviving the long hunts. The East saw it all as a drama in which they had no role; merely as readers of newspaper reports.

The official Extermination Policy was decided to be a failure by July of 1871. The American just couldn't kill Indians fast enough, and, unlike the Germans in the twentieth century with their fully scientific approach to the murder of civilian men and women and children by gas poison and Krupp furnaces, the Americans tried to do everything with only guns and burning. They lacked the ardor and the ordered science of the laboratories of the Germans to see people as mere items and numbers (usually tattooed on the skin of the arm), and to be liquidated as impure. The Americans began to work on a Policy of Conciliation when it was apparent they lacked an inhuman rancor for full and final extermination of human beings—even of a different skin-color.

The ideal of solving problems by war is a splendid game and a deadly one. It proceeds like a malignant growth. The wars of the Southwest had brought about a gradual escalation of Army forces. In 1860, there had been ten thousand soldiers actively engaged in the Indian policies of force. By 1862, it had risen to fifteen thousand, and 1865 established the total of twenty thousand; always the demand for "the final victory" for more men, guns, horses, cannon, supply wagons. Some of this was used against Confederates and white guerrillas.

The Frontier was served by brave and hard-schooled officers at most levels, with the usual proportion—always high—of drunkards and sadists. Many good officers did their duty and often died as a result of it. The military problem of the Frontier was that none of the major high-ranking officers was really of the brilliance that the Civil War seemed to bring out in Sherman, Grant, Thomas, Jackson, Lee, and some of the others. None of these served in any important way against the Indians; most never got west of the Mississippi. Grant as a captain had peacetime duty in a California fort; Custer as a good leader of horse in the Civil War was not a major talent and, embittered and embroiled with problems, not of the highest mental calibre.

So what the Frontier fought with mostly were hard-riding, loyal fighting men. Miles, Crook, and others—good as they were—were not the Civil War's top-drawer generals. Money, too, was hard to get for the Frontier fighting units. It cost millions (in the real money of the period) to keep troops, horses, wagons, cannon, and forts active.

During the Civil War, or, as the Confederates called it, the War between the States, the South recruited a brigade of Indian troops from "The Five Civilized Nations" and used them in Arkansas and Indian Territory against United States troops with indifferent results.

General Sherman, making a tour of the West, 1866, saw the Indian when "hemmed in by settlers, the poor devil naturally wriggles against his doom . . . All the people west of the Missouri look to the Army as their legitimate field of profit and support."

Lots of people certainly did; traders, agents, contractors, suppliers, bankers, freighters, railroaders—all derived hefty profits from Federal expenditures in supporting reservation Indians, or mounting expeditions against the tribes. It was on a small scale, in comparison with what politics and business made so rewarding among American industry in our later Asian wars; a giant outpouring of assets and resources undreamed of in the West a hundred years ago.

Chapter 6

THE REAL CHIEF COCHISE

Forts and troops in the West were often moved, but not necessarily where most needed, but, rather, where special interests could make a good thing of the buying and supplying. The exaggeration of the Indian troubles was already almost a cult.

General Pope wrote of fake wars being blown up into big ones. "Troops were immediately demanded, and then began an Indian war which greed of contractors and speculators interested in their continuance, playing upon the natural apprehensions of a people and influencing the press, makes it very difficult to conduct successfully or bring to an end."

Wrote General Sherman: "Each spot on every road, and each little settlement along our five thousand miles of frontier wants its own regiment of cavalry or infantry."

All this transpired while Cochise of the Chiricahua Apache was still on the loose. One of his major opponents in 1871 was an odd and dedicated figure, a Lieutenant Howard B. Cushing, given to strange immediacies of behavior. He fought, not so much for the United States, as in memory of the death at Apache hands in 1869, of his dear and close friend, Lieutenant Franklyn Yeaton. Whatever exotic dilemma was the basis of their friendship, certainly it was not a healthy one, and Cushing brooded and acted pretty much like the dedicated psychopath in his ferocious revenge against the Indians for killing his buddy. In three years of mental turbulence, he led his men on the thousands of miles of hard pursuit, and no desert, no mountain, could or did stop him. He fought to destroy any Indian he ran into on sight, obsessed with killing, burning camps, even stopping to stomp down and destroy the little patches of corn and beans tended by squaws. In those pre-Freudian days this sick man was looked up to, and a modern historian states he was: "one of the ablest, most tireless, most successful Indian-fighters of Arizona."

On May 15 with twenty-two troopers, Cushing was as happy as an unchained bloodhound on the trail of Chief Cochise up toward Bear Springs in the Whetstone Mountains. It is hard to believe, but the experienced Indian fighter led his men into the old Indian ambush: The Apache, waiting on the lips of a canyon he had to pass through. A sergeant said there were Indians about, but before the soldiers took any action, the Apache poured a volley of rifle fire, from hiding, onto the detachment. Then they charged on the run through the brush, crying out their terrible war yell as they came in for a fight to the death. There was a hard hand-to-hand fight with knives, rifle butts, tomahawks, and only the sergeant and a few men escaped. Cushing and the rest were left for dead to be mutilated and scalped. The mesmeric compulsions of poor Lieutenant Cushing were at an end.

General Grant moved toward an Official Policy of Conciliation aware that if you can't beat them in battle—you may outsit them at the conference table. On July 21 he sent a representative with powers to settle the "nomadic tribes upon suitable territories, and bring them under control of the proper officers of the Indian Department." (Colyer Commission, 1871.)

It was perhaps true—the official report states, "The Indians may have always desired peace with the Americans when they first knew them . . . until the Americans adopted the Mexican theory of extermination and by acts of inhuman treachery and cruelty make them our implacable foes . . . this policy has resulted in a war which in the last ten years has cost us a thousand lives, and forty millions of dollars, and the country is no quieter nor the Indians any nearer extermination."

Cochise was one of the few chiefs who smoked the pipe of peace with General Gordon Granger at the Canada Alamosa meeting. They talked in Spanish. He was offered the mountains he now occupied as a home for his people. We have an eyewitness report of this meeting, set down by Dr. A. N. Ellis, who took notes:

"Returning to the council-place they all, with the exception of Cochise, seated themselves on the ground. He remained standing to make his talk. While he was talking, we had a fine opportunity to study this remarkable man. Evidently he was about fifty-eight years of age, though he looked much younger; his height—five-feet, ten inches; in person, lithe and wiry, every muscle being well-developed and firm. A silver thread was now and then visible in his otherwise black hair, which he wore cut straight around his head about on a level with his chin. His countenance displayed great force of character and his expression was a little sad. He spoke with great ease and gesticulated very little for an Indian. As soon as everyone was quiet, he began his discourse by saying:

"'The sun has been very hot on my head and made me as in a fire; my blood was on fire, but now I have come into this valley and drunk of these waters and washed myself in them and they have cooled me. Now that I am cool I have come with my hands open to you to live in peace with you. I speak straight and do not wish to deceive or be deceived. I want a good, strong and lasting peace. When God made the world he gave one part to the white man and another to the Apache. Why was it? Why did they come together? Now that I am to speak, the sun, the moon, the earth, the air, the waters, the birds and beasts—even the children unborn—shall rejoice at my words. The White people have looked for me long. I am here! What do they want? They have looked for me long; why am I worth so much? If I am worth so much, why not mark when I set my foot and look when I spit? The coyotes go about at night to rob and kill; I can not see them. I am not God. I am no longer chief of all the Apaches. I am no longer rich; I am but a poor man. The world was not always this way. The Apaches were once a great nation; now they are but few and because of this, they want to die and so carry their lives on their fingernails. Many have been killed in battle. You must speak straight so that your words may go as sunlight to our hearts. Tell me, if the Virgin Mary has walked throughout all the land, why has she never entered the wigwam of the Apache? Why have we never seen or heard her?

"'I have no father nor mother; I am alone in the world. No one cares for Cochise; that is why I do not care to live, and wish the rocks to fall on me and cover me up. If I had a father and mother like you, I would be with them and they with me. When I was going around the world, all were asking for Cochise. Now he is here—you see him and hear him—are you glad? If so, say so. Speak, Americans and Mexicans. I do not wish to hide anything from you nor have you hide anything from me. I will not lie to you; do not lie to me. I want to live in these mountains. I do not want to go to Tularosa. That is a long ways off. The flies on those mountains eat out the eyes of the horses. The bad spirits live there. I have drunk of these waters and they have cooled me; I do not want to leave here.'"

Leave he did, however, when later orders came for them all to pack up—never mind what the general had promised—ordered to a hell-hole called Tularosa Reservation. Their answer was war, as more than half of the Apache followed Cochise into the mountains. Cochise, in a year, attacked fifty-four times, killed nearly fifty settlers and he captured women, cattle, and horses.

Few American writers of the period touched in any great detail in their published works, on the Indian sexual morality (or lack of it) as it differed from the white man's piously worded moral and social systems. Julius Froekel, a German, in his book, *Seven Years Travel*, is franker in his text on prostitution among the Plains Indians and their unihibited attitude toward sex. Of one Indian meeting, he writes:

"He had his wife with him—a fat, elderly woman whose face retained the traces of some beauty and the type of the better class of American families. This person had probably been stolen in her childhood; she did not dismount but sat astride upon her horse, like all Indian women, taking no part in our conversation with the old Indian chief. Some young females of the lower class of Indians, however—one a very pretty girl—kept up an animated chat with our drivers, and evidently tried to turn their coquetry to profit.

"Amongst the crowd we saw many stolen Mexican boys and girls who seemed on the whole to be not badly treated. A light-haired, blue-eyed boy, with a fair complexion and an open brow, must have come from a German settlement in Western Texas. When addressed in German, however, he did not answer. Another boy told us, in Spanish, that some years since he had been carried off with his sister from Mexico, and that his occupation during his detention consisted in herding his master's horses.

"In the fort I saw an old Iowa, the ugliest Indian I ever beheld. I can compare the expression of this fellow only to that of a hyena. But he had a beauty of his own: his mouth was drawn up on one side; one of his eyes was half-closed by the drooping eyelid, the other unusually wide open. He had a young Mexican woman with him whose whole face was daubed with red paint. She begged us to purchase her—her husband asking only two mules in exchange. He had, probably to enhance her value, expended so much red paint upon her face. It is characteristic of Indian bestiality that the hind part of the horse which the old brute rode was painted round the root of the tail as carefully as the face of his wife.

"On our journey the next day, a Kiowa, riding over the plain, came up to us, his wife and son remaining at a distance, until, seeing there was nothing to fear, he fetched them also. The man and woman had a clever and good-natured physiognomy; they then came up to me, inspected my carriage with much curiosity and asked whether I, too, had not a wife. On my replying in the negative, they offered to fetch me a girl out of their camp; at the same time depicting in a lively manner by signs and words her charms and beauty. At last the man placed the forefinger of one hand on that of the other, added an expressive '*Bueno!*' (good). 'This woman,' he said, pointing to his companion, 'is a mere common woman—*mujer car . . . a,* the other, young, good—*otra chiquita buena!*' So saying he held his fingers pointed before his breast. I replied that we were travelling further, without delay, and that I could not wait for a girl; to which he answered that his wife would fetch her, and in two days they would overtake us. On my positively declining the offer they both laughed and rode off. Probably their intention was to sell me the girl, perhaps a Mexican whom they had made prisoner. I might doubtless have had her for a few cups of well-sweetened coffee, as companion in our next camp; for these procurers brought us the next evening a woman, richly bedaubed with red paint, who first tried her fortune in vain among the gentlemen of our party, and whom I afterwards saw amongst a group of our drivers by a camp-fire.

"From numerous enquiries I made respecting the customs of the Indians, I believe that most of the tribes keep prostitutes on purpose; either prisoners, or women whom some peculiar circumstance had reduced to this degraded state. It is these women who are offered to strangers."

A fine description of one contact with Indians is given by Robert White:

"Mr. Anthony and I thought we would take our chances again, and burn lime on the Buckner, or middle branch of the Pawnee, about thirty miles north of Fort Dodge. We were well aware that the government could not furnish us with a guard. But the Indians were now supposed to be peaceable and not on the warpath. They had only captured a few trains, burnt a number of ranches, and murdered small parties of defenseless emigrants on the trail; still, they were *not* considered at war. All the whites were forbidden to kill or molest an Indian in any manner, although it was perfectly legitimate for them to murder us.

"Our positive instructions from the commandant at Fort Dodge were: 'Under no circumstances, no matter how aggravated, you must not kill an Indian first; let them kill you; then it will be time enough to retaliate.'

"Late one night, the quartermaster, Lieutenant Bassett, and his chief clerk rode into our camp and told us that the Indians were killing everybody over in the Smoky Hill country. They had travelled all night and laid by during the day, as they were unable to get any escort, all the troops being out in the field after savages. They left for Fort Dodge early the next morning, warning us to take the utmost precaution against surprise and attack. After the departure of Lieutenant Bassett and his clerk, Jim Wrighting, an old wagon-boss, and I started for a load of wood. We had to go about four miles down the creek for it, but still in plain view of our camp. Suddenly we saw a dozen bucks, each with a led horse, rise over the top of the hill. The creek was between us, and we knew it was exceedingly boggy; it could only be crossed at certain places; if these places were missed, it would mire a saddle-blanket. I said to Jim: 'What shall we do? There are some of the very lads who have been murdering the women and children over on the other river; shall we try to make it back to camp, or go right ahead and pretend that we don't see them, or don't care for them if we do see them?' He replied: 'We will take our chances and go ahead. I hate to run, and have the boys laugh at us.' 'Here's with you,' I answered.

"We had only revolvers with us, and away they came lickety brindle. I thought: 'Laddie bucks, you are tender-feet, or young ones, or you would not come tearing down the hill that way. You don't know the creek like your forefathers, and if you keep at that gait, and don't tumble into a mire-pit up to your necks, never to get out again, then you can call me a horse-thief. Then Jim

Wrighting and I will go down and chop off your heads just even up with where the mire strikes them, as did Jack the Giant Killer.'

"They left their led horses back on the hill with two guards so they were free to ride at will. But when they arrived at the creek, they stopped short with a little jerk-up, and I think one or two of them—those in the lead—got a taste and the other had to pull them out. Now they began to slowly and carefully hunt a crossing, which was difficult to find. Then they tried other tactics; they rode along and commenced yelling and gesticulating, motioning for us to stop, but our eyesight was not very good in that direction and then we lost them altogether. I said: 'Jim, these fellows have given us up or else have tumbled into one of these mire holes and we will have a time chopping their heads off when we go back.' Jim answered: 'No, them 'ere fellows was born on the prairie, and is as true to instinct as a buzzard is to scent carrion. They are sure to find a crossing and be down on us in a holy minute, like a hawk on a chicken, and we are bound to have fun.' You see I was beginning to get very ticklish myself—scared nearly to death—but did not want to let on for fear Jim would get scared, too. I knew I must try to keep my courage up by keeping up his, and I said to him: 'Jim, maybe they're only youngsters, and don't know how to shoot; they appear to be by the way they charged the creek.' Jim replied: 'Youngsters, nothing! Them is the worst kins.' Said I: 'Jim, perhaps they only want to pay us a friendly visit, and want us to go to camp with them and help eat their grub; what do you think?' Jim answered: 'More than likely they will take us into camp, but I will be at the taking.'

"This was just what I wanted. Jim's metal had 'riz', and I knew that he was ready to fight a stack of bobtailed wildcats. As the savages reappeared, I turned to Jim and said: 'Here they come.' 'I knowed it,' he replied. 'Don't waste any ammunition; we have got twelve loads apiece, and there are only eight of them.'

"Four of their number had remained in the rear to guard the led horses, and the eight had only delayed to find a crossing; but they trimmed themselves up besides, to be ready for any emergency. Four of them now dashed ahead, two to the right of us and two to the left, making a detour wide enough to keep out of range of our pistols, which they could plainly see in our hands. Then the first four come in, while the others closed up behind. We kept right on, however, until they finally surrounded us and we were obliged to stop. They held their six-shooters in front of them, but we had a decided advantage of them for we were in a thick, heavy wagon-box. They wanted to know where the main big camp of the Indians was. We told them they have been camped at the Cimarron cross-ing, but the soldiers had got after them and they had gone south. Then we pointed out our tents—we have five of them and they made quite a respectable figure at a distance—and told them it was the soldiers' camp. They evidently did not believe us, for they went over to the camp, bound the cook securely, whom they found asleep (why they did not kill him is a mystery), cut open every valise and took several revolvers from our tenderfeet, who had left them in their grips instead of strapping them on their persons. They carried off all the ammunition they could find. All the horses, mules, ropes and everything else that seized their fancy. Mr. Anthony and the remainder of our men were quarrying rock up in the bluffs, and had their rifles with them.

"'These young bucks were certainly of those who had been con-cerned in the murder on the other river, for we noticed dry blood on their hands and clothing and, as there was not an antelope or buffalo in the country then, it could not have been the blood of game. They had evidently strayed away from the main band and were very anxious to find them, or get back south of the Arkansas River, where they were better acquainted with the country. They were a little out of their regular beat where they now found them-selves, and that fact undoubtedly deterred them from committing further acts of deviltry.

"I have seen with my glass from the lookout on top of my build-ing at the ranch (Cimarron) two hundred or three hundred wagons and two thousand head of mules and oxen, all waiting for the river to go down so that they could cross; and I have watched a band of Indians charge upon them like an avalanche, kill the poor, panic-stricken Mexican drivers as easily and unmercifully as a bunch of hungry wolves would destroy a flock of sheep. Then the savages would jump off their horses long enough to tear the reeking scalps from their victims' heads and dash away after fresh prey. They, of course, drove off many of the horses and cattle. Sometimes the owners would succeed in getting the majority of their stock into the corrals and for days and weeks afterward, the miserable muti-lated oxen would struggle back to the river for water, some with their tails cut off close, some with ears gone, some with great strips of hide stripped from their bodies, others with arrows sticking out of them, the cruel shafts sunk deep into their paunches half-way up to the feathers. The Indians did not care anything for the cattle as long as there was plenty of buffalo; they mutilated the poor creatures to show their damnable meanness. The horses, of course, they valued."

Chapter 7

PORTRAIT OF AN INDIAN FIGHTER

The Indians called him *Nan-tan Lupan*—Chief Gray Wolf. General George Crook was not much to look at—a little, hammered-down man with crispy, unkempt whiskers. He was a skilled Indian fighter and he knew their ways. In July 1871 he was made Commander of the Arizona field. He was also a realist. He knew nothing is too fantastic in real life.

Of the Apache, he simply states: ". . . his villainies arise more from a misconception of facts than his being worse than other Indians. Living in a country . . . which will not support him, he has either to cultivate the soil, or steal—and, as our vacillating policy satisfies him we are afraid of him, he chooses the latter . . . being more congenial to his natural instincts . . ."

All the general had were five companies of horse soldiers and a troop of scouts. He prepared his men for some hard going. Crook enlisted Indians as scouts for the Army in numbers never before used—a sort of Foreign Legion of ruthless Navaho, Opata, Pima, Yaquis, Pueblo, even Apache, with a scum of half-breed Americans and Mexicans. As with the Legion, believing in nothing but booze and women, they had no codes, no future. They made very good soldiers when under stern control.

Crook also depended upon the mule, organizing pack trains better than they had ever been in the Western military service. (One packer, seeing him at inspection once, tried to hire the general as a mule driver.)

Crook, in size and skill, resembled the British North African general of World War II, Montgomery; with less ego, but with an idea that if supplies and more supplies were in order, he could fight a war. Attention to details made the two men effective generals.

Crook ordered an expedition, set forth a policy. His troops would move at once "to punish the incorrigibly hostile." He liked to fight in cold weather, when life was at its hardest and the smoke from the Indian campfires in the mountains visible. On November 15, he moved out for Tonto Basin, a plateau huddled among the high peaks of the Sierra Ancha, Mogollons, and the Mazatals.

The Indians there were not resigned to martyrdom in their alienation. It was a cold, bleak start for the Army; the small streams already solid ice and no water for the mules and horses. Bugles blew at two in the morning and, after the common indecencies of preparing for the day, and coffee and hardtack, by four the men were marching in the dark to meet the dawn. No halts were permitted until the sun was setting in the west. Crook moved firmly forward with no trepidation.

Attacks would be made all along the Tonto Basin by several columns, under the general plan of taking Indian prisoners if they gave up. Orders were to kill them if they didn't. No soldier was to leave the column. If his horse couldn't make it, he was to follow on foot. He finished with the usual last line: "Try to keep from killing the women and children." But it was not a firm, official negative.

The Indian chief Crook wanted was Chief *Chuntz* of the Tonto Apache—a cruel and splendid raider and dedicated killer. A turncoat Apache of *Chuntz's* band was to lead Major Brown and a battalion of the 5th Cavalry to his hideouts. There were also in the march the old enemies of the Apache—a hundred Pima Scouts under Chief *Bocon*—Big Mouth—and forty Apache sellouts. The attacking force came to three hundred and twenty fighters. Against these, the chief could muster ninety-four men, women, and children. The soldiers spent Christmas Day moving into the freezing mountain heights. The next night, they were picking their painful way up the dangerous gorge of the Salt River Canyon. The weather was deadly cold, and all extra gear and clothes had been left behind. Then the command came to lie low and stop talking. Scouts had seen fires ahead.

The scouts reported an empty camp except for some worn-out horses. The soldiers went ahead in the dark, always in danger of murderous falls down the steep slopes. Near dawn, a scout smelled woodsmoke. The turncoat Apache Nantahe moved ahead and led them to surround a cave where the chief often rested. A detachment that climbed up over the precipice sighted a group of Indians below, engaged in a domestic scene of cooking and at play. In front of the cave, there was glee and dancing in the biting cold. Indian village life in illusory indolence lay below them—as targets.

The soldiers began firing, killing six Apache; they never knew what hit them. The Indians at once made for the cave, leaving nothing in sight but the corpses. Nantahe called down to the cave for the Indians to give up. All he got in reply was a howl of rage. To make a direct attack by climbing up to the cave was too dangerous. Army sharpshooters were placed across the canyon facing the cave fifty feet away. The angle, however, of fire was ineffective and they began to shoot at the roof of the cave, hoping their bullets would be deflected down onto the trapped Apache. Men, women, and children were hit. The Indians began to return the fire. After a half-hour with no surrender in sight, there was heard the introspective death chant of the Apache.

Nantahe cried out: "Their death song! They're going to charge!"

Two dozen Indians, nearly nude, came pouring up over the lip of the cave, daubed in war paint, decked in their red headcloths and turbans. It was nearly a breakthrough, but rapid fire from the soldiers and hand-to-hand fighting leaving numerous dead stopped the charge. The survivors retreated into the black cave mouth. One lone Indian, who refused to go back, found himself facing twelve aimed carbines. He howled out: "No, no, *soldados!*" before a volley cut him down, his struck body bouncing about from the force of the mass firing. The shooting into the cave continued. Return fire grew weaker. Soldiers climbing up above the cave saw that below them a kind of natural bowling alley existed. Down this groove the soldiers began to hurl large, heavy stones which gained speed, then smashed into men, women, and children, mashing them into fearful lumps of the dead and dying. It was a hellish ten minutes of howling against human beings as ninepins; then the remainder of the soldiers began to swarm up and into the cave. Only eighteen people—all women and children—were still alive. Seventy-four Indians were mangled, broken, and flattened into death. One survivor was covered and masked by dead Indians. He was overlooked by the soldiers and later crawled out with a mangled leg, and escaped.

Chief Chuntz's band now belonged to the ages. But the chief, himself, had escaped being trapped in the cave. He and a few warriors were not in the cave at the time of the attack. They, with six of their women, joined the band of Chief *Del-she.*

Crook figured the two big bands of Apache left were on the topmost point of almost unclimbable Turret Butte, and on the crumbled landscape of Superstition Mountain. Reconnoitering units took up this hunt. Attacking via the mountain, Crook kept on the move, almost catching his prey. But the big bands evaded him. He settled for three Apache males and thirteen women and children.

The soldiers were suffering from the deadly cold—their long mustaches became frozen amber tusks, colored by their chaws of tobacco. The tight, ever-moving pursuit went on. A dozen Apache scouts with the Army, hearing trail sounds, captured an eight-year-old boy. He said he was sent down from the tribe with a message for the commander of the soldiers. He was frightened, but he blurted out his message. It was that the Apache wanted the war done with . . . they wanted peace.

The boy was fed and offered a pipe of Army tobacco which he gravely smoked. In the cruel weather he was given a soldier's jacket to cover his naked torso and told to go back and have the chief send a full-grown messenger. They would talk only to such an emissary. In an hour the boy was back with an old witch of a squaw, dirty and venomous. The soldiers still refused to talk to anyone but a warrior. The squaw was well-fed on beans and sent back. The third messenger was a very feeble old man of perceptible senility. Leaning on a stick, he came stumbling and tottering.

Major Brown decided to talk to him. His ultimatum was that either the Indians give up, or every last one of them would be hunted down and killed. Surrender—and *now*—was the only answer. The old Indian said it would take time to bring all the scattered folk together and it was cold here—not much of a place or room for everybody. If the soldiers would move out for Camp Grant, the Indians would collect themselves and meet them at the Gila and San Pedro rivers' junction.

At the river spot no Indians came in and it looked as if another mistake had been made in trusting a cornered Indian. Just at dusk, the old man (he was chief, it seemed) came tottering into the camp with a few Indian warriors. What would be done, he asked, once the Apache gave up? Major Brown answered that General Crook would decide that. The old man smoked his pipe, mumbled, and went off with his escort—a funeral procession of very cold Indians.

Next morning as the soldiers marched an Indian appeared and

joined the scouts. Soon more and more Indians appeared, and took their places in the ranks as if playing some kind of special game. They came out from among rocks, cactus, sage, and mesquite—many whispering: "*Sisquism, sisquism* . . . (my brother, my brother)." The chase of Superstition Mountain ended with a hundred and ten men, women, and children marching with the soldiers into Camp Grant.

But Turret Butte, with the combined bands of Chuntz and Delshe—a mixed group—was a problem still to be resolved. They had been raiding toward Wickenburg where they surprised a party of Englishmen (younger sons from stately homes) who had come to America to raise cattle and to mine the wealth of the New World. Most of the white men were killed, two being saved for torture.

"They tied two of them to cactus and proceeded deliberately to fill them with arrows. One of the poor wretches rolled and writhed in agony, breaking off the feathered ends of the arrows . . . but each time he turned his body, exposing a space not yet wounded, the Apache shot in another arrow."

No one balanced this deed by cruelty with the crushing of men and women to death with huge boulders. "War is kind," ironic Stephen Crane was soon to write.

The band returned via Bradshaw Mountain to Tonto Flat Basin. The soldiers were just a day behind them.

The basin is a huge, round mesa with steep walls and the way up —even today—is hardly accessible. The site could withstand a siege of months, far from any source of an attacking force's supplies.

Major George M. Randall and the 23rd Infantry set themselves to the task of climbing toward Turret Butte and on the night of April 22, 1872, were at the base, looking up, tired after the long trek. Dropping heavy gear and baggage, the men—in the sooty darkness—began to inch their way up the steep slope. It was impressed on them not to make any noise and all were warned to not break silence. It took hours of punishing effort, at a slow pace and crawl, to move to the top, which was reached at midnight. The Indians felt sure of their isolation. They had not posted guards. The glow of Apache fires was plainly seen, locating the Apache camp. Randall decided to rest his forces and attack with the first color of the dawn to the east.

Bugle calls rasped out the signal for attacks coming in on the Indians. The Apache could only cry out and try to seek escape.

There was none. The soldiers fired several volleys and a few Indians picked a quick exit by leaping hundreds of feet to their death, slamming as they fell into the base of the precipice. All the rest gave up, including the two chiefs, Chuntz and Del-she.

The remaining Apaches seemed to sense the handwriting in the smoke-signals. The Mojave Apache under Chief Chali-pun gave up, because the new cartridges captured from soldiers would not fit the muzzle-loading Indian weapons. As he shook General Crook's hand, a chief said, *"Demasiados cartuchos de cobre"* (Too many cartridges now of copper).

Crook, proceeding with a civilizing program, put the Apache to work farming, digging irrigation ditches under the watchful eyes of soldiers on several reservations. Each Indian wore a numbered disk, tagged like a branded Army mule. The Apache objected to the tagging, but had no say in the matter. The feel of the trap, they discovered, was the full measure of despair.

The worst problems on the reservations were the politically powerful white agents and traders who were there to get rich off the Indians. Tucson was the headquarters of the political ring of Federal contractors and officials. As power-endowed racketeers, they objected to the Indians being able to grow their own food. This sensible approach could destroy their fat income from rotten food and sick cattle they sold the government for Indians' use at very high prices. ("Hell, they'll eat anything they can bite through!")

These men pulled political wires; an order came one day removing the Camo Verde Indians from their fields and ordering them to the sterile waste of the San Carlos Reservation—that dreaded Indian Siberia. Policed by troopers, they were marched out toward their barren new site. The old, crafty look of Apache killers came into their eyes.

Chuntz, Chaun-desi and Cochine (*not* Cochise, as is often mistakenly written) were involved in an attempt to stab an agent named Larrabee for some official hanky-panky at San Carlos. They did kill a lieutenant. After this crime, the three took it on the run to the mountains. General Crook insisted that the chiefs left at the reservation go bring in the killers.

Worse was to happen. Freighters of supplies found it fun to get the Indians drunk. When refused more whisky, a group of Apache killed seven men. Their heads were sent to General Crook. By this time most of the Apache were back on the loose. Indian scouts caught up with the freighter-killers, shot them on sight, cut off all *their* heads and brought them in to empty the gory objects from a bag at the general's boots.

The three chiefs were all hunted down and shot. Chochine, in May 1874; Chaun-desi, in June, and Chuntz, in July. Del-she was killed in the same month by his own people, who had become part of the U. S. Army.

The Tucson Ring, powerful in Washington, continued its criminal activities against the Indians. General Schofield, in an honest huff, reported to the Secretary of War: "Indians paid for a large part of their rations . . . by supplying hay and wood [at] much less than before paid to contractors and that the contractors, their employees and customers, this lost the profits heretofore realized. It has been suggested that this may explain the Camp Grant massacre."

As members of the War Department were part of the supply system, wined and dined and paid off by lobbyists, suppliers and manufacturing firms, no action of any real value was taken to stop the graft. The reservations were eventually transferred from the War Department to the Department of the Interior and its Indian Bureau began to lean hard on the reservations. Cochise made a treaty of peace. General Howard took an oath that the Chiricahua Apache would be permitted to stay in their mountains. Howard died in 1876 and the treaty was broken. High-ranking Army officers in the West were, in the main, fair to the Indians on reservations—but powerless.

Bitter over the white man's lies, the Apache looked for new leaders after the death of Cochise. Everyone's eyes were on two chiefs living in the Ojo Caliente Reservation in New Mexico; Geronimo, and Victorio. Geronimo's true image has been distorted by publicity, flashy fiction and motion pictures. Actually, Geronimo was never a real chief—men merely followed him as a leader-type. Victorio was the greater man with genuine military talent. His military prowess (while not rivalling exploits of Hannibal crossing the Alps in his harassment of the Romans) was that of a skilled general. The tendency to ignore his feats in many histories is hard to explain.

At Sulphur Springs, the station of the Overland Stage in the Dragoon Mountains, the agent, one Rodgers, sold whisky to the Indians, and damned rotten whisky it was, too. By 1876, he had been frequently warned by officials about bootlegging to the Indians, but it brought in money, and he was greedy. The Chiricahua Apache were permitted to hunt in these mountains to fill out their rations, lean times having come on the tribes. Rodgers' bad whisky didn't help their mood. Harassed, tagged, cheated on their supplies, the chafing acid booze on their empty guts brought on the old Apache madness and, to make matters worse, they began to fight among themselves.

Two men and a child died in a brawl. Morning brought on the epitome of all hangovers along with a tribal lament for the dead. Two Indians went down to Rodgers' place to get "some of the hair of the dog" for a recovery-drink to still the tremors of hangover. Rodgers only gave them three fingers each in shot-glasses and refused any talk of a few bottles of the brew. He was worried: the Indians looked miserable and mean with bloodshot eyes and they also looked murderous and sullen.

They managed to frighten him out of a few more drinks, but Rodgers held out against providing enough bottles for a debauch. Rodgers told them to get the hell off the property; they weren't getting another drop of whisky. The Indians shot Rodgers, and for good measure, killed his assistant. Indians and whisky were a deadly mixture.

The Apache looted the station, taking whisky, horses, and ammunition and lit out for their hunting camp. There, Chief Eskina and the hunters were still feeling the results of the crackskull alcohol of the night before. Everybody got very drunk again that night and in the morning they rode out, howling war cries and ready for war. They killed whites, wounded, stole horses. The Apache Whisky War was on. They raided ranches and tried to get the reservation Indians to join them. When Chief Tah-sa refused, there was an intramural fight; half-a-dozen men died and Chief Eskina was left a corpse.

When the rest of the tribe was ordered to the evil San Carlos Reservation, eighty warriors and about two hundred women and children took off for Mexico, led by Chiefs Geronimo and Juh. On the way, they killed about two dozen whites.

In 1877 Geronimo was captured and locked up in the guardhouse at San Carlos. Luckily for him there was a political fight in progress inside the Indian Bureau. The honest head of the Bureau, one John P. Clum, sick of the dishonesty and stealing, was forced out and in the mixup that followed, somehow Geronimo was set free.

The Mescalero Apache were also in trouble: White cattle-rustlers were active among the settlers' growing herds and the blame was always put on Indians, supposedly raiding from their reservations. Reports to the Commissioner of Indian Affairs indicate that these horse thieves were also stealing Indian ponies, leaving the Apache on foot, where he was—he felt—helpless. Another thing that rendered them horseless at times (one report reads) is that when an Apache wanted drink badly enough he would trade his horse in for a quart of the most deadly and cheap whisky around. This sacrifice took place in a day when most general stores had a bucket of whisky and a tin-dipper on the counter for the customer to help himself, *if* he weren't an Indian.

The whites massacred Indian women and children on such provocation and when the tribe ran away after such an event, soldiers sent to bring them back usually shot to kill when they found them. The stealing of the horses of the survivors continued.

The Mimbreno Apache chief, Victorio, had been trained by Mangus Colorado, but he was a much greater man and more extraordinary as a warrior-leader. His deepest hatred was for the concentration camp at San Carlos, the name of which the Indians feared as later peoples were to fear the names of German death-factories.

In April 1879 Victorio and his people were ordered to San Carlos. Instead, he moved off into the desert with thirty warriors. The soldiers came after him but Victorio swung south into the dust of El Paso, crossed the Rio Grande to the Big Bend country south of Fort Quitman, Texas, and escaped into Mexico. He was joined there by three hundred runaway Mescalero Apache off the reservations. With a force of a hundred men, he began the long series of running-games with the United States Army that proved him a military genius. He made steady forays but protected his bases and outwitted the soldiers. Colonel Grierson reported to the War Department: "There seems to be a tacit understanding between Victorio and many Mexicans, that so long as he does not make war upon them in earnest, he can take whatever food and other supplies he may need for his warriors."

The system was a simple one. Herders and ranchers were permitted to exist in peace, as long as they furnished Victorio with a tax in food, weapons, and ammunition. The *ranchos,* the adobe *casas* paid up and co-existed, while both Mexican and American military forces planned Victorio's defeat. Victorio's scouting system was splendid. One historian declared: "It never had its superior in the history of any warfare."

After playing hide-and-seek with armed forces, as yet too large for them to face in battle, the Indians raided New Mexico. In need of horses they attacked the camp of the 9th Cavalry near Ojo Caliente in the night, killing eight soldiers and stealing forty-six horses with the loss of an Indian. For three days there was calm, then a posse of miners and ranchers was hit near Hillsboro, New Mexico, by a wild, howling, painted charge in which ten whites died and all their horses were captured. Warriors began leaving the reservations to join up, for this was a recruiting drive by Victorio. His band soon numbered a hundred and fifty men.

Lieutenant Colonel Dudley ordered two troops of the 9th Cavalry on their trail and rode into an ambush at the head of Las Animas Creek. He found the Indians waiting for him among the boulders. At the first shots two more companies of horse soldiers, under Captain Charles Beyer, joined the fight. Outnumbered, the Indians still held their positions. A daylong fight went on and by dark the soldiers had lost eight men and thirty-eight horses. The Indians had suffered no losses. Before morning, Colonel Dudley, carrying his dead and wounded, retreated. It was a clear-cut victory for Victorio.

Major Albert Morrow then took up the chase with about two hundred men. A series of running fights took place, one lasting two days. Three Indians were killed. Night camps of soldiers were continually attacked and sentries killed. A captured squaw led the soldiers to an empty camp. On October 1, 1879, Morrow followed Victorio across the border into Mexico. (As late as 1912, General John J. Pershing was also to follow another Indian raider of the U.S.A., Pancho Villa, across the border into Mexico.) The troopers were worn out. They were without water for three days and nights, down to their last bullets. On the Corralities River, the Americans lost a scout and two men were wounded. Their endurance was at an end. The soldiers began to retreat across the border, worn down by fatigue and more like ghosts than men. They staggered into Fort

Bayard on November 3, more than a month after crossing the border. Victorio was growing more powerful every day.

In Texas and New Mexico they hoped that Victorio was in Mexico for good. It was an unreciprocated hope.

Chapter 8

THE WAR GOES ON

"The weak have no rights," Nietzsche has said, and the Indian would have agreed with him.

The problem in fighting an Indian genius was well stated by a Texas Congressman, Volney Howard. "The Indians were well mounted and the most expert riders in the world—not excepting even the Arabs. You could neither fight nor pursue them with infantry nor artillery. Out of reach of the guns of the fort and these corps might as well be a thousand miles' distance. They never come up with the enemy."

Well—hardly ever . . .

The unshod Indian pony lived off the land or the desert. The U. S. Army mount was a grain-fed animal which had to be shod and cared for. A regiment of mounted men cost a million and a half dollars a year to maintain in active service, not counting cost of horses, pay nor weaponry. It can be seen that the economy and the strength of sudden attack were all on the Indian side.

The daily rations of a U.S. trooper took up bulky space and was hard to supply, while the Indian, if he had to, lived off parched corn, jerked or smoked dried beef or whatever could be swallowed and kept down. The soldiers' daily ration per man was nearly a pound of pork or bacon or one and one quarter pounds of fresh or salt meat, eighteen ounces of bread or flour or twelve ounces of hard-bread or hardtack, or one and one quarter ounces of corn meal.

Every hundred rations also called for eight quarts of peas or beans, or ten pounds of rice; six pounds of coffee; twelve pounds of sugar; four quarts of vinegar (to make spoiled foods eatable); two quarts of salt; four pounds of soap; one and one half pounds of tallow (candles or weatherproofing wax). And whatever loose chicken was around. Also eatable was the wild game, if there was time to hunt it. There are a lot of *or's* on that list, and the crooked army contractors almost never fulfilled their commitments properly. Much spoiled and rotten and dirty food was shipped to the troops.

Constipation was a problem, sometimes helped by Indian herbs or the Army medical man's pills. Needless to say, not all soldiers listed were fighters. There were blacksmiths, farriers, drivers, saddlers, wheel-makers, wagon repairers, gun machinists, herders, packers, and plain goof-offs and officers' servants in the Army. These never used a weapon regularly.

All the hard-riding Indian carried on one pony was himself, his weapons and a bit of dried food. If, when chased by the horse soldiers, he killed everything in his way, he had had his object lesson set by the no-good whites among the settlers.

Victorio now came up from Mexico to carry on his war against the whites. The stagecoach from Fort Davis was attacked, the driver and passengers killed and some of the horses and the coachwork used as a pin cushion for arrows. Telegraph wires were severed and the poles cut down or burned. War was back in the Big Bend. Water was also an Indian problem and Colonel Grierson sent a force to Fresno Springs, posted a thousand troopers, concealed around the waterhole, hoping to lure the Apache in as they went caroming around the land.

Next day at ten in the morning, Apache scouts were spotted. But a wagon hoved into view and the Indians at once set up an ambush for it. Grierson's troops came out of hiding to save the wagon crew. The Indians pulled out quickly and the whole band started for the border. Grierson took up the chase but he could not catch the swift Indian riders. They hid out in the wild Candelaria Mountains after raiding a few fat ranches. Victorio had food, water, horses, and temerity of purpose. Two Mexican forays against him led to the massacre of all hands by Victorio's men. Texans looked on indifferently at what the Indians did down there among "the hifalutin' dons," and a writer from Texas, C. G. Rath, even wrote out some unlikely folklore. "Neither wild animals nor birds had touched the bodies and it is said to be strange fact that no wild animal nor bird of prey will ever touch the body of a Mexican. If it had been Indians, negros [small *n*] or whites, the coyotes, bussards (*sic*) and carrion crows would have eaten them the first day and night." So much for racial nonsense of that period. (As a mountain-trapper said of a case of cannibalism: "Meat's meat!")

Early in a January day, Victorio and his people crossed the border into New Mexico. Every soldier within a couple of hundred miles took up the chase. Two sharp engagements took place between Victorio's band and Major Morrow's small force, first at the Puerco River, and next in the San Mateo Mountains. Then Victorio disappeared and no one knew where he was. Three months' search in wild land did not bring on a confrontation. But wherever Victorio found a ranch, a miner's cabin, a lone wagon, he killed and burned. He seemed in a black rage against the whites, murdering women and children without pity. A hundred people, by the records, were killed, and there were scores who never were listed.

After some brushes with troops, who finally caught up with him, Victorio headed for the Mescalero Reservation. In some mood of heightened sensitivity, in a catatonic state of killing, he needed contact with other Indians.

The dismal reservation folk had it hard both ways. The Army plagued them as dangerous and Victorio pressured them to join his war. The agency supplies often did find their way to Victorio, but not in the bulk that the Army claimed. He was alienated from all prevailing order.

The Army ordered all reservation Indians disarmed and their horses taken away. This cruel absurdity was official. Eight hundred soldiers marched to Mescalero to disarm the Apache, although the starving Indians had obtained permission from the agent to go hunting along the Rio Tularosa. Garrison was about to attack their camp when a messenger arrived, saying these were reservation Indians hunting with permission. So massacre of these innocents was averted. (To be judged innocent in time of trouble was often a sign of guilt—of not taking the proper side.)

Even the disarming of the Indians was muddled. Shots were fired by soldiers and the Indians suspected a massacre. Several Indians were killed. "Those who surrendered were placed in a large stock-pen in which horses and cattle had been kept. The refuse from these had not even been removed, and the disconsolate Indians were forced to put up with the indignity . . ." One historian wrote: "As many as could, here and there, ran off to the wilds."

Now a two-nations' International Agreement was drawn up for the largest organized manhunt in the West. General Edward Ord of the U.S.A. and General Treviño of Mexico joined forces to get Victorio. Victorio's raiders totaled two hundred and seventy-five warriors against two thousand American and two thousand Mexican soldiers, with uncounted posses of miners and ranchers.

Grierson was resting at the Tanajas de las Palmas Springs when he heard Victorio was on the warpath again. He called on available troops, only about twenty men in the immediate vicinity. On the morning of July 31 the scouts of Victorio were coming closer and *closer*. Victorio moved in for a quick kill. Grierson's son, home from a Eastern college for the summer, was with the soldiers.

Firing began, but the Indians did not close in. They felt they had a lot of time on their hands and could amuse themselves killing off the whites. In less than an hour a horse soldier troop, with Captain Charles Viele at its head, appeared from the direction of Fort Quitman. The party under siege mistook their relief for Apache and fired on them. Everyone was firing at everyone else as another company of cavalry showed up. Victorio—now badly outnumbered —pulled out of the fight. Seven Indians had been killed and an enlisted man was dead. It was a kind of deadly low-comedy battle, all confusion and all thumbs. Victorio made for Mexico but in four days he was back, ready for more fighting.

Victorio appears erratic but not cantankerous; a man who was rambuctious, predatory, full of turbulence. Of his true inner nature little can be known. He was now sixty years old and feeling it. Since youth, he had led a dangerous, beset life, hunted for years by large forces of horse soldiers—by Americans, by Mexicans—by civilians—ranchers and miners and any settler who could join a band and get a crack at "the Indian sonofabitch." His life was a dichotomy of terror and power. Victorio had been harassed from mountain peak to canyon mouth, had crossed vast spreads of arid desert, survived by finding water in almost impossible places. Back once more in his Mexican hide-out he wanted to rest.

But his warriors demanded action. They lived like pirates on booty; their only means of existing was to take what they needed by force. As the historian, Twitchell, wrote: "If Victorio had been permitted to remain at Ojo Caliente, it is more than likely that the terrible devastation following his removal to San Carlos would never have occurred."

Victorio's record was impressive and deadly, the historian continues: "He outwitted two generals of the American Army and one in command of Mexican forces. He captured from the Governor of Chihuahua, in one campaign, over five hundred horses. He and his warriors killed over two hundred New Mexicans, more than one hundred soldiers and two hundred citizens of the Mexican Republic . . ."

Victorio, with his best men away on a raid, made for a canyon in the Tres Castillos Mountains. There he walked into a trap laid by General Terrazas and his Tarahumari scouts. Victorio's party was composed largely of old men and women and children. As they entered the basin they were met with volleys of rifle fire. It was a battle to the death, the Apaches fighting on as their dead piled up. With nightfall, the firing went on. Dawn still saw the Indians fighting, but their bullets were now few. The Mexicans charged. Victorio, wounded, still led the fight. An Indian scout, Mauricio, crept forward and got Victorio in the sights of his rifle. One well-aimed shot rang out. The chief dropped. He was dead on striking the ground. Few of his band escaped alive from Tres Castillos. Mauricio was rewarded; presented with a fancy nickel-plated rifle for his deed.

With Victorio's death, the Apache lacked a great leader. Old Nana, twisted by rheumatism, carried on, raiding, fighting, retreating into Mexico when the chase got too close and hot. The Apaches had no great chiefs and they met stronger and stronger opposition on both sides of the border. It was merely a grinding-down process, the final merciless ritual of tragedy in sun and dust.

On July 29, 1882, a treaty was signed between the United States and Mexico, officially permitting forces of each country to cross borders when in hot pursuit.

Chapter 9

AN INTERVIEW WITH GERONIMO

General Crook, who had put down the Sioux in the Northern Plains, was back. He reorganized the Indian Police. Riding his favorite mule, Apache, he went and talked to the Indians. He listened to grievances; he got them to plant crops. He began to move all white miners and squatters off the reservations. Crook managed to get dishonest agents fired. He even went after more important government officials who condoned and shared in the graft. The Tucson Ring fought him with its strong political power.

He was a remarkable man of stringent principles, this General George Crook, and he has been too easily forgotten. Lesser figures, like Custer and Buffalo Bill Cody, have captured the attention of the makers of myths, who seem impervious to the reality.

Crook also had to deal with Geronimo, another historic figure who has been distorted by romantic writers of fiction and films. Geronimo's name was actually *Goy-ya-thle*—He-Who-Yawns. He was a small, comic-looking little figure, but only on the surface. General Crook labeled him "the Human Tiger." General Nelson Miles added that "Geronimo was the worst Indian who ever lived." Born about 1829 at the source of the Gila River, Geronimo was a member of several Apache groups.

In 1878, a scout named Tom Horn, who spoke Apache, went with two others to talk terms with Geronimo. (If this sounds foolhardy, it should be recorded that Tom Horn was later hanged for murder by white men.)

Here is part of Horn's report of his Geronimo adventure:

"Just as we were crossing the Bavispe River, we saw an Indian coming down a ridge on foot toward the Terras Mountains. While our horses and mules were drinking in the river, the Indian came and stood on the bank and leaned on his gun and looked at us, but did not speak a word until our animals were through drinking, and we rode out on the side he was on. Sieber and Merijilda spoke to him, and I did the same. He said to me: 'Who are you? I know these two men, but I never saw you before.'

"Merijilda told him who I was and told me, also who the Indian was. In talking to an Apache, you may never ask his name for no Apache buck ever pronounces his own name, and when once you know the custom, you will never ask his name. You may ask who he is, and he will tell you what band he belongs to, but his own name he never speaks.

"Well, this man turned out to be the one sent by Nana and Geronimo to meet us, and his name was Hal-zay. He was the first hostile Indian I had ever seen, and he sure looked the brave that he was. Tall, slender, and smiling, he stood there looking as unconcerned as you please. He was dressed in a low-cut breechclout and a handsome pair of moccasins. For ornaments he wore a belt full of cartridges with a long Mexican knife. Sieber said he was a half brother to Natchez, and that he was one of the worst Indians there was in the entire tribe. As he appeared then, now smiling good-naturedly and now laughing, he did not seem to be the bad man Sieber said he was. I will write later on of his death at the hands of an old man in Pedro's band.

"Hal-zay said Nana and Geronimo were waiting for us up on top of the Terras Mountains, and he told Merijilda to go to a place in the Terras Mountains called by the Indians Tu-Slaw. We asked him if he were not going back with us and he said, no. We then started on to where he had directed us to go. Sieber and Merijilda said that his fellow would watch to see that no soldiers were following us to trap the rest of the hostiles.

"It was about 10.00 A.M. when we saw the first Indian, and it was night when we got on top of the mountain and to the main Indian camp. There must have been one thousand or twelve hundred Indians in camp. Camp-fires were burning everywhere. Just when we got to the edge of the camp, an Indian boy about ten or twelve years old spoke to us and told us to follow him, and for the first time in my life, I saw this man [Geronimo].

"Certainly a grand-looking war-chief he was that morning as he stood there talking to Sieber: six feet high and magnificently proportioned, and his motions as easy and peaceful as a panther's. He had an intelligent-looking face, but when he turned and looked at a person, his eyes were so sharp and piercing that they seemed fairly to stick into him. Anyhow, that was how they looked to me, but I was a little shaky, anyhow.

"'How are you, young man?' said he to me in Apache.

"I told him I was all right. I might as well have told him I was a little shaky, for he knew it anyhow. He asked us to come over into the center of the circle, where we had the talk, and then he said to Sieber: 'Who will interpret for you?' Sieber told him I would do it.

"While Sieber could talk Apache very well and understand it very well, still he could not talk anyways near well enough to take in all that a man like Geronimo said. Geronimo then said to me: 'I speak very fast, sometimes. Can you undertake to interpret as fast as I talk?'

"I told him he had but one mouth and tongue, that I could see, and for him to let loose. 'Well spoken!' said he; and then he asked Sieber what he had come down there for, and Sieber said to hear what he (Geronimo) had to say. 'I want to hear you talk,' said Sieber.

"Well, the big talk was on; and how that old renegade did talk! Of all the wrongs done him by the agent, and by the soldiers, and by the White Mountain Apaches, and by the Mexicans and settlers, and he had more grievances than a railroad switchman and he wanted to go back to live on the Reservation. He wanted to be allowed to have a couple of Mexicans to make mescal for him and he wanted the government to give him new guns and all the ammunition he could use. He wanted calico for the women, and shoes for the children when there was snow on the ground, and any and everything he ever saw or heard of he wanted. Geronimo was the biggest chief, the best talker, and the biggest liar in the world, I guess, and no one knew this better than Sieber.

"Geronimo must have talked an hour or two and Sieber never said a word in reply. At last, Geronimo stopped talking, for he had asked for everything he could think of, and he was a natural born genius at thinking of things."

Geronimo had begun life as a pleasure-loving Indian, preserving a good appearance. He had married at seventeen, an Apache girl named Alope, who presented him with three children. While he was raiding in Mexico, the tribe was massacred by Mexicans. Geronimo returned to find ninety women and children had been carried off to be sold as slaves. His own mother, a wife and children had been brutally murdered. Only eight warriors were left. Nearly mad with grief, he hid his emotions. As he remembered that dreadful moment he said: "I did not pray nor did I decide to do anything in particular for I had no purpose left. I finally followed the tribe silently . . ." He did not say that he had just returned, himself, from murdering women and children. Geronimo was never the same again. He raided and killed as usual, but his nature was meaner. In 1876, he led a war against the Americans and was later arrested and taken in chains to Fort Apache. As previously noted in the mix-up of Indian-agent trouble, he was inexplicably set free and went back to the war-path. He was described by an eyewitness as "compactly built . . . dark-faced . . . one hundred and seventy pounds, five-feet-eight in height . . . Crueler features were never cut. The nose was broad, the forehead low and wrinkled, the chin full and strong, the eyes like two bits of obsidian with a light behind them. The mouth was a most noticeable feature—a sharp, straight, thin-lipped gash . . . without one softening curve."

When Geronimo accepted reservation life, he bided his time. In 1884, a new agent named Chase was installed at San Carlos. The Apache were drunk on *tiswin*, a foul forbidden brew. In May, Geronimo and his chiefs, forty warriors, ninety-two women and children, slipped off the reservation.

Chase caused some bloody fighting. Indian men and women were hunted down like wolves and Geronimo led his band into Mexico.

Indian raiders went out under Ulzana, a former Army scout. He avoided guarded waterholes by using the intestines of slaughtered horses which he filled with water, at least forty feet of them, wrapped around a warrior's pony. Such portable water supplies made them free of the necessity of seeking springs and waterholes. After wild raiding and killing, Ulzana started for the border, with two thousand troopers after him. He got away in a snowstorm and entered Mexico. In four weeks, accompanied by ten warriors, he had traveled 1200 miles with enemies on every side, killed thirty-eight persons, stolen and worn down two hundred and fifty mules and horses, and even when twice dismounted, managed to get fresh horses. His losses were one warrior, killed by the White Mountain Apache. This record is both amazing and appalling. The Apache had a moral deformity.

Crook began to experiment with new ways of fighting Indians. He began to depend more heavily on his Indian scouts. Most of his scouts now were Mimbreno or White Mountain with some Chiricahua Apaches. The scout usually wore hand-me-down Army jackets and a knotted loincloth, his legs clad in sagging legging-moccasins, his hair wound in a turban or held back by a headband. They made remarkably good soldiers and trackers and fought their brothers as keenly as they had once fought the white man. Whisky, gambling, women were their pleasures when not on an expedition. Their lives were without true identity; dispirited, mean, and sterile.

Captain Crawford led a mixed force into Mexico in November. Crossing the Sierra Madres, he penetrated deep into the country. But Geronimo had gone even deeper—on into Sonora. Crawford, leaving most of his baggage and supply mules behind, decided to keep going south. The Indian scouts held a medicine dance and each scout kissed the sacred buckskin of the old medicine man No-Wa-she-ta to the sound of evangelical chants and pleas to the Great Spirit. Most armies have this innate characteristic of assuring themselves God is only on *their* side.

By morning Crawford was on his way, mounted on mules with seventy-nine men, across the Haros River, and on the trail that led south. It was a grinding, dreadful expedition, traveling after dark, forcing themselves and the mules up the Devil's Back-bone—the *Espinosa del Diablo*—they struggled over the cruel crags, to kip into a hot, tropical stretch of palms and jaguars where snakes loitered in the lime-colored sunlight.

They went on like somnambulists, leading one another, to the brusque *he-haw* of the mules. The chief Apache scout sent back news at twilight, January 9, 1886, that there was a *rancheria* . . . an enemy village ahead. Both the Indians and Crawford moved up in the dark, crossing and recrossing a river, teetering along dangerous trails, until Crawford staggered out of line overcome with a stupefying fatigue. He had to be helped along by two scouts, his arms around their necks.

The hope of surprising the *rancheria* deep in the canyon failed when a burro's braying warned the villagers of the approach of the attacking column just as the sun rose. The villagers began firing, then moved on, leaving the empty village in Crawford's control. It was a gloomy prospect, to have come so far, with such effort, to have killed one enemy horse.

An old crone of a squaw approached Captain Crawford and said she came from the chiefs, Geronimo and Nachite, who wanted to have a talk. Crawford said he'd be pleased to set up a meeting for the morning of the next day. One wonders just what would have come from this conference which never took place. That morning, a company of *Seguridad Publicos*—Mexican militia—ran into Crawford's scouts and, thinking them the Geronimo people they were looking for, began shooting, wounding three of their allies. Captain Crawford came rushing over to the sound of action, lifting his hands and yelling, "Don't shoot!"

"*No tiran,*" replied Major Corredor, to stop the firing.

But some of his Tarahumari scouts, eager to join the action, had arrived on the scene, and one of them lifted his rifle and fired, drilling Captain Crawford through the brain. The American force began firing back. Major Corredor took a bullet in the heart. A Mexican lieutenant was riddled like a sieve and two Mexican soldiers died in the exchange. The rest proceeded to retreat at once out of rifle range. Crawford, amazingly enough, was still alive, but with his brain matter draining down over his face, death was near.

Placing the dying captain on a litter and a wounded scout on another, the American Indian scouting force, outnumbered two-to-one, headed north. Lieutenant Marian F. Maus, who was now in command, went over to talk to the Mexicans who had asked for supplies and food. Maus was held as a prisoner by the Mexicans, but was ransomed in exchange for six mules.

The party, in a sweat of mutual distrust, moved north carrying the two litters, making only two miles the first day. At nightfall, Geronimo himself came into the American camp to talk things over. The chief was in a fine position to make his points; this expedition was no menace to him so he laid out his grievances. Maus promised to set up a meeting with General Crook to confer with the chief in San Bernardino Springs. Later that night, old Chief Nana came in to surrender with eight Apache, among them, Geronimo's wife, suggesting some kind of domestic drama. This polyglot group crossed the border with the sad expedition. Captain Crawford had died on the torturing trail.

On March 25, General Crook, with a staff of scouts and interpreters and a couple of tamed chiefs, was at the Canyon des Embudos southeast of San Bernardino Springs, just across from Sonora. Geronimo, with chiefs Chihuahua and Nachite and a few followers, appeared. They didn't look too confident of their welcome and hung back, all but Geronimo, who was in a good talking mood. Everyone talked—hours of talk. The chief again repeated all the wrongs done the Indians and done to him, personally. There was some fantasy and some truth in what he said. Geronimo was a showman and he gave a dramatic performance. There was no debility, no lassitude, in the dry old body; no sense of sin or wrong-doing, either.

"I have, several times, asked for peace, but trouble has come from agents and interpreters . . . whenever I meet you, I talk good to you, and you to me, and peace is soon established; but when I go to the reservation, you put agents and interpreters over us who do bad things . . . what I want is peace and good faith."

Not much of his full day's talk made as much sense as this, but Crook let him ramble on. The next meeting took place two days later. Nachite and Chihuahua also spoke for the Indians. The meetings deteriorated into phlegmatic, dense, monosyllabic grunting. The official transcription of the meetings states that Geronimo finally broke in. He said: "Two or three words are enough. I have little to say. I surrender myself to you."

He held out his hand to the general, who shook it. The chief went on: "We are all comrades, all one family, all one band. What others say, I say, also. I give myself up to you. Do with me what you please. I surrender." (The chief was in his talking-stride again.) "Once I moved like the wind. Now I surrender to you and that is all." Handshakes around again. It looked like peace.

That night, a whisky-peddler named Tribolet wriggled his way into the camp and began dealing whisky to the keyed-up Apache. They had various bits of gold and silver loot to pay him with. Just before dawn, a committee of chiefs came and told General Crook the Indians were howling, dangerously drunk. Could the Apache please take care of the bootlegger in their own way? The General said respectfully no. When the officers got to the camp, the Apache drunks had set the grass on fire and were riding through and around it, crazy drunk, on their horses and mules. A heavy rain came in time to cool them off a bit, but in their morose, hangover stage, they were even more dangerous. Geronimo, figuring there might be big trouble, decided this was no time for peace or moving to a reservation with so small a band—thirty-three men and women and six children. He took off to the high Sierra Madres. Most of the drunks continued on to the reservation and Fort Bowie, envenomed by the whisky.

General Crook was also in trouble in Washington. General Phil Sheridan, not too bright off his horse, was now handling Indian problems in the capital. (There is always the problem: How does one employ a general in time of peace?) He canceled General Crook's terms already offered to the Apache. Sheridan telegraphed that the only terms were: UNCONDITIONAL SURRENDER, breaking all Crook's promises to the Indians.

Neither compromise nor mercy awaited either side.

The Indian experienced in war the fantasy of complete release, and in loot, prisoners and scalps, the practical rewards of victory. By the end of the nineteenth century, the Indian was an anachronistic survivor in a white world of empty pieties, resolute exploiters of a splendid nationalism, bolstered by the victors of the Civil War having won a country undivided.

The native white could face his political scene and its voices and shouters, aware of politics' breeding emotional sterility and moral emptiness—the excuse was that an expanding nation could not stop for niceties, for neat discriminations of good or bad, honest or dishonest—*that* did not create frontiers, expand the boundaries of a nation.

There is no doubt that the Indian toughened the white man when their cultures rubbed together in friction. The settlers and the soldiers on the Great Plains were not natural Indian fighters. The records of panic, massacres, and ambushes that plagued the white men in the early days of the wars tell us that. But soon the invaders were adapting dress, gear, thought, war processes from the Indian enemy, and it must be remembered that Indian scouts and police served their white masters well. It was often the Indians' own methods that were turned most effectively against them. Americans were capable of turning on women and children and committing atrocities with the best. Records on the Plains (and in Asia) show that. Old shadows do have substance and heirs. All native people begin to look alike.

Chapter 10

THE HUNTING OF GERONIMO

The crooked Tucson political ring of government contractors and grafters had beaten down General George Crook's original hopes of humane justice for the Indians. General Sheridan, acting as the ring's unwitting stooge, was not himself dishonest, but he stuck to his order for Geronimo and the Apaches: Unconditional Surrender. Sheridan has been labeled by some historians as the man who created the proverb: "The only good Indian is a dead Indian." He may have revived the line, but it doubtless goes back to grim colonial days, the fight for Kentucky, and other Indian country.

Discredited and besmirched, General Crook sent a message to Sheridan of which these are the last lines:

"I believe that the plan upon which I have conducted operations is the one most likely to prove successful in the end. It may be, however, that I am too much wedded to my own views, in this matter, and as I have spent nearly eight years of the hardest work of my life in this department, I respectfully request that I may now be relieved from my command."

Sheridan wasted no time nor entertained any thought of softening the blow to Crook—a dedicated soldier. The next morning, he appointed General Nelson A. Miles as Commander of the Department of Arizona. Miles did not like it; he was a good friend of Crook's. But as a soldier, he followed orders. Miles was a competent Indian fighter who knew the Plains, the desert, the tribes—he had filled the reservations with Sioux, Comanche, Nez Percé, Kiowas—most of whom he had run down and conquered.

His job now was to trap the wily Geronimo. He issued an order: "Commanding officers are expected to continue a pursuit until capture, or until they are assured a fresh command is on the trail."

Miles continued Crook's method of recruiting Indian scouts and of light traveling in fast-moving columns. His best hope lay in Captain H. W. Lawton, and a signal device, the Heliograph, which with reflecting mirrors in the clear desert air could send detailed information in Morse code across fifty miles of desert. Invented in Kipling's India, the device amazed primitive peoples. With a series of twenty-seven stations on mountain peaks, the Army could send a message eight hundred miles in four hours—something that would take a dispatch-rider a couple of weeks in the face of dangerous risks. In four months, Miles's heliograph handled over two thousand messages.

Geronimo was on the warpath again in the Santa Cruz Valley, invading the Peck ranch, killing the cowhands and outraging Peck's wife, torturing her in front of her husband until he lost his mind. As Indians respect the insane as holy, the rancher was set free, but the marauders carried off the thirteen-year-old Peck daughter. Captain Lawton took after the band, which was wedged between the Americans and a band of Mexican irregulars. The Peck girl fell off a horse shot from under her guard. She crawled into the brush. She was later found and returned to her father who, in time, recovered his sanity.

The Apache got away, with the exception of the warrior who had been carrying the Peck girl, who found himself without a live horse. He held off the Mexicans, killing seven of them with amazing marksmanship, hitting each one of them in the head. Then he escaped.

Geronimo went on to the border, killing miners, woodchoppers, ranchers, anything alive and human in his path. Captain Lebo, with a troop of the 10th Cavalry, ran him down in the Pinito Mountains. The Apache were shooting at Lebo from the heights, and the troopers pulled back, leaving Corporal Scott badly wounded. Lieutenant Clarke, a shavetail fresh out of West Point, made a run for the wounded man. Apache bullets were buzzing all around him. He got the wounded soldier up in his arms and carried him to safety while the target of every Indian in the neighborhood. The sharpshooter was certainly not there that day for both men reached safety. Geronimo's band moved on again and the soldiers didn't follow. The unique energy of these desert Indians was a phenomenon to the Army.

It was now a deadly serious hunt, out in force. Five thousand soldiers, five hundred Indian scouts—no one counted the hundreds of Mexican irregulars, ranchers and civilians who wanted to "get themselves an Indian"—were all after Geronimo. The situation was rendered gruesomely comic by the fact that the Apache band numbered only eighteen warriors, with their women and children an added burden.

On May 17, Captain C. A. P. Hatfield confronted the Indians in the heights between two rivers—the Santa Cruz and San Pedro. Hatfield charged and ran off all the ponies, but in herding the horses out, the Apaches ambushed him in a canyon, killing two soldiers, wounding two more and grabbing back all the lost ponies.

Lawton took over the hunt, moving his men a full twenty hours a day, with no time out, eighteen hours without a drop of water for man or horse. Without the heliograph tale-bearers reporting their tracks, the Indians could have holed up in a concealed place, but no sooner were they in camp than some signal pinpointed out their stopping place, and the chase would be on again. Geronimo kept on dealing death. General Miles quotes Lawton's reports of finding at least ten murdered Mexicans a day during the chase. Governor Torres of Sonora claimed the last stages of the chase cost the lives of six hundred people, which sounds like the usual official casualty lists issued in a war, for propaganda purposes only.

Months passed, and Geronimo was still at large with his few men, leaving behind human calling cards, disfigured, murdered, tortured in the most fiendish ways. He was still a cantankerous and deadly foe.

On June 6, Lawton again sighted Geronimo. A detachment had seized his supplies, much of his ammunition and the spare ponies. Geronimo was in serious trouble; coming up behind him was the bloodhound, Lawton, determined to pursue him as far as Mexico, and even into Sonora. The soldiers and scouts went through torments in that chase.

Part of an unknown soldier's poem gives us an idea of what it was like:

> The rattlesnake bites you, the scorpion stings
> The mosquite delights you with buzzing wings;
> The sandburs prevail and so do the ants,

And those who sit down need half-soles on their pants.
The devil then said that throughout the land
He'd managed to keep up the devil's own brand.
And all would be mavericks unless they bore
Marks of scratches and bites and thorns by the score.

It may not be of the quality of Milton's *Paradise Lost* but it's much realer.

The heat in the summer is a hundred and ten—
Too hot for the devil and too hot for men.
The wild boar roams through the black chaparral
It's a hell of a place he has for a hell.
The red pepper grows on the banks of the brooks . . .

Lawton went on climbing peaks nine thousand feet high, going down to prickly heat-parched desert areas with a Death Valley temperature; no one could touch the metal parts of their weapons without getting a bad burn. Pack trains were abandoned as the mules died in the fearful heat. How humans stood it no one could understand. But Lawton refused to turn back. He was one of those heroic figures the Army has produced from time to time who have the virtues of duty-first, and a determination—almost a desire—to sacrifice themselves and the men under them.

There was no water, and as supplies ran out, they went five days at a time without food but for desert varmints they could capture. General Miles, in his *Personal Recollections,* writes that their thirst was so dreadful at one point that some of the soldiers opened their own veins and set their lips with the blood of their arms. A slow loss of contact with reality seems to have seized Lawton.

On July 13, Geronimo was seen in a village near Tornababu, and while he again slipped away, most of the dwindling supplies and ponies of his small band were captured. Geronimo was making for the Torres Mountains, hoping that among the rocks, he could throw the Americans off the trail. But Lawton's Indian scouts—wolflike in the urgency of the chase—always managed to find a clue and the exhausted soldiers slogged on under the demon drive of Captain Lawton, who was ready to expend every man in his command, including himself, to get a whack at the Indians.

Meanwhile, back at Fort Apache, General Miles had decided

to move about five hundred Mimbreno and Chiricahua Apache out of the country and up into Indian Territory. A plan was suggested to him based on the fact that the Indians always came to the post corral when an Apache raid was reported, so that they could not be accused of being part of it. Why not, he was advised, pass out a fake report of an Indian raid, and when the tame Apache reported to the corral ring them with troops, herd them to the railroad, and ship them East like ranch cattle?

General Miles said of this suggestion: "Why, *that* would be treachery. I could never do that." (Never?) General Miles was also advised by Washington that his plans to move the Indians was against existing laws. Miles sent a delegation under Chief Chato to Washington to talk to the men around the Great White Father to listen and understand why they should be moved.

The Indians stayed in Washington, remained expressionless, and doubtless knew less of what was going on around them than ever. They refused to submit to being told where to go and demanded their rights to go back to Arizona. When Miles heard of their stubbornness, he ordered the train bringing them back to take them to Fort Leavenworth Prison. He instructed the outraged delegates that they must either act like "good, treaty Indians," or be treated as prisoners of war.

Washington, in a sagacious and tactful mood for once, wired Miles that the Indians on the reservation could be safely taken care of in Fort Marion, Florida. Miles reviewed his moral code, *then* spread the story of a false Indian raid. When the Apache reported to the corral they were at once surrounded by soldiers. They recognized the trap but could do little more than rage and cry out. They were ordered to sit down and it was explained to them that they were going on a journey.

Herded into the train, the men were silent and the women and children set up a clatter and a howling, a weeping. The train carried them off to the dismal prospects of the hot, unhealthy Florida swamps.

Geronimo and his band were not among them. For three months, Lawton and his tattered ghosts had trailed them. Not one Indian in the band had been caught nor shot down. Mounted on newly captured animals, the Apache made for Fronteras. They, too, were tired. Squaws came into the town and announced that the Indians wanted to give themselves up. The message was delivered to

General Miles, for Lawton was still toiling somewhere on the trail that, hot or cold, was never in sight of the prey. Geronimo was worn down but still free.

But he was willing to talk. Talk could be restful. His frenzied animalism was becoming tattered.

General Miles sent Lieutenant Charles Gatewood and a small party of friendly chiefs and scouts to contact Geronimo. There was also a Mexican plan to get the Apaches into town, get them roaring, falling-down drunk and do away with them in a Latin Massacre. General Miles may have thought this, too, was "treachery" so Gatewood was ordered to find the Indians before the Mexicans did. The peace party, with squaws as guides, carried a flour sack tied to a stick, hoping Geronimo knew what a flag of truce was.

For three days they traveled and approached the Apache camp on the Bravispe River. The squaws and the scouts walked in and delivered their message to the old chief himself. Geronimo announced he'd talk to Gatewood, alone.

Lawton had now caught up with Gatewood and warned him of the danger. But the lieutenant, with two men, went out alone to meet the chief, sending up smoke signals and firing rifles to indicate they were ready for the talk. Indians appeared, and at last the chief himself, looking very sour and more of a human tiger than ever. Peace pipes were brought out and were puffed. The chief asked what General Miles had in mind.

"Surrender and you'll be sent with your families to Florida, there to await the decision of the President as to your final disposition. Accept these terms, or fight it out."

The chief passed his hand over his brow and eyes and the officer thought he saw the hand tremble. Geronimo held a caucus with his Indians and came back with an offer of his own. They'd go back only to the reservation to be given some land. If not, they would fight to the end. Gatewood explained that their friends were already in Florida, which set the Apache back on their heels. More Indian talk among themselves took place. Then Geronimo put it this way: "We want your advice. Suppose you were not a white man—what should we do?"

"Trust General Miles, and surrender to him."

Geronimo said he'd have to sleep on it. He could be as full of deceit as a lawyer.

Next morning the Indians said they would go with Gatewood

to meet Miles and give up. On August 25, the journey back began. But a Mexican force of two hundred men appeared on the scene and it looked as though a fight between them and the Americans for possession of the Apache would transpire. Lawton fended off the Mexicans and Gatewood and the Apache took to the hills. The Mexicans let themselves be talked out of their prey under the guns of the Americans, and again in a grave, hesitant spirit, the start north was made by the soldiers and Indians.

On September 3, Miles and Geronimo stood face-to-face in Skeleton Canyon. There was talk, and the next day the last Apache war chief and his band gave themselves up to the agencies of the American government.

What Miles won was a motley band as he remembers them: "They were clad . . . to disguise themselves as much as possible. Masses of grass, bunches of twigs or small branches were fastened under their hatband . . . and also upon their shoulders. Their clothing was trimmed in such a way that, when lying upon the ground in a bunch of grass, or at the head of a ravine, if they remained perfectly quiet, it was impossible to discover them as if they were a bird or a serpent . . ."

At Fort Bowie under the eyes of armed troops the Indians were loaded on a train and their strange journey began. Several friendly Indians—scouts—who had helped the Army in the surrender were also—to their shock—loaded onto the train and sent off to Florida. (Two of them were held prisoner for twenty-six years. In 1931 they sued the government to collect back pay as Army Scouts at $2 a day. The Secretary of War admitted their claims but added, "There were no funds available to pay them.")

One daring, unquiet Apache prisoner escaped from the train after it passed St. Louis. By lying low and traveling in great misery and hunger, taking a full year for his trip, he managed to work his way back to the San Carlos Reservation without a map and without being seen by a single white man. Here he kidnapped an Indian girl, lived with her in the mountains for a few months, and then murdered her. He appears to have been a remarkable brute. He came back for another girl, and in all, repeated the girl-stealing several times, with the same cruel results. Only one girl escaped and got back to tell her tragic story. In time, he was reported killed.

And Geronimo?

After several prisons, he settled with his survivors at Fort Sill, Indian Territory. At the St. Louis Fair in 1904 he was on exhibition—sold the brass buttons from his coat and photographs of himself; even put on a top-hat and posed behind the steering wheel of an early motorcar. He died in 1909, already a garrulous legend.

The last Apache war party on record took off in April of 1930, the year of the Great Depression under Hoover. A newspaper item records that "riding out of their wilderness hide-out, high in the Sierra Madre mountains, a band of wild Apache scalped three persons on April 10th, in a settlement near Nacori Chico . . ."

V. M. White, a mining engineer, said they were led by Geronimo III, the grandson of the original Geronimo, the old war chief. One wonders if some place today there is not a Geronimo IV or Geronimo V . . . If so, he has, it appears, become too smart to go up against napalm, air bombings and Army helicopters with heavy-caliber gun power.

III

Uprising in Minnesota

We vew this passage across the continent as affording immence advantages to the fir trade but fear that advantages wich it offers as a communication for the productions of the East Indias to the United States and thence to Europe will never be found equal on an extensive scale to that by the way of the Cape of Good Hope. still we believe that many articles not bulky brittle nor of a perishable nature may be conveyed to the U'. States by this rout with more facility and less expence than by that at present practiced.

*— Captain Meriweather Lewis
to President Jefferson,
in his own spelling . . .*

Chapter 11

A CHRISTIAN INDIAN

A look at the maps or the endpapers will show that the wars on the northern plains began in 1862 in what is now Minnesota, around a fort called Ridgeley, located in a large section denoted as the Department of the West. This region was mostly forest country with hunting trails and a few wagon paths cut through the brush and big trees. It was sparsely settled by farmers, each of whom had—with his sons, if he had them—cut down the trees, piled them in heaps, burned them, plowed the land and put in crops. There were cattle and horses and houses—a primitive yet satisfactory frontier way of life. The Indians in the north were Chippewa, and all around were the proud Santee Sioux, who lived under a treaty to keep the peace in return for supplies and food. There were few forts, for the Indians were seen to be friendly. The main line of forts was further south, beyond Minnesota—Fort Laramie, Fort Kearny, Fort Leavenworth. The farmers and settlers were mainly hard working, "from sunup to sundown." The soldiers at Fort Ridgeley, bored by duty and drill, were not expecting any trouble nor wanting any.

Some of the Indian chiefs had become churchgoing Christians, not merely for show, but because they felt the white man's God might have magic, and the Indian believed in magic. Some even wore white man's clothes, for clothes, too, have magic.

If the soldiers and the settlers did their work, performed their duties and wanted peace, the Indian agents and traders, who exploited the Indians, wanted only profit. They were political appointees and the government in Washington did nothing to change a situation that smoldered and was set to explode into open war.

"If they are hungry," said Andrew Myrick, Indian agent at the Lower Sioux Agency near Fort Ridgeley, Minnesota, "let them eat grass for all I care."

It is downright unlikely that he knew a French queen had once said that about cake. This sally got a good laugh among the frontier hangers-on at the agency. But one who didn't laugh was the Indian Chief Little Crow, son and grandson of Sioux chiefs and of famous warriors who had been forced to accept the Mendota Treaty of 1851 where the best hunting-grounds had been lost. This larceny was called "ceded land" and the grafters and bagmen the government in Washington sent out to run the agency cheated the Indians through the promised food they never got. As for the wormy, mealy flour, the rancid bacon they did get—fortunes were made on that. The whisky sold them was doctored and miserable stuff. The women of the tribe, too often seduced, had turned into sluts and whores, so that the camps were crawling with fatherless half-breed children. There was little hope things would improve. To the land-greedy white man, the Indian was expendable and in the way. The dreamers and makers of the nation were looking westward to an expanding continent of settlements, mines, orchards, great vistas of wheat. The thunder of the buffalo herds would soon sound fainter in the hungry lodges of the treaty-tied Indians.

It was August of 1862, and while deadly civil war between the white men held the North and South gripped in a gigantic and ferocious struggle on the other side of the mountains, Chief Little Crow sat brooding in despair, in hurt pride, in anger, at the indignities heaped on the Sioux.

He had tried to change as the times had changed—the white man's way seemed best—had given up the drinking of whisky, had insisted the tribes give up the drinking, too, of traders' rotgut, that firewater that melted the Indian brain and made him foolish and helpless in dealing with the whites. Little Crow had even sent for the Reverend Williamson, a Christian missionary, to come to teach the Indian "the white man's way" of that Jesus Christ the soldiers used as an oath. A last insult had been visited on him when Little Crow had gone to Indian Agent Myrick to ask where were the promised supplies for the hungry Sioux. The answer was painted in pain on Little Crow's brain: "Let them eat grass for all I care."

Little Crow made no unconditional surrender to destiny. He gave up his white man's dress, turned his back on the New Testament. (As a later philosopher was to say, he had seen Christianity but met no Christians.) He tore off the black broadcloth coat, the high, white, starched collar and dark cravat in which he had been photographed by a frontier cameraman. He had kept his two heavy braids of soot-black hair and now he became again a blanket Indian. The word went out. *It was to be war against the whites.*

Along the banks of the Minnesota River, bands of painted bucks moved in impenetrable darkness full of tense expectancy, armed with bows and arrows, a few smooth-bore trade muskets, a stolen horse pistol or rifle, lances, clubs, and tomahawks—many of good English steel brought down from Canada. So war came. Painted, lean, hungry, savage rage was unleashed.

The farms had been hacked out in the wilderness; many Germans had come to the edge of the frontier. They were hard-working, phlegmatic fertile people—not given to drink and horseplay like loafers at the agency, the pelt hunters and the frontier ne'er-do-wells. It was Sunday and the farms were forty miles from the agency near the fort. The folk sat at dinner—as the midday meal was called—the evening meal was called supper.

Three of the German families ate together—blond, burly, solemn. They sat at the rough-hewn table piled with the best available version of the old country cuisine. One of the diners was a woman accompanied by her little girl. She was the wife of one of the farmers present. The sound of unshod pony hoofs drummed on the hard-packed earth outside. The slab door was banged back and four painted Sioux crashed into the farmhouse room. Rifles were fired into the surprised Germans and knives flashed. It was brutal, savage murder. The bodies of the farmers, the woman, the child, were hacked; scalps were peeled off heads after a circling of the skin with a blade point. Mouth still held unchewed food. It was barbaric, direct and dreadful. The Minnesota Massacres had begun and the pattern was the usual Indian reaction when their emotions passed the pressure-point.

It was the first of many such attacks carried out that day by war parties, slashing and slaughtering among the clearings. The main attack was destined for the Lower Sioux Agency. All night the war parties of Sioux had been moving into position around the cluster of huts and wagon-sheds, stores, piles of timber, hay rakes, manure piles, corrals—all the usual frontier post buildings cluttered, carelessly put together, slovenly cared for. Monday came with signs of a good, rosy day of early August at its best.

Just as dawn made the sky clear and crystal to the east, the howling war cries of the Indian war party broke the agency's morning calm. The sound of rifle fire woke sleepers. There was little comprehension among the agency hands of what was going on. The traders, clerks in nighshirts ran to the doors of their cabins to see what was happening in the packed dirt street. Most of them died there, tacky with sleep; died from the fire of a well-planned ambush. Andrew Myrick, whose cynical remark had been the spark that set fire to the revolt, was slaughtered in the doorway of his store. His mouth, when he was found later, was stuffed with grass.

Clerks and traders—eight in all—died across their counters among their trade goods. Blood from stained calico bolts dripped on yardsticks. The Sioux, heavily painted, were whooping and screaming, hideous to see in their war colors, hysterical in delight as they began to break open food packages, rummage for ammunition. There was always a shortage of powder and lead, of cartridges, and of good rifles. They also found the whisky. This free drinking gave the stunned white survivors of the dawn attack time to reach the river on the run. Fifty white men, women, children fled toward the ferry, run by a Hubert Miller, who brought his rough barge into position. He took most of them across in several trips—they, chattering or cursing in fear; he, himself, dying from an Indian bullet as the Sioux began to organize the chase of the fugitives. All the agency people who had not made it to the ferry crossing were hunted down by howling bucks and killed and scalped.

Fort Ridgeley was fifteen miles away. It was for the agency personnel a journey through an August hell, as the panting, half-naked people, bush-torn survivors, ran, mostly on bare feet, ahead of the Indians whose doeskin moccasins came closer as their war cries echoed in the thickets. Seven whites were overtaken, chopped down and left, crumpled and broken shapes on the trail.

The stragglers came up to the fort wide-eyed, crying out the dreadful details of what they knew of the Indian uprising that had begun with no overtures. The telegraph key at the fort clicked off the news eastward and the citizens there nodded and clucked their tongues and repeated the old saw: "Only good Indian is a dead Indian."

Meanwhile, the chasm between the two races was too wide for jumping across. Raiding increased among the white settlers. Men, women, and children died as bands of Little Crow's warriors con-

tinued to raid farms, to cut off startled settlers, ambush woodcutters and herdsmen. They put rifle and knife and tomahawk to
full use. Horses and women they took captive when they could,
for these were the prime natural booty of Indian warfare. Some
children were killed. A few were permitted to come along with
their screaming mothers, carried off for gang-rape, slavery, concu-
binage in some Sioux lodge. The Indian, long before napalm, made
total war. It was his ritual right, his sense of tribal sportsmanship to
take horses and women—in key with his vision of the world, his
guiding spirits.

Deadly work was done in Renville County, Lake Shetek. Every
white—no matter what age or sex—was hunted down near the Lower
Agency. More than two hundred victims lay mutilated and dead in
mass slaughter, or in isolation and inertia, surprised alone.

At the Lake Shetek gathering of cabins, one family, the East-
licks, suffered dreadfully. At first they hid out in the lake rushes.
Then the Indians, braying like bloodhounds, ran them to ground
and killed the father and three of the five sons. Mrs. Eastlick managed to hide the baby, Johnny, in the reeds, leaving him in the
care of the only other surviving child, her young song, Merton, making him promise: "Never leave Johnny, even if you die together."

The Indians flushed her from cover, carried off Mrs. Eastlick.
Merton escaped, carrying the baby. He went on wandering the
wilderness for days, living off berries—emaciated, feverish, but
carrying Johnny. The two children were found by white scouts
forty miles from the place the massacre had happened. The flesh
was worn from the soles of Merton's feet. For days he could not
utter an intelligent sound. But baby Johnny was fine. Mrs. Eastlick later escaped from the Indians and was found by a mail
rider madly muttering to the trees that her family was dead, *dead*.
She survived to be reunited with her two surviving sons. They
were tough people, these pioneers. Their sense of pain and agony
was like ours, but unlike our neurotic age, they expected little help
but from neighbors and they saw the futility of long lamenting or
debate.

Frontier figures of the number of dead settlers in the Little Crow
uprising are hard to come by. Many of the dead were never found;
many a solitary farmer or hunter was never missed by anyone.
The Minnesota Historical Society figures list the dead settlers in

Renville, Dakota Territory, and Big Stone Lake, Brown County and Lake Shetek and other frontier counties as 644.

Of captives of the Sioux, there were supposed to be several hundred. After one battle against some Sioux war bands, two hundred and sixty-nine horrified, tormented, crazed prisoners were rescued. A hundred more were later recovered. The story of rescued wife or daughter, pregnant with an Indian child, were dramas that never found a William Faulkner. No one knew how many just vanished to become concubines, slaves, sport for torture, staked out to die by bits, screaming (staking out was an Indian spectator-sport), and some whose scalps, twisted and smoked on willow hoops in the lodges of Little Crow's warriors, became fringe designs, décor for shields, lance shafts, and legging trimmings.

So began the great wars—the settlers' martyrdoms—of the prairies and the plains, the wars of the white and the Indians. It was not to end formally until 1907 when the last of Geronimo's Apache band in exile in Florida and Alabama were permitted to return to settle on the Mescalero Reservation in New Mexico. The very last of the old war chiefs who had fought and killed whites was old Chato, who died in August 1934 at the age of ninety.

There was to be a great deal of fighting, bravery, cruelty as the ever-tightening ring of white man's pressures crowded in on the tribes, the Sioux, Apache, Cheyenne, Nez Percé, Comanche, Kiowa, Arapaho, Modoc, and all the others. Long years would pass before what was bad would be better, and what was unfair to the Indian would be somewhat tempered by a little wisdom, free of politics and dishonesty. The Indian had to learn to live by dispensing with hope.

Meanwhile, there was a lot of history to be consumed before the weapons and gear of the Indian wars became wall decorations in museums and collections. Little Crow and the Sioux had only started their war. And the horse soldiers and white settlers were recovering their breath and loading their weapons.

Chapter 12

WAR WITH THE SIOUX

The Minnesota uprising went on—the sneak attacks on the settlers by Little Crow and his bands—beyond the destruction of the Lower Sioux Indian Agency. The refugees from the agency found Captain John S. March in command of Fort Ridgeley. When the captain heard their story he sent a rider hell-for-leather to Fort Snelling a few miles away with the news of the massacre. He, himself, mustering most of his men—forty-six in all, with an interpreter, Peter Quinn—started out for the agency in wagons, leaving the fort thinly defended. They soon met panting, screaming fugitives and passed by bodies of dead whites, scalped and mutilated. Captain March was brave but no Indian fighter. Leaving the wagons, he led his apprehensive force to the ferry, across from which the bright orange flames of the burning agency licked at the sky. Perverse human impulses of wonder, fear, the sudden disparity between being alive and dead held them.

Except for the crackling fire, the brush sound, there was a great silence. Captain March saw a figure that stood out against the fire. A man. The soldiers knew him as a minor Sioux chief, White Dog. He now made friendly gestures, urging them to come on over to his side. The captain hesitated. White Dog then made a sweeping signal and suddenly there was flanking fire poured into the soldiers and the sound of hair-raising Indian war whoops. Captain March had walked directly into an ambush of two hundred Sioux. The poor interpreter died at once, riddled by slugs. Five soldiers were killed with him at the first volley. After a return of fire by his men, March ordered a quick pullback in the dense white smoke, away from the howling thickets of warriors. The soldiers stood firm among some trees by the river but their position was deadly. The Indian fire kept up. Men were pop-eyed with shock. Captain March had courage, if not sense or knowledge of Indian fighting.

He decided boldly to move over to the other bank. The men shrugged at the idea. To show his men how easy it would be, Captain March plunged alone into the river. The fast current grabbed at him and his men, in horror, saw him drown before their eyes; an arm of blue, a swirl of eddies and he was gone. Without a leader the men started for the fort, firing into the brush, harried every foot of the way by Little Crow's bucks. Half of the soldiers—twenty-four of the forty-eight men who had started from the fort—were dead.

Terror, not discipline, held Fort Ridgeley that night under Lieutenant Tom Gore. He had few men left and too many women and children on his hands, all in a fort no one had yet tested by direct assault. It seemed reasonable that the Indians would capture the women by morning. Most of them begged to be spared rapacious dishonor—rape being part of tribal culture—by the mercy of a bullet in the head from a friend or soldier.

Morning saw more fugitives coming in, bringing dreadful tales. Still, Little Crow did not attack. At the fort in charge was a Captain Gere, taut, waiting for the war cries, the direct assault. The women stared or became hysterical; the children cried. A few—very few—like an old soldier, Sergeant Jones, expected overwhelming disaster.

What delayed the expected Indian attack was that the chiefs could not get the Indians to give up looting and mass in force for the united attack on the fort. Now it was too late for the Indians. The message had gone through to Fort Snelling and the first reinforcements were seen approaching from the north under Lieutenant Tim Sheehan. A cry of: "Thanks to God! the Army!" went up from the fort. Other messages had gone to other nearby forts. Would they send help?

Soon another detachment of soldiers came, dog-tired, to the fort after a forty-mile all-night march from the south. The soldiers were mostly fuzzy-faced young recruits, not trained fighters. But at least Sheehan could now command a force of 180 rifles to protect the 250 settlers packed in the fort. The Indians would attack soon and he placed his men on the ready for the Indian rush being planned out there among the shrub and timber. The day was hot; the humanity grew rank in smell as many stared over the walls.

On the morning of August 20 a red horseman came up to the west side of the fort and signaled for a parley. It was Little Crow gesturing. He wanted to talk. But it was a ruse: He was detracting attention from an Indian rush on the fort from the other side where an outpost had been set up. War cries and rifle fire announced that attack, and Little Crow—slightly wounded—sawed his horse's head around and rode fast for shelter. The savage, loud Sioux rush overran the outpost and captured houses outside the fort. Sheehan was losing men inside the fort from intense Indian fire. He found his newest raw recruits beginning to panic. Cursing, haranguing in anguish, he tried to rally them as the Indians attacked the walls. The younger soldiers, in utter confusion and fear, began to pull back to the south buildings where the refugees were packed together, bug-eyed and in terror. The Indians were at the walls and would soon be inside.

The old hard-tack soldier, Sergeant Jones, was a gunner with wife and children in the fort. He had found some ancient rusty cannon, obsolete and in bad repair, and he had spent the dull weeks of summertime, the entire past season, repairing these cannon and training a crew to use them. Now as the Indians had the fort almost in their howling power and the screams of the women begging for death ran through the demoralized fortifications, Sergeant Jones rallied his makeshift gun crew and ordered the old cannon loaded.

The Indians were in the fort, the recruits lost to resistance were moving to the south side of the fort. Sergeant Jones cried out, "Aim for their center! Rapid fire!"

The motley collection of old iron spewed out a blasting of nails, cannon balls, solid shot, and canister. The white, choking smoke of gunpowder whirled up to hide detail and Sergeant Jones exhorted the men with curses to reload in a hurry. Twice more the cannon boomed out, spewing the old iron at the Sioux. At the last discharge, they broke. They never liked to face "wagon guns." Little Crow, because of his wound, set a minor chief, Mabkato, in command. He had no heart for another whooping rush into the cannon's mouth.

The Indians attacked again in the haze of morning, but the cannon kept them from overrunning the entire place. Fort Ridgeley was not to be taken. Indian losses were high. Little Crow had taken his first defeat in his war against the whites who were shaky of the horror of war cries, the dreadful appearance of the painted Indians, the stories of torture and rape. The settlers remained behind the fort walls. The Sioux bands roamed the brush just out of rifle range with a mocking temerity of purpose.

A handful of miles downriver was a town—the German collection of buildings called New Ulm. The day after the agency was over-run, hostile Indians in war paint were seen there and were fired upon. Help came to New Ulm with a company of volunteers under a Judge Flandrau, and an ex-sheriff, Boardman. The Indians were still busy at the fort. By the 23rd of August, the smoke columns of burning homes of settlers under cumulus clouds and thunderheads, signaled the Sioux were approaching New Ulm. (What is clear—as we read old letters of these early days of the Indian wars in the West—is the panic and terror of the whites. Later, while horror was always present, both settlers and soldiers—knowing what was ahead—were grimmer and less keyed to outright hysteria.) New Ulm, fed by panicked refugee stories, was jumpy and full of weeping women and children and catatonic, sorrowful men.

Judge Flandrau, a fiesty character, was voted to command by the defenders of the town. He had about a hundred and fifty men with rifles, pistols, and old swords. He sent them, with a stern order, out a half-mile into the brush. At ten o'clock, there was firing in progress—smoke, cries, howling Sioux, and cursing, worried settlers.

The Sioux came out of the forest in fine array, precise cruel images, five hundred strong, riding from the trees, splendidly mounted and painted, feathers high, waving lances and rifles held up as threats—every Indian throat screaming death to the whites. They fanned out to engulf the outpost defenders, riding hard. The Judge tried to rally his men, but the untrained, outnumbered volunteers in those early days of the war didn't stand up to charging Indians on horseback. Later in the wars, a square of determined sharpshooters could have done much damage to the yipping Sioux.

The defenders pulled back. The Indians took over the houses on the outskirts of the town and began pouring a deadly fire into the heart of the village. The judge managed to stop the panic and his line of riflemen held off the main attack in the incessant noise of the battle. The Indians were outflanking the town and soon seized the lower end and set it on fire. The houses of wood and shakes burned briskly. In the thick smoke, the savages advanced into the town at a lope, crackling flames all around them. The streets were murderous; slugs of lead were coming from all directions. One of the defenders, a Captain Saunders got a slug right through his body and went down, critically wounded.

In the smoke, Little Crow was massing for a final assault on the town. The whites, however, were beginning to recover their breath. Grimy-faced, grim, they waited. As Judge Flandrau was to put it later in his legal tones: "There is something so fiendish in their yells and terrifying in their appearance when in battle that it takes a good deal of time to overcome the sensation that they inspire."

The judge refused to let the Indians seize houses he couldn't hold and he had forty buildings burned down after a countercharge of his drove the Indians out of the town. He ordered everyone to dig trenches during the hot, worrisome night—and dirt flew. The largest brick house in town was dubbed a fort, provisioned, and made into an ammunition dump. Morning came. Some last surviving cock crowed, and the gamey, worried defenders looked out from trench and brick house and waited for the terrible war cries, the rush, bark of rifles, battering in of doors where women and children were.

The Sioux never came. They had enough booty and prisoners.

Little Crow had pulled back against a very gallant defense and Judge Flandrau's firmness. Little Crow and his war parties went off, deep into the wilds to smoke and tan scalps, count wounds, sort out the booty and, if it was whisky, drink it up. Also to torture prisoners in ghastly fashion, pleasure themselves with the white women captives, bounce at victory dances, and to howl they had won back their hunting-gounds. Little Crow was much Big Man in their eyes.

But it was not victory, only first success.

Minnesota rallied to the war against the Sioux. Colonel Henry Sibley was put in command of public forces. A hard-eyed, long-time soldier, he had been around the frontier, spoke the Dakota Indian tongue as well as French, and he was—as they said—"savey to Injun ways."

He commanded fourteen hundred raw, tobacco-chewing volunteers. He sent out calls for Indian fighters and they came in; farmers, pelt hunters, horse handlers, frontier boozers, riffraff, good solid citizens, pig gelders, leather tanners, blacksmiths; also outlaws from the East; embezzlers and busted gamblers, young boys eager for adventure, men bored with family and marriage, or those earnestly ready to defend themselves and their broods. On the frontier, one didn't ask too many questions about a man's past, as long as he could load and fire a rifle and not let you down in a closer corner.

Sibley, marching out for action, spent a lot of his time burying the dead he found in his path. By August 28, he was at Fort Ridgeley being cheered by survivors. He moved on next morning to the charred ruins of the agency, interning Captain March's dead soldiers and twenty civilians. Indian scalping marks and tomahawk blows were plentiful on dead whites, but no living Indian was seen. J. R. Major Brown was sent out to find Indians—he took a party in wagons up river, two hundred men, burying dead settlers on the way, camping at Birch Coulie on the night of September 1.

At dawn, Little Crow and a band of warriors in full cry came roaring down through the birch trees on Major Brown. Soon there were dead men, dead horses, screaming, maddened mounts with broken bones. All was in confusion after the first hard assault. Every horse was down and only Colonel Sibley, hearing the firing and rushing up just in time, saved Major Brown's men . . . (There were a lot of local "Majors" and "Captains" in these wars, but few had any real Federal military training; just titles.)

Sibley drove off the Indians. Dead and dying men and animals littered the place; the wagons were shot to bits. Twenty-four men were dead. Sixty-seven bore wounds. Sibley and the survivors retreated.

Colonel Sibley saw he didn't have the fighting men he needed so he began to drill them, stiffen them, make soldiers of a mob. This left Little Crow free to roam, attack, kill; to go back to his camp with more booty and scalps, where he already had hundreds of prisoners.

Chapter 13

THE DESTINY OF CHIEF LITTLE CROW

Colonel Sibley's purpose, beside defense, was to rescue the women and children held captive in Little Crow's camp. Any warlike move would mean fearful massacre. The western and eastern press attacked Sibley for his wary care in making a move.

"A snail who falls back on his authority and assumed dignity and refuses to march," the papers said. He was also called, "The state undertaker," as he was burying the hundreds of dead, "with his company of gravediggers."

The main village of the Sioux was scouted out as being on the northwest side on the Yellow Medicine River. With 1600 men and two fieldpieces, on September 18, Colonel Sibley moved out to attack. His ace weapon was the artillery. Indians broke before the sustained fire of what they called the "wagon guns." Cannon and shellfire seemed to them an unsporting use of a terror weapon.

Little Crow, aware of the advance, planned an ambush in a thickly wooded gorge of the Yellow Medicine River, still primitive forest country. The whites' advance under a Major Welsh was just past Wood Lake when they were attacked by Sioux, wounding four scouts, one fatally. Moving up half a mile behind, the main body heard the firing and a company came forward to save the scouts.

Many Sioux were in front of the advance and in ambush on both sides of the gorge. To the whites, it looked easy—just clear the hostiles blocking the way ahead. The order to charge was given and into the thick brush rushed the company. The old Indian ambush trick had worked again. Suddenly, Indians were firing from all directions while still hidden in the thick growths. (At this period, the whites had the innocent assumption ambush was not fair, a carry-over from General Braddock's British idea soldiers fought in the open.) They were plagued and nettled by the use of this trick, but were slow to learn to avoid it. Their minds were still cauterized by formal, respectable battle logic.

Major Welsh was a stubborn man. A rider came up with orders from Colonel Sibley to pull the scouts back to the main body. It took a second angry message before Welsh admitted he was trapped and called for retreat.

Meanwhile, Colonel Sibley, taking no chances, was establishing the main body of his forces on a low hill. Welsh and his battered men and wounded began to pull back, at which moment the Sioux came in yipping to attack—painted, quick-moving, a terror to unseasoned soldiers.

Welsh's men panicked and ran. If Little Crow could have massed all his forces, he could have overrun Colonel Sibley. But that officer counterattacked with five companies and the Indians pulled away to mass for a major attack. For two hours they sent charges against the low hill and once nearly succeeded in stomping the left flank into the ground. The artillery began to shell Sioux hidden in the gorge, and they broke and ran from the fire of these two guns.

As often happened when roughly handled, the Indians decided to call it a day, and melted away into the timber. The Indian brave had a low breaking point. Any omen or odd turn of events or a bit of action gone sour could throw him off his stride.

The recruits cheered themselves nearly into "conniption fits" and went out to scalp the dead Indians left on the field of battle. This was a frontier habit in some sections, but it horrified Colonel Sibley, who, burdened with the wounded as he was, still had time to issue an order forbidding scalp-taking.

"The bodies of the dead, even of a savage enemy, shall not be subjected to indignities by civilized and Christian men."

It should be recalled that both British and American had, in the past wars, offered cash and trade goods for white settlers' and soldier's scalps—the British at one time insisting the ears be included with any colonial hair brought in for payment because some Indians were cheating by dividing one scalp into two.

Meanwhile, Little Crow was facing the external problem of most Indian generals—his forces had lost interest in the war. It had been grand fighting, massacring and pursuing attending sports—but now, with loot and captives, they wanted to disburse, talk over victories and personal triumphs in battle.

At first small bands, then larger ones, began to break off from the main body. Little Crow had insisted all captives be killed at once, but the other chiefs felt the prisoners had value as "hostages." With these words, Little Crow knew he was deserted. The other chiefs hoped to sit down to negotiate with the whites for terms, using the captives as pawns.

Colonel Sibley in the next few days offered amnesty and pardon to all Indian sinners who turned in their captives. On September 26, he got a batch of battered, soiled captives—269 persons, mostly women and children in tattered Indian garments. Sick, wounded, brutalized and—as one historian put it—"some refined and educated women." But there were . . . "others . . . ignorant, immigrant settlers . . ." rescued. The implication was that refined and educated women minded rape and beatings more than ignorant, immigrant wives. Many were dazed and in hysterics. Some cried. Others danced and sang to dramatize their freedom.

Colonel Sibley moved on; no organized fighting resistance was left among the Sioux. He arrested fifteen hundred Indians who hadn't accepted amnesty and filled the prison blocks at Fort Snelling and Mankato. The First Indian War of Minnesota was over. The *angst* and agony left many scars on mind and body.

Now it was time to kill a few more Indians by court martial and sentence. As one letter home put it: "The Indians are common as whale shit—can't kill 'em fast enough!" So all that was left was to punish; an Indian was an Indian, and if you couldn't prove one crime on him by witnesses—then hang someone else's deed on him. But there is no doubt that most of the Indians court-martialled had, in one way or another, taken part in the Little Crow War.

The charge against the nearly four hundred prisoners was "extreme barbarity." Three hundred and seven Sioux were sentenced to death by hanging before public witnesses. Sixteen got lengthy prison terms. President Abraham Lincoln in reviewing the courts' sentences commuted the death penalty for all but thirty-nine Sioux. The participation of these thirty-nine in the most brutal of the massacres was testified to by eye-witnesses.

With full military colors and drumtaps, on a cold December 28, a great gathering of settlers and soldiers massed before a huge gallows. They were to witness the "turning off of the Indians to dance on air" on the freshly erected gallows. It was a memorial mass execution. The lapsed Christian convert, Little Crow, was not among the limp bodies left dangling in the cold winter breeze.

Rumors were that Little Crow was organizing a new war—recruiting and planning an ever-bigger series of attacks. Stories and gossip, false reports circulated, but actually Little Crow had dropped out of sight of the settlements, where fear of a renewed war kept many settlers from returning to their land and what was left of their houses, gear, and cattle.

By July of 1863, the betting on when Little Crow would start another war was full of wild guesses.

The settlers did not let themselves sink into any dolorous hangover. The hostiles were out there *somewhere.* Nat Lampon and his boy, Chauncey, were out after deer meat in the north woods, hoping to pack back to a hungry family some fat haunches of venison. In a berry thicket they suddenly ran into two Indians busy picking the fruit off the bushes. Two Indians' horses stood by. To Nat all Indians were "the enemy" and he poured a load of deershot into the nearest one. The other Indian tried to push his wounded comrade onto a horse but the wounded man tried to aim a gun at the whites. Young Chauncey just took quick aim and shot him dead. The surviving Indian flung himself onto a horse and was off into the brush.

Nat Lampon scalped the dead Indian and packed the body back to the village of Hutchinson to show hostiles were in the neighborhood. The gamey corpse was dumped into the cesspool of the local slaughterhouse.

Later at Devil's Lake, among a group of Indian prisoners, a teen-aged boy asked to speak to the commander of the soldiers. Part of the statement the boy made consisted of this news: "I am the son of Little Crow. My name Wo-wi-nap-sa, sixteen years old. Father hide after soldiers beat us last year . . . we were hungry . . . Father and I picking berries near Scattered Lake. He shot in side just over hip. He shot again, in side over shoulder. This shot kill him. He say to me he killed now and ask me for water . . . He die then . . ."

Colonel Sibley, reading an elaboration of the boy's statement, had the Indian's body removed from the foul cesspool. If it were indeed Little Crow, the body would have a deformed right wrist, the result of an early tribal feud when he took a gunshot wound in the arm. The dishonored corpse had a deformed wrist.

It was announced that Little Crow, War Chief of the Sioux, was dead of deer-hunter bullets, and had ended up a very dead Indian in an offal-pit. He, who was once the most Christian of converts, the wearer of white man's broadcloth and starched collars, put upon by dishonest Indian agents, told to feed his hungry people grass; then, a merciless leader, the producer of one of the most deadly massacres of all the Indian Wars, was thus ignominiously dispatched.

From incomplete records we know nearly seven hundred white settlers had been massacred and tortured to death and nearly eight hundred soldiers had died. Many captives were never heard of again.

Westward and south across the western map the Indian wars began to spread. On a frontier there are no disassociated outsiders, nor in a wild landscape any refinement of sensation. The wars that began with Little Crow's raid were to run their long course, in a world where violence and action would take the place of sensibility. The cry of the loon, whoop of bittern owl and hawk would often bring on the notion that Indian calls were close. The Sioux and Cheyenne would join the pesky mosquitoes, blackflies, and snakes as things to be put up with. Fear, anger, cruelty ran through the Tetons, Pierre's Hole, Utah Lake, along the Cimarron, the Platte, the Snake, the Great Basin. And war made on supplies of salt, bacon, hominy, Indian corn, squirrel stew, dried jerky, *and* the Colt's Root of 1855 and the Christian Sharp's single-shot loaded buffalo gun.

The settlers who came from beech and butternut tree clearings made with a hickory-helved ax never understood the Indians of the Plains or his culture.

The Teton Sioux belonged to the Dakotas, feeling themselves lords of that earth long before the white man came, roaming after buffalo in the vast grasslands. Their domain merged into the Black Hills and the Rockies where beavers built dams, deer ran in herds, and a chief could get bearskins and the fat bear-meat for feasting. The Teton Sioux were meat-eaters and hunters of meat and not a lean and hungry people who relished only a succotash of beans and corn.

They had to be strong for they had many enemies: Crows, Flat-heads, Pawnees, Blackfeet, Shoshones—all who wanted scalps—the scalps of enemies. For, without enemies to kill, the Indian had no existence; work was for squaws. The Good Spirit provided—he whom they called *Waka-Tanka-Great-Unknown.* He gave them the Plains, the mountains, the fine valleys for their lodges.

Around 1822, into the Ogalalla branch of the Teton Sioux was born a boy-child to be called Red Cloud. His father was an alcoholic, a distinction on the Plains for only an exceptional Indian, that early in history, could manage to get the big habit and the drink to carry it on. We know little else about him.

Indian names are often mysterious to us. There is no record of why the boy was called Red Cloud. Early in life he was already a tribal leader, a bold raider, splendid horseman, an expert with all weaponry, strong, brave. In accomplishment he was like many Indian braves, but he stood out as a leader.

Much time has been wasted trying to explain why some men are born leaders; why others follow them as if they were gods. Whatever virtue or special aura it is that makes a leader, Red Cloud had it. In his early twenties he was head of his own loyal band of warriors doggone set to enjoy the miscellaneous pleasures of war.

All the Sioux were brave: the Teton Sioux were among the bravest and, of the Tetons—who were made up of the Ogallalas, Unkpapco, Sansarcs, Brules, Minneconjous—Red Cloud's band raised as many war parties as any of them.

Some historians write of the Sioux as if they were part of a system like the Knights of the Dark Ages, with loyalties, chivalry, oaths, deeds, and a love of the bravery in their enemies. Perhaps so. The Sioux had no other lives but their war games and hunting—both directed and based on visions and omens. Medieval man—even at his darkest—made some progress in church building, in art; sheltered monks studied, could read and write, produced some kind of medical knowledge, cherished connections with philosophy, and recorded history. All this, to any real extent, was missing from the Sioux, for all his formidable personality.

An Indian carried a coupstick—a sort of shepherd's wand—which in battle he used to touch an enemy; this supposedly gave him a distinction like an award of the Legion of Honor ribbon,

1. Chief Hand Shaker. The strong features explain the
kind of people who refused to be pushed aside by "progress."

2. Horse soldiers of the western Plains—tough, good, and loyal. Many were veterans of the Civil War, outlaws, drunks, and rootless men.

3. Chiefs at Fort Curtis, Montana, wearing Indian garb with white man's hats, shirts, and vests. Note calico dress on squaw.

4. The Indian scouts who served with the U.S. Army were dissolute and ruthless turncoats but were fine trackers.

5. General George Crook in the full dress he hardly ever wore—and with his whiskers in order.

6. Powder Face, Arapaho Indian chief, in full battle dress with coup stick. The feather headdress was seldom worn unless the warrior was on horseback.

7. Buffalo Bill and General Miles. The general was a tough soldier but was usually very fair to the Indians.

8. Chippewa and Sioux peace treaty talk with Buffalo Bill at Ashland, Wisconsin.

9. Custer in 1872. Always a bit of a dandy,
he designed his own uniforms.

10. Custer and friends at an outdoor party.

11. Fort Laramie peace treaty, April, 1868. General William Sherman is the balding man near the center pole. Few, if any, treaties were upheld once gold and silver were discovered, or when cattlemen and settlers needed land.

or the Nobel Prize. But our awards have some small value, given for some honorable work. Coupstick touching meant only needless bravery. The Sioux had no military system of order, reason or deep strategy. Young men followed the prestige of a famous, or popular, but always brave chief. The war party was autonomous, directed by its own aims alone, and while several bands would often combine, the merger was only for the one action. It would take time and the menace of the white in great numbers to bring together two to four thousand Sioux for battle.

The Sioux were courageous, with a tenacity that amounted to genius. Or race suicide. They paid little attention to the growing number of whites passing through or stopping to dig for some foolish metal—except to steal their horses, ambush a few fur hunters, bushwhack a gold-seeker, barter for whisky, sell a squaw to some horny roisterer.

To the south along the Fort Leavenworth-Fort Laramie trail the whites were sending out huge wagon trains, with many long lines of horses, cattle, mules, muddying the waters. Indian raids on those wagon trains brought war to western Kansas and Colorado—so any Indian, no matter what his tribe, was in danger of being killed on sight. Worst of all, the buffalo were unhappy and in panic, and where the wagon train moved, the expected buffalo migrations were thrown out of order.

After one bitter and brutal massacre of the Cheyenne at Sand Creek in 1864, the Cheyenne sent the warpipe to Sioux to smoke with them, and enter into battle as allies against the whites.

Among fugitives from Minnesota had been the Santee Sioux after the dismal destiny of Little Crow. Major General Dodge, in the summer of 1865, commanding the Missouri section of the Department of the West, was after the Santee Sioux with four columns of troops moving in the summer heat, rein chains clanging, horse soldiers stiff in the saddle, mules bringing up the camp gear and supplies.

From Army reports can be put together an outline of events, some clear, some unclear, some vivid, some vague, where the information is missing. History is not neat.

Red Cloud and the Tetons joined the war, attacking white detachments as partners of the Cheyennes. They jumped a supply column under Colonel Sawyer staking out a military road to the Montana gold diggings. A hot engagement took place and it all ended ingloriously for both sides when Red Cloud accepted as a bribe a wagonload of coffee, rice, and sugar to let the column proceed. There was a disagreement as to the dividing of the indemnity. Indians staggering in late for action felt left out and the column had to shoot its way out through greedy Indians.

To settle these road problems, a new treaty, called the Harney-Sandborn document, was signed in 1865. Red Cloud was laid up with a Crow arrow wound; he had been hit in the back, the arrow going right through his body with the arrowhead protruding from his chest. A medicine man cut off the head and feather of the arrow and drew the shaft out with an Indian prayer. Red Cloud was against the Harney-Sandborn treaty.

In his place, Spotted Tail and Man-Afraid-of-His-Horses (actually a mis-translation for He-Who-Is-So-Fearful-In-Battle-Even-His-Horse-Causes-Fear), and other chiefs, made their marks on the treaty.

Red Cloud fully recovered, saw that the treaty would destroy the Indian hunting lands. So his bands of yipping warriors were soon burning anything white-made and scalping their way to a wave of such terror that early in 1866, Washington felt it was time to offer the Sioux a new treaty. The government was trying to seize the Indian lands through a barrage of paper documents.

This treaty council of civilians and Indians collected at Fort Laramie and this time, Red Cloud was on the scene. Even as peace was talked, the Army intruded one of those deficiencies and uncertainties of military thinking. General Henry B. Carrington, a fort builder, rode up to the fort, with troops moving into the Powder River County to set up a series of forts on Indian land! The council and the military were in direct action *against* each other. The Indians at first remained taciturn.

General Carrington dismounted and slapped dust from his military jacket and began to shake hands. Red Cloud, seeing Army, felt a betrayal, became boiling mad, jumped to a platform, set up under cut-pine boughs, and shaking a finger at the general, cried out: "This is the White Eagle who is here to steal the land for a road through our Indian land. This we will not have. I go now and fold my tepee!"

And off went Red Cloud to sweep his people out of range of the fort and onto the Plains. The Council was dead and knew it. Some chiefs lingered, but the warriors slipped away, carrying weapons, riding their best horses to join Red Cloud. The old chiefs were discredited. Red Cloud now led the Sioux nation—war chief of *all* of them.

Chapter 14

TIMBERS OF FORT KEARNY

General Henry B. Carrington lived by orders. If the Army wanted a fort in the Powder River, he'd see they got it. The Bozeman Trail was needed—it would see thousands of gold-seekers rushing into Montana and Idaho as soon as the word *go* was pronounced. Two forts went up: Fort Phil Kearny at Piney Creek (always pronounced *crick*), and nearly a hundred miles to the north, Fort C. F. Smith.

This meant war. Red Cloud rode, made talk, smoked tribal pipes—all for war against the whites. He enlisted Crazy Horse of the Ogalallas, High Backbone, and Black Shield of the Minneconjous.

Among the fuzzy sumac, cottonwood, bunchgrass, berry patches it was a gathering of forces, the largest Indian crusades of the West—spread for miles on both banks up and down the Little Goose River. The lodges rose, horse herds gathered, weapons were burnished—No. 3 Harper-Ferry rifles, Leman percussions, French *Lebels* —even a Remington-Hepburn here and there. Wood smoke and war talk filled the air. Fifteen thousand Indians, all hating the whites as destroyers of forest, the buffalo grass, and frightening the great herds; setting up forts on Indian land they had promised never to touch.

Of warriors, Army historians estimate there were four thousand mounted and armed. No such force had ever been collected into one war party by the Sioux. The earth shook as they rode past, war bonnets fluttering, lances high, buffalo-hide shield on one arm—firm limbs and bodies streaked with earth and berry reds and soots and ghastly clays.

As an Army, it was much like Cromwell's Roundheads—a cavalry of amazing power. Generals like Benton and Crook called it the light cavalry equal to any in the world. Its faults were that it lacked routine disciplines, tight organization and staff work. A deep science of warfare (perhaps a myth, anyway) did not exist for Indians. The ambush was about as far as they went into maneuvering. Siege lines could not be maintained. Yet, Red Cloud led most of this force—at least, that under his direct command—with remarkable dash and skill.

By the middle of July, General Carrington was shaping raw timbers for his first fort—Fort Kearny. Axes replaced weapons in soldiers' hands. Two days later at dawn, the Sioux attacked the fortsite. Historic change was locking the whites and Indians together like the protons and neutrons of the atom; a small change could cause an explosion.

Horses were lost; there were two dead soldiers, three wounded. First round. The Indians went off to overrun a traveling sutler as a supply of dismal food and other items to soldiers was named— a sort of primitive PX in wagons. Six dead. In the next two weeks, five wagon trains were under attack. Fifteen dead. Great loss of cattle and horses.

General Carrington bowed to the situation and wrote a message: *Send reinforcements.* The fort was deep in Indian territory and the hostiles roamed and scouted all around it. Herders and sentries were killed. Night and day the Indians watched and waited. Patrols had to fight their way out and their way back in. Over fifty attacks on the fort are recorded.

Winter came. In the miserable, bone-freezing cold, the siege held. Score, from August 1 to January 1: 154 dead in or near Fort Phil Kearny. Wounded, twenty. (The list of wounded is deceptive; many of the dead listed died of wounds under the grim impact of military doctoring.)

The ledgers also carefully list the loss of seven hundred horses, oxen, and mules. And add to the Sioux scalping knife, silent death in the night, winter blizzard, loss of toes and fingers to frostbite.

General Carrington went on building his fort. The nearest good timbers began seven miles away. And the fort was planned on a grandiose scale by some military chair-holder safe in Washington. The building was to be 1600 feet long, 600 feet wide with corral and stables for nearly a thousand horses and mules. All that needed immense amounts of timbers. Woodcutters and haulers worked in gangs of 150 men—guarded, armed; yet casualties occurred. Soldiers were carried off for torture at leisure.

But build one must. The rigid laws of necessity and consequence governed national growth with all those assumptions of responsibility.

General Carrington, records show, was the builder-type. In November, a fire-eater named Captain William J. Fetterman came to Fort Phil Kearny—a veteran of the Civil War, aching for a fight, for battle, promotion—and a desire to kill hostiles. He thought General Carrington a do-nothing for letting the Sioux harass him. After all, there were women in the fort to protect.

On December 6, flag signals at a lookout point on Pilot Hill announced a fort woodcutting party was under fierce Indian attack two miles or less from the fort. Captain Fetterman charged out with forty men, including a captain and three lieutenants. General Carrington, with twenty-five horse soldiers, rode out toward Piney to surprise the Indians from the rear.

In the crisp cold air Fetterman's force moved on until they sighted Sioux, mounted—and they exchanged fire. Rifle, carbine slugs made ugly sounds all around the two parties. Then the Indians pulled their horses' heads around and rode fast down the valley. Galloping hard, the soldiers following, yelling in glee.

They passed the woodcutting party and rode on five miles, never managing to reach the Indians, prancing just ahead of them like lures on fish lines.

The fort was lost from sight. The Indians pulled up their mounts. New Indian riders poured out from all sides. Now the soldiers ran as the hare and the Indians were the hounds.

The old simple Indian ambush had worked again. Some of Fetterman's soldiers got clear away, but he and two dozen men were surrounded, outnumbered four or five to one. It was one of a thousand times when a small detachment was cut off and hemmed in. There was nothing to do but fight. Before things got too deadly, General Carrington came up, riding hard, with his handful of troopers. Surprise confused the Indians and, suspecting he had the entire fort force with him, the Sioux pulled back. Score: one lieutenant dead, one sergeant dead, five soldiers wounded.

Captain Fetterman, when chided for his foolish action, replied,

"Look, give me eighty men and I'll ride through the whole God-damned Sioux Nation!" Of such ideas are Little Big Horns made. By December 21, the fort was nearly finished. A cold sunny day, men's breaths sending out streams of vapor, the fort dogs trying to get near the wood fires, snow over all the landscape outside. One more cutting of good timber and the general could write: "Fort Phil Kearny completed as ordered."

Fifty-five men left gamey but warm quarters to cut the last of the timbers. Eleven o'clock saw bad news signals from Pilot Hills. *Wood-party under heavy attack.*

A brave bugler put a freezing metal mouthpiece to his chapped lips and about fifty men of the 18th Infantry and over two dozen of the 2nd Cavalry went out to save the woodcutters. Captain Fetterman, eater of Sioux empires, headed the foot-sloggers. And Lieutenant Grummond (leaving his wife in their warm bed) led the steaming horses and riders.

Records show also a Captain Brown was involved—an early Ernest Hemingway type who saw Indians as animal-game, and is recorded as "crazy to get a scalp." A couple of old Indian fighters, Fisher and Wheatly, brought along two new Henry breech-loading rifles to "try on the redskins." Actually, ammunition at the fort was low and the men were not overburdened with fire power.

The general looked Fetterman in the eye. "*Just* relieve the wood train, drive the Indians back. On *no* account pursue Indians beyond Lodge Trail Ridge. I'll repeat that."

And he did. Captain Fetterman said, "Yes, sir."

He led his men not to Sullivent Hills, where the woodcutters were in trouble, but directly to Lodge Trail Ridge. The wood-cutters got free and went on to the fort. Captain Fetterman broke orders twice repeated to him. He led his men over the Ridge and out of sight and into another Indian trap. He couldn't resist the tempting bait.

A half dozen or more Indians or ponies were lazing along. They looked easy catchings. These Indians were led by Big Nose —a Cheyenne who rode back and forth in front of the soldiers, ducking bullets as if begging "come on, try to catch me."

Riding hard, the soldiers charged after the few stupid redskins who rode on in two parties, crisscrossing each other.

Hundreds of Sioux and Cheyennes were hidden in ravines and gorges along the route of the chase. With a treetop-shaking series of war cries, they rushed out from ambush (the game was becoming tiresome!) and circled the soldiers, some Indians, riding clear through them. Soldiers died of knife stabs, by tomahawkings, by rifle fire. The cavalry managed to make use of the top of the ridge, cut off on all sides, arrows and bullets doing damage.

A cavalry officer was knocked or shot from the saddle. The foot soldiers began to sweat in cold fear and tried to climb higher on the ridge. One great, engulfing rush of Indians went over them, screaming, weapons finding flesh, skulls, arms hacking at limbs. The Indians lacked the fire power; they depended on clubs and arrows, the lance and tomahawk. It was fiendish body-to-body contact for killing.

Every man that Captain Fetterman had led from the fort that morning including himself was soon dead. It was the moment for scalping.

There was no mercy, even for the dead. Both sides lived in shatterproof, merciless structures of "no quarter."

And Captain Fetterman lay dead, unseeing eyes staring at the treetops.

Chapter 15

THE TRIBES AGAINST THE FORTS

The massacre resulted from a failure in communications and orders between the fort and the Fetterman group. It was also an end result of a contempt that the whites had for the Indian in many such situations: to accept the aboriginals only as feral and brutal, not alert or human enough for the most simple military planning. "In all societies, commonsense gives way first," La Bruyère wrote and commonsense in the military mind—as Tolstoy showed in *War and Peace*—often simply does not exist.

General Carrington, behind the uncongenial raw walls of his fort, was unhappy, aware that Fetterman had flaunted orders and gone out of sight behind the ridge. He heard heavy firing, desperate expenditure of treasured ammunition. The noise grew in volume; obviously, this was a major engagement. A surgeon was sent out to see if the men under attack needed his aid but he came back quickly, crying out the hills were loaded with Indians.

Captain Ten Eyck, a fort officer, was then ordered to muster up fifty-four men, mount and gallop to the sound of the firing. The general, through his field glasses, watched Ten Eyck's detachment reach the peak, just as the firing died down. Then Ten Eyck, too—as if in a planned drama—went over and out of sight behind the cursed ridge. In a matter of minutes a soldier came riding back to the fort, carrying a hurried penciled message from Captain Ten Eyck:

The Valley on the other side of the ridge is filled with Indians who are threatening me. The firing has stopped. No sign of Fetterman's command. Send a Howitzer . . .

There was the omen of ignominious defeat and there were no spare horses to send a howitzer. Forty men were rushed toward the Ridge and the fort began to arm any and everyone who could hold a rifle, even releasing guardhouse prisoners. The situation was grim, the atmosphere hysterical.

As Captain Ten Eyck headed over the ridge with his men, he saw two thousand enemy warriors in the valley below him. It was a chilly day. There were signs of a blizzard in the blue-gray air. The Indians were dancing and howling and running about but there was no sign of the actual battle any more. Ten Eyck must have shivered and gone grim-faced at the sight and, being more trained to obey orders than to use his head, he waited until the reinforcements came up before moving down into the valley.

But now the Indians were no longer in sight. Even their war cries were stilled. They were gone, leaving the soldiers with an incomprehensible kind of uneasiness.

Ten Eyck's detachment moved on, with caution and wonder, down the crude woodcutters' road. Then, in all its horror, they saw the terrifying, unmoving setting of a bloody disaster. Among great boulders lay the bodies of Fetterman and Brown and their dead soldiers—tossed about like bundles of rags. Nearly every man had been scalped, mutilated by knife and spike-studded clubs, pincushioned by arrows. Not all of them had died of Indian weapons or by Indian hands. The two officers had neat bullet holes in their left temples and, from the powder burns on their skin, it was clear they had used their last shots on themselves, either in desperate regret of their blunder or (more likely) to avoid the torture and dreadful games Indians practiced on captives. Wagonloads of bodies, forty-nine in all, were carted back to the fort in a chilling twilight. The cold was marrow-freezing.

Attack on the surviving whites was expected in the bitter cold night and the fort stood "to arms," stamping freezing feet, peering into the blue-black dark, seeing lurking savages in every distorted shadow.

No attack came.

A strong imminence of death gripped the men and women in this cold wilderness.

Dawn came, cold and silver; the blizzard was close. Thirty-two men were still out under Lieutenant Grummond. His wife was frantic with despair. General Carrington marched out with eighty soldiers to see if there were any signs that the troop might still survive. His orders to the fort officer left in charge were stern. He worried over the women and children. All forts usually had married officers and men who brought their families along. It was a tradition that Army wives followed the flag to these rough forts set by—by Washington's orders—on trails to protect the settlers, keep the trails open, and police the Indians.

"Put every woman and child," ordered General Carrington, "in the powder magazine and on an officer's honor, promise none of these will fall into hostile hands alive." Once the Indians were over the walls, resistance at an end, the officer was instructed to blow up the powder supply, and the women and children with it.

This was hardly an order of reassurance or of hope.

On the road, General Carrington soon found signs of the overwhelming attack on the soldiers. Cavalry mounts, dead or dying, were piled here and there, thin limbs pointing to the leaden sky. Now and then the body of a soldier was found with his blood like varnish, frozen and shiny on his body. Beyond the place where Fetterman had been overrun lay the body of Lieutenant Grummond. Just beyond twelve dead bodies were bunched in a huddle that suggested a last defense. Brass cartridges were scattered around. The frontier scouts, Fisher and Wheatley, had gone off to one side for a personal last stand and their discarded cartridge shells showed they had done deadly work with their repeating rifles before dying. They seemed to have felled the only Indians who died there. Loose, riderless ponies were milling about and seventy puddles of blood from Indians, wounded, killed or carried off, were observed.

The dead soldiers were mutilated and scalped. Indians used enemy ears, fingers, and genitalia as décor. They also—as believers in spirits—felt a well-cut-up corpse would lose respect in the next world.

The score of the Fetterman disaster was eighty-one American dead accounted for. Tribal legend agrees that Indian losses were between sixty and seventy. Indian historians do not agree as to which chief led the attack. Red Cloud is rarely blamed. Most historians speculate it was Crazy Horse—a rising young fighter of the Sioux. Others mentioned, but never proven, were the Minneconjou chief, High Backbone; Black Leg, and/or Black Shield. The massacre was the result of no great military plan but the usual simple, easy-to-arrange Indian ambush—the luring of the enemy with decoys into a heavily grouped mass of warriors. That this plan worked so well so often suggests the white soldiers were slow to learn.

The furious blizzard broke after General Carrington got the dead back to his fort. A temperature of thirty degrees below zero was recorded. The snow drifts began to cover the fort wall, so that work details had to be organized to keep shoveling it away before an Indian raid could walk in over the drifts. Keeping careful watch was almost impossible. Men froze in a matter of minutes, no matter how many fox pelts and buffalo robes they bundled into. Sentries had difficulty lasting a twenty-minute round of duty before ears, nose, fingers, and toes lost all signs of life. Frostbites for weeks afterward brought discomfort and danger to the men.

The blizzard and bitter cold no doubt saved the fort. It was the Indian plan to overwhelm the defenders in several great rushes according to memoirs, but Indians freeze also in subzero weather and the fort was spared an attack. Mrs. Grummond, a loyal Army wife and new-made widow, looked down in grief upon the corpse of her husband. The fort remained in danger, as it was low in manpower, low in amunition, horses, and food. And the terrible weather continued without mercy, making it impossible to send out parties to cut firewood.

Fort Laramie, the nearest point of help lay to the north—236 rough country miles away—all Indian-infested. The only hope of relief was to get a courier through to Laramie. Volunteers did not leap forward at this chance of a lingering, freezing death, heroism notwithstanding. The old hand—the hard-bitten plainsmen, fur trappers, and deft veteran scouts—shook shaggy heads. You couldn't see anything a hundred yards in front of you. The storm was still at its peak and hostiles were all over the whole shebang: General, don't look my way for this duty!

These men knew the horror of wandering in snow so thick there was no visibility, of freezing solid, and maybe even encountering Indians foolish enough to be out, prowling in the blizzard. You could bet five hundred to one no one could get through with his hair or his life.

However—enter a touch of romance to the cold misery—one soldier, John "Portugee" Phillips, was sighing over the plight of the fresh-made widow, Mrs. Grummond. He saw a chance to make a gallant gesture and perhaps save the life of the woman he secretly worshiped as a love image beyond his reach.

Phillips stepped forward to carry the message. It is of interest to note that Mrs. Grummond later married General Carrington and not the gallant "Portugee." There are entries in journals and diaries of the day that picture an atmosphere of passionate love affairs, broken marriages, and sexual melodramas that existed among men and women confined to the pathological and inert dullness of a remote Army post. We often forget they were human —not just characters in history.

"Portugee" was no raw recruit but a skilled trapper and raw-hide-tough Indian fighter and scout. He took the general's own horse, Kentucky, a big buffalo coat, a pocket of Army hardtack, a bag of horse feed and, we hope, a smile from Mrs. Grummond. He walked his mount out of a side gate into the bull-roaring, icy world of a Plains' blizzard. He led the animal through the drifts for a long time, wondering if the Indians had observers watching the fort. When at last he mounted he rode as fast as the wind and snow would permit, past frozen lakes, the sticky snow covering him and the horse.

Morning, hidden in the whirling storm, "Portugee" stopped to feed the animal and himself and to gulp snow. Even as a trained plainsman, he could find no landmarks—the twenty-foot drifts had wiped out the largest—and he proceeded more by instinct than by knowledge. Another night and morning and he was at Horse Shoe Station, forty miles from Fort Laramie and nearly two hundred miles from Fort Kearny.

At Horse Shoe there was a telegraph key and a message went out to Fort Laramie of the disaster at Fort Kearny. "Portugee" had really never trusted this newfangled signal system, so he rode on to Laramie—freezing, ice-coated, the horse under him staggering under every drift.

He figured it was Christmas Eve by now at Fort Laramie. And it was.

The people were celebrating the birth of the Son of God with dancing and drink. The "Bedlam Officers' Club" was gay with candle and oil lamps and full cut-glass punchbowls. Records show that a very grand ball was in process. Uniforms shone, still crisp and gaudy with their full-dress braid, piping and yellow stripes for horse soldiers, and other bright colors for the various branches of the service. The fort ladies were in their best finery and inherited jewels and felt part of "civilization" once more. The fort band, with an honored fiddler, sawed away at fashionable dance tunes and the guests were active. There had been no alarm, no mustering of troops, for the telegraph message from Horse Shoe Station had *not* come through. Storm or Indians had severed the line.

There was the cry of a sentry on duty outside; the rush of an Officer of the Day. The dancers crowded to windows to see what the commotion was. A panting horse, his nostrils flaring, lay dying on the parade ground and a buffalo-robed figure was helped indoors. After a good belt of the officers' whisky, "Portugee" told the dreadful story of the Fetterman massacre to the Fort Laramie commander. Then "Portugee" collapsed, falling like a jackknife closing: exposure, exhaustion, too long a time in the saddle, had gotten to him at last. He was bedded down in the hospital.

Four companies of infantry were dug out of their warm quarters and sent away from their own holiday wassail. Ammunition and other stores were packed and off they went in the whirling snow to aid Fort Kearny. And, in their turn, to be besieged by the Indians.

"Portugee" Phillips remained in bed for weeks in the fort hospital trying to recover from his rugged feat. Later he was paid $300 for his ride and scouting duties. He married, not his beloved Mrs. Grummond, of course, started to raise steers, lost them to the Sioux and years later, after his death in 1883, the government finally got around to reimbursing his widow—$5000 for the stock he lost to the Indians.

General Carrington was made the scapegoat for Fetterman's misadventures and was shunted off to Fort Casper. He was replaced by a Colonel Wessells. General Carrington, quite innocent of Fetterman's madness, asked for a military investigation which took a full twenty years to conclude and exonerate him. The Fetterman disaster showed the nation it had a tough, mean, and quite real Indian war on its hands.

Red Cloud had no idea of pulling away from the siege of Fort Kearny. All winter he and his band watched the fort. He lived in a cold and windy lodge, encouraged the Sioux to stand fast. Colonel Wessells found the weather too cold for a counterattack and Red Cloud was finding it hard to buck the envious chiefs who felt he was gaining too much power. Man-Afraid-of-His-Horse even tried to talk to the whites about a peace commission. But Red Cloud remained the popular war leader. When summer came, the fort people glimpsed the Indians lurking on every side.

In August, the Sioux attacked a fort woodchopping detail. There were fourteen wagons under a Lieutenant Powell who, at the first war whoop, had the ironbound wagon beds removed from their wheels and arranged in a circle for defense. The soldiers had new rapid-fire Springfield-Allen rifles, a supply of cartridges, plus Colt revolvers. The lieutenant's smart stratagem persuaded the Indians to run off all the wood cutters' horses.

The attack came on foot with infectious exuberance, the usual Sioux high spirits. They infiltrated the brush. Many more Indians were armed with guns than the year before. A detail of woodchoppers, who were making for the shelter of the wagon corral, were overrun. Arrows killed four. The wagon circle enclosed thirty-two worried defenders. Wagon seats, oat sacks, ox harness and tree trunks were used to strengthen the defense. The sharpshooters were given three rifles each and special men were assigned to them as loaders. Silently the wagon-box circle awaited the attack. The most nervous soldiers (or, perhaps, the most calm —there is no way to know) attached a rawhide thong to their triggers so they could fire a slug into their own heads, using a toe as a finger, should the fight become hopeless and Indian torture session inevitable.

The charge came on, led by High Backbone, Crazy Horse, Crow King, American Horse, Big Crow. Just names as yet, but soon to be famous. The chief who gave the signal for the charge was Red Cloud himself. A general staff college of Indian leaders hurtled against the small force. Mounted and screaming war cries the Indians rushed toward the circle of wagon beds—lances, rifles, and coupsticks forward.

Deadly return fire brought many out of their saddles or, rather, the buffalo or deer-hide contraptions they used instead of saddles. Then they experienced a surprise. The fire did not diminish as men reloaded. These soldiers kept up steady firing. The repeating rifle was in action. This weapon was subsequently described by an admirer: "You load 'em on Sunday and they fire all week!"

Horses and warriors dead or mortally hurt littered the ground. Surviving Indians charged on, their howls growing in fury. They split to engulf the soldiers on each side and rode to meet behind the corral. The deadly rifle fire never let up.

The Sioux felt that a small army was hidden behind the wagon beds; they had underestimated the number of soldiers. Inside the wagon circle casualties included an officer and two men. The Indians signaled for reinforcements with trade mirrors. More Indians came up for a fresh attack. Indians with rifles were sent forward on foot to infiltrate the scene of action and keep up a hot fire. Little fire was returned and, when the main attack was launched, the Indians were sure most of the soldiers were dead. The charge was a ferocious surge of painted bodies, of open mouths screaming, and the white man's fire took deadly toll. But the Sioux never stopped rushing the charge, feathers flying, until they were face to face with the defenders. Knives were out to make the attack a death-slashing to a finish.

The repeating rifles kept up their consistent damage, mowing warriors off their feet like wheat being cut. The foot charge fell back and a mounted one rushed forward. Howling Indians, their ponies' hoofs unshod, came thudding into the leafmold clearings; the carnage was frightening. Sheer power and weight seemed able to blow away everything in sight. Again the rifles broke up the Indians' charge. More copper-colored bodies fell. The sun in the west was sinking fast and the fierceness of battle was maneuvering in shadows.

The Sioux wavered and began to try to recover the dead and wounded and to move off quickly. A covering Indian fire was launched to hold the attention of the soldiers. Lariats were attached to Indians' limbs, prone bodies dragged off the field. The quick and the dead were unceremoniously removed from the vicinity of the wagon boxes.

Nearby there was the sound of cannon fire and a detachment of soldiers, under a major, appeared on the scene to clinch the Indian defeat. The soldier-survivors (loss: seven dead and three wounded) came out to hurrah the relieving force. Fear and apprehension gave way to cheers and even frenzy.

Three great Indian charges, it was estimated, had cost the Sioux about a hundred and eighty of their braves. Both sides, of course, made preposterous claims. The whites claimed as many as fifteen hundred Indian casualties (more than the entire attacking forces) and the Indians later said only six were killed and half-a-dozen wounded. Battle casualties, historians note, as reported "officially," are often nonsense.

For the time being Fort Kearny survived. Red Cloud, losing prestige, went off on a tour of various tribes to talk up the war. Only Ogalalla kept his war parties harassing the fort, and inside, the soldiers redigested their experiences and added new tales to them.

In the spring of 1868 there was the routine peace commission. In April, at Fort Laramie, Red Cloud and the Sioux chiefs met with the peace talkers. Red Cloud stated his terms grimly: *Close* the Bozeman Trail that led to the gold fields of Idaho and Montana, abandon the U. S. Army forts along the route.

To this the commission agreed if the Sioux would permit the building of the Northern Pacific Railroad to proceed. The Powder River and the Black Hills, were to be Indians alone . . . One officer present wrote: "Did anyone remember Machiavelli's line? 'Bitter foes today; sugared darlings tomorrow, kissing and scratching in a breath . . .'"

Red Cloud opposed the treaty, insisting he'd not make his mark on it until the soldiers were all pulled out. In August, Fort Kearny hauled down the flag. The troops departed and, as the last bluecoat left the fort, looking back and thinking of their dead comrades, of cruel and freezing nights and hard summer fights with the woodcutters' detail, the Sioux rushed into the fort from the other side. Black plumes of billowing smoke went up to smudge the summer sky. Red flames licked and crackled on the bullet-scarred logs. The bannerless flagpole fell. The white man was gone. For good—or so it seemed to the Sioux.

Red Cloud finally approved of the treaty on November 6. The Indian had recovered an integral part of life; pride in the great pulse of being free. The primordial plains and the forests that hemmed his existence were his again. The Indian was sustained (for a pause there) as a red Spartan living in a pure relationship between himself and the existing universe. It was a major Indian victory at the time. The Indian experienced a time of common effort, common force. Red Cloud had won a war.

However, he failed to improve his strength and his methods; to create the organization for mobilization and sustained military strategy. He made no conscious adjustment to the great changes the whites would set up as they increased their pressures against the tribes. The time would come when it would be necessary to break the treaties. To the white man, the Indian remained little more than a fractious horse who would have to be domesticated—or liquidated.

Chapter 16

MASSACRE AT SAND CREEK, U.S. STYLE

The southern Cheyennes, unblunted belligerents, liked to winter among the sagebrush and soapweed, the barren expanse between plain and mountains. They congregated in the bend of Sand Creek, thirty miles north of Fort Lyons, in the area which is now Colorado. The Cheyennes liked war, but Black Kettle (*Moketavata*), their chief, had instructed: "No trouble with the whites!"

Chiefs White Antelope and War Bonnet, also southern Cheyennes, aware they were on the periphery of vast change, had backed Black Kettle up and November of 1864 was peaceful. The smoke rose from the top of the warm buffalo-hide lodges. Hunting was good. They had been promised protection by the soldiers as long as they remained at peace. Thus, they had even turned over half of their guns and rifles to the fort, keeping only enough for necessary hunting. How could an Indian show his faith better than that? After his conscience had been so often made highly soluble in alcohol?

Now, perhaps, peace would stay, the raids by the Sioux and the Kiowas would peter out. The soldiers would not again attack Cheyenne villages, as they had been. They even promised to attempt to keep the wagon trains from frightening off the game. Skepticism was calmed. Black Kettle hoped for the best.

But bigotry, intolerance, and the Old Testament rode out with Colonel J. M. Chivington of the 2nd Colorado Cavalry. The colonel was, when not in uniform, a Methodist preacher, an antislave fanatic and bushwhacker in the bloody border gangs. In time, he became the presiding elder of a church in Denver, but in the Civil War, he had refused to go as a chaplain but had cried out: "If I go with the soldiers, I am going to fight!"

He was given the rank of colonel.

Now, as he rode on a chill November day with his troop there was a half-breed prisoner along with his hands tied to a trooper's saddle pommel. Colonel Chivington must have relished the speech he made just before they had started this expedition: "Kill and scalp all Indians!" He had spoken to a sea of faces—some of them religious zealots like himself, hot in their purposeful narrowness. "Big and little—scalp them all. Nits make lice!"

He looked now at the half-breed, Jack Smith—nephew of the Cheyenne chief Yellow Horse. Jack's father was a famous trapper and trader; his mother was a Cheyenne.

"Well?" the colonel yelled.

The trooper said, "This breed—he won't go no further."

As reported later, Jack Smith had spoken up: "Wolf howl, Injun dog, he hear wolf howl and he howl, too. Injun hear dog howl and he listen. Hear something. Run off . . ."

The colonel was a big, rough man—belligerent and oblivious to mercy, mean for all his preaching.

"Jack," he said as he touched his pistol holster, "you fool with me and don't lead me to that camp . . ."

Jack, the half-breed, decided, under this obvious threat, to lead the cavalry. They were hunting the camp of Black Kettle on Sand Creek. It was a tough company. On the other side of the colonel rode an even more dedicated Indian hater—Major Dowling, who, he had insisted, found it easy to get *any* information out of an Indian just "by toasting his shins over a small fire . . ."

All night the soldiers moved, leading their horses at times, then, at morning, mounting them and inspecting their arms. Below them, in the heightened perception of dawn, lay the sleeping Indian village. Orders were passed down the ranks. The troop broke into a gallop. An Indian woman, still half-locked in sleep, hearing the roar of hoofs cried out that a big buffalo herd was stampeding through the village. Indians—buck-naked—appeared at the openings of their lodges and saw the troopers tearing down the ridge. Black Kettle rushed out and held an American flag over his tepee with a white rag under it. He had been instructed by the Army to show these banners to prove he was friendly.

The Indians made no move to defend themselves. They milled around and grouped themselves in little clusters as if for gossip, wondering what would happen. What happened was deadly, heavy shooting into their ranks.

A few Indians seized their arms and one trooper was shot from his saddle. The first volley of the soldiers took deadly toll of women and children. "You go get after hostiles, them womin and children wuz allus in the way . . ."

The surviving Cheyennes looked for shelter in a shallow creek bed. The massacre continued. Black Kettle got away. Indians could melt away into the landscape.

Colonel Chivington murdered the few remaining braves, fighting a lost rear-guard action as if brushing insects aside. Nearly a mile from their camp the surviving Indians dug holes and pits. Here, men, women, and children huddled, waiting for the attack. In the captured village the troopers were cheering, howling their delight beyond control. Firing squads executed any Indian found alive. Looting of the camp went on. Fugitives discovered in the brush were murdered. There was a great taking of Indian scalps and mutilation of dead bodies.

At a Congressional Investigating Committee hearing, later on, there was eyewitness testimony of a lost Indian baby, naked, toddling down the trail when sighted by a soldier who missed it with rifle fire at seventy-five yards. Another trooper said, "Let me try the little son-of-a-bitch." He, too, missed his target.

A third marksman got the baby with a splendid shot. The ferocity of the colonel had seeped down into his men.

In the foxholes up the creek, the surviving Indians shivering in the November chill—men and women—were holding out. At high noon the two howitzers were wheeled into position and began shelling the foxholes, at point-blank range. The survivors of that bombardment, leaving their fragmented dead and dying, pulled back. The guns kept firing at the Indians every time they tried to dig in. Five miles of merciless target practice went on.

Meanwhile, Jack Smith, the half-breed prisoner, with wary instinct, eyed the colonel, who ordered him shot. It is recorded that when members of the troop appealed to him to protect the half-breed, Colonel Chivington replied: "I have given my orders and have no further instructions to give."

A preacher forgot to ask Jack Smith to prepare his soul for God. That preacher only turned away as the prisoner was murdered. The preacher was Colonel Chivington.

Pleased as King David bringing in the foreskins of the Philistines, the colonel returned to Denver with seven women and children prisoners and a hundred fresh scalps. The hair was exhibited during performances in a local theater. Colonel Chivington had massacred three hundred Indians who had been flying the flag of truce—mostly women and children—for only seventy-five of his victims were male. The troopers had lost fourteen dead, forty wounded.

The government, in regret over these events, paid the few ragtag-and-bob remains of Black Kettle's band a large indemnity and, in a seventy-two-day hearing of evidence condemned the actions of Colonel Chivington, who couldn't have cared less. He had done God's will and in time, returned to Ohio, became a newspaper publisher, and ran for the legislature. News of the Sand Creek massacre turned the voters against him, however, and he, a proud man, withdrew from the race. He died full of years, preaching the words of a stern Jehovah.

General Nelson A. Miles in his recollection wrote of Colonel Chivington's deed as "perhaps the foulest and most unjustifiable crime in the annals of America . . ."

The ferocity of this action against peaceful Indians caused a rethinking: had the white man betrayed them again? The tribes regretted having handed over half of their weapons. Now their war pipe was carried north on news of Sand Creek, seeking allies, and one of the smokers was a young man just coming into power, as one close to the Great Spirit. He was called Sitting Bull.

As one historian has put it: "The Little Big Horn had its roots in Sand Creek."

In January of 1895, a large assemblage of warriors—Cheyenne, Sioux, and Arapahos—met near Julesburg, Colorado, on the Overland Stage Route. A few Indians scouting in the morning light, took after a few field workers outside Fort Rankin. The cavalry bugle sang out the call to mount up and a pursuit began that lasted for over two miles.

It was the old, old game. Lured from their fort by a few casual Indians, the horse soldiers suddenly faced a huge, savage war party. Captain O'Brien, who was in command, pulled back just in time to avoid a complete disaster, losing eighteen men in the race for the shelter of the fort.

Meanwhile, the inhabitants of Julesburg had all run for the fort and the Indians looted the town, capturing the Army's paymaster's iron box at the stagecoach station. The box contained thousands of dollars, the payroll for the troops. The Indians, ignorant of paper money, scattered it far and wide in the wind. Hunting parties of soldiers later recovered about half of it in a real "paper-chase." Shopowners and homeowners put in claims of $40,000 in goods lost to the Indians.

Raiding and killing continued wherever a ranch or stage station could be overrun. One unfortunate turn of events concerned the capture of nine soldiers who had been discharged from the 3rd Colorado Cavalry which had taken part in the massacre at Sand Creek. In their baggage the captors found Indian scalps taken at that terrible massacre. The soldiers were promptly hacked to pieces. The Indians, after a prolonged spree of killing, burning, and looting, returned to Julesburg and burned it to the ground. This time, the soldiers watched from the fort but did not come out to play tag with the Cheyenne.

Another gruesome story deals with a Lieutenant Casper Collins who had a run-in with a war party. He tried to lead his men to safety over a bridge and got an arrow in his head. Reports indicate that he was still alive when captured. The Indians filled his mouth with gunpowder, put a fuse to it and lighted it.

A wagon train was attacked by one band led by a six-foot-three warrior who weighed about two hundred and forty pounds. The huge man appeared to be solid muscle. He bore the Indian name of *Surt* (the Bat) but, as his nose was very large and hooked, the soldiers called him Roman Nose. He chose the Indian version of that name—*Wogun Woguini* (Hook-Nose)—as his fighting name. Wogun was the fortunate owner of a sacred war bonnet blest by tribal priests, which he put on with great ritual piety. It was believed that the bonnet made him absolutely invulnerable in battle. No arrow nor bullet could strike him. Many Indians desired this brand of magic from the tribal necromancer, but the medicine man was chary concerning whom he provided such token of immunity. (Of course, if the charm failed, the medicine man could always decide the wearer had been impure or a warrior of little faith.) Roman Nose was always in the forefront of the battle, exposing himself recklessly under his sacred feathers, safe in his own mind from the haunting presence of death.

All during the summer of 1867 the Indians raided, killed, and mutilated. A first in history was recorded when, in early autumn, the Cheyenne found the new-laid iron rails of the Union Pacific east of the North Platte in Nebraska, where it cut the inherent emptiness of the Plain in two, as with a pencil line. A heavy log was laid across the tracks and the Indians retreated to the nearby brush to watch. Instead of a roaring steam engine, two men came down the line pumping a handcar. They saw the Indians and pumped harder to get by the hostiles at greater speed. This spurt derailed them when they hit the log. The Cheyenne closed in for the kill on the helpless railroadmen who died, hysterically, on the new iron ribbons.

The Indians then pulled out the spikes holding a rail to the timber ties and with log levers managed to bend the rail out of alignment. Again they waited, looking down the wide, flattish distance. Dark came and there was no sign of the great iron horse. From down the tracks finally sounded the *chug* of the engine and the vibration on the rails of the turning wheels. The headlight appeared—a blazing eye moving closer. The train, never slackening speed, hit the molested rail, shuddered and ran off the tracks, the engine turning on its side. The first train wreck in the West by sabotage could be chalked up to the American Indian.

The warriors bore down on the steaming, broken-backed monster and murdered every member of the train crew, including the brakeman who had dropped off with a red lantern from the rear end as required by railroad rules. The train was partially looted but the plunder was too sizable even for the Cheyennes to carry off.

Western Kansas was now Cheyenne-held—day and night. Fear stalked the countryside. The white settlers huddled for safety in the forts and the soldiers rarely appeared in time, for the raids were so heavy and consistent the Army found it difficult to cope. It was a transitory power the Indians held but it was, briefly, complete.

About this time a figure soon to become legendary and much fought over since by historians, appeared on the frontier for the first time. General George Armstrong Custer, hero of the Civil War, a gallant commander of horse, an egotist with a good sense of soldiering, Custer was daring and brave. Some of the later accounts do not give him credit for his excellent if risky actions throughout the Civil War. He had come west with his young, adoring wife, his wolfhounds and a feeling his reputation was slipping. Needing new accolades, he was ready to dare anything. If his faults have been emphasized by history, it must also be noted he was possessed of the courageous naïveté and stern military sense of duty.

The Indian with his illusory feeling of permanent life and invulnerability, if pushed, was always ready to fight. Trained soldiers were necessary to hold him at bay in battle. The white settlers were badly organized as fighting units, and the professional soldiers were often undersupplied and inexperienced. Two major Army problems were whisky and women mostly Indian women. Alcohol and females demoralized the frontier soldiers, according to journals, diaries, reports, and post newspapers.

Peter Garrioch, a trader whose prose style remains one of minor Jonathan Swiftian touches of Western history, writes of the soldiers and the sexual responses of the Arikara, Gros Ventre, and Mandan tribes: "The women come, not so much to cohabit with the whites for the pleasure of the thing as much as the remuneration they expect after the business of rutting is over . . . Never, perhaps, since the days of Adam, nor since public markets were first instituted, did the species of animal or goods prove more marketable, nor meet with more general demand and ready sale than the hindquarters of these ignoble and prostitute females."

Here speaks a faithful husband or a Malthusian, seeing some profit in Indian wars.

A Sioux chief, Little Bear, refused as trash the beads and other gifts offered at Fort Pierre and asked in return for all the Indian women pleasured by the whites, that items of like value be given in return. "Behold, you have lived with women of our tribe long enough! We want, in our turn, a thousand young girls—virgins all and of white skin," stated Little Bear.

There is no record that this order was filled, nor even considered seriously. Yet later historians have concluded that thousands of New England spinsters might have leaped at the trade. Not all the Indian favors were as acceptable to the whites as their women. The Plains Indians were, for one thing, eaters of dogs, which they fattened and served in a kind of unseasoned stew. One white man who fed upon it reported dogmeat was "fat and tender, like mutton chops, maybe . . ."

Indian reaction to whisky did seem eccentric. "At the end of a meal, having the mouth full of whisky, they pass the contents to the mouth of their neighbor, the greatest act of politeness and of good manners among the Sioux," one man wrote.

Chapter 17

SOLDIERING IN THE WEST

The soldier, in foreboding and disenchantment, led a miserable life on the Plains, among the dusty, dirty forts, where life's amenities were few. Winter could be an agony for survival. The shoddiness of Army-issue clothing was shocking. Greatcoats and caps and hats were not suited for winter blizzards; where gear never seen elsewhere was needed by Army forces. Temperatures of thirty to forty degrees below zero were recorded regularly on the Plains. The survival kit became the Indian method of wrapping oneself in buffalo robes and sleeping curled up in the warm woolly pelt. An Indian would sell buffalo robes for about three dollars each and let a tanned deerhide go for a dollar. Many soldiers began to live and dress Indian-style in self-defense, wearing buffalo and bearskin coats, beaver gloves, and mittens. In the dead of winter the soldier hugged his bread ration to his person. The ration could freeze as hard as stone if left outside the sleeping robe. Winter on the Plains was no joyous pagan affirmation.

With spring, the soldier could put on Indian leggings, take to blanket-wearing, play at being Indian. Life was dull between battles and some soldiers became white Indians in dress and habit if the fort commander was not a stern ramrod for discipline. Most of the officers, according to their personal journals and diaries, were deep in alcoholic escape themselves. Captain U. S. Grant is the best-known of the frontier officers of the period, whose heavy drinking forced them to resign from the Army. According to these records, Grant was the rule rather than the exception when it came to demoralized officers.

Historical records are replete with the jokes played on Indians who asked for papers proving their fine character and noble love of the white man. One such surviving endorsement is probably typical: "Beware of this Indian, Big Crow. He is a thief and a liar and will murder you if he gets a chance. Take warning."

Frontier service could produce a reasoned derangement of the senses. To keep boredom at bay the soldiers not only dressed as Indians, war-painting their faces and beating drums, but staged plays. When there were enough white women in the neighborhood there were balls and dances. One letter, written by a Colonel Francis Lee, begs the Adjutant General for the return of a chronic alcoholic trooper and deserter, one Thomas Gilmore:

> I would very much like to get him back for I am informed that he probably is the *very best* Clarinet player in the Army and our Band needs the instrument badly.

Hard liquor was not permitted to be sold in the fort to the rank and file. The canteen run by a sutler (one sutler was a cousin of Mary Todd Lincoln) could offer a soldier a daily ration of a pint of beer or ale, or a gill of wine. The sutler could freight in cargos of spirits "for personal use" and sell his private stock from under the counter to anyone with the price to buy. One enterprising wife of a soldier fixed up a small still in her quarters and made corn whisky, which she sold to soldiers secretly with irrational ease.

The Indians became alcoholics. They were willing to beg for alcohol, tossing aside all dignity and pride.

"Crying whisky, whisky . . . the Gros Ventres were ready to give anything they possessed—even their wives and daughters—for whisky . . . in less than an hour, the whole Gros Ventres' nation was gloriously drunk!"

An excruciating uneasiness and monumental lusts, existed. A fort poet, Captain Enoch Adams, wrote:

> In this fort, we are like Adam,
> 'Ere he had obtained his madam.
> Butter, cheese and women's eyes
> Would make this place a paradise.

This poet could overlook the cheese and butter when he crossed the river with a pint of whisky, or some other trade item, to visit an Indian tepee brothel run by Fool Dog for the pleasure of the soldiers and serviced by Indian girls.

Wrote the poet, nevertheless:

> All we lack in this vicinity
> Is a stock of femininity.
> Sutler bring it to Fort Rice
> It will fetch an awful price . . .

Fool Dog's wenches might be lacking in white women's femininity, but, they made do.

The settlers, gold-hunters, and soldiers were never tightly united against the Indian. They disliked each other at times even more, and after the Civil War when rootless Southerners—hopes and homes destroyed—came West, an Army fort newspaper, *The Frontier Scout*, rasped out in an editorial: "Treason dislodged from its home in civilization is pulling out like Jeff Davis for the brush . . . The boats are crowded with the debris of the Rebellion putting for up-the-river, trying to outrun their reputations . . . Missouri is emptying its Border Ruffians into the lap of Montana . . . ladies singing 'Stonewall Jackson's March' and 'Bonnie Blue Flag' . . . Will it [the Government] allow the Missouri to be the sewer to float such a population off—not even allowing their feelings to be hurt by requiring them to take the oath of allegiance? Let the bayonnet and the sword propel civilization into the Territories . . . and if taking the oath makes them pucker their mouths worse than a dose of castor-oil, so much the better . . . unless treason is stamped out, it will take root . . . assisted by the character of the country to the West it would make us a vast amount of trouble." Newspapers don't write editorials the way they used to.

It appeared the Army would prefer to face Indians than former Confederates. The same newspaper came out against the unsavory habits of the traders and their cheating of the Indians, expressing a vituperative opinion of the political figures and lobbyists that backed dishonest Indian agents. General Grant, having become President Grant, permitted or did not care to recognize the cesspool that comprised the Indian Bureau he appointed.

The Frontier Scout, describing Indian agents and traders and their power over the soldiers stated: "Troops are kept here at vast expense to the Government to act as bodyguard and menials for these men, generally disloyal and always rapacious . . . The Indian Bureau is the Slave Power of the Territories!"

A Colonel C. A. R. Dimon disagreed that the Indian agents should be punished. He believed a White Terror could cow the tribes and for reprisals he recommended "that for every soldier killed by treachery, kill twelve men or squaws, and meet any hostile acts with immediate punishment . . . The Indians are not governed by as strict laws among themselves as the whites." Aware that his ideas were in advance of their time (perhaps the Germans learned from him), Colonel Dimon did add that there would be opposition to his plans. "The treatment of Indians in the present state of affairs is a very delicate subject," he noted.

In all fairness, the colonel's suggestions on how to treat the common soldier balanced his ideas of how to control the Indians. The volunteers, recruited as soldiers in a time of trouble to help the regulars, had homes and families in most cases. During dull time with no action, instead of rotting away drinking and fornicating with Indian women, they decided to go on home without official permission.

Colonel Dimon wrote officially: "The battalion of the 4th U. S. Volunteers is fast mustering itself out by desertion. I have caught a great many of them and have them in the guard-house . . . I require permission to execute those guilty of desertion . . ." It does not appear that he got such permission to slaughter either Indian hostages or white volunteers. The soldiers could only return to exploration of dissipation under such officers.

Colonel Dimon seems to have been trouble-prone. Captain Adams, the poet, showed a remarkable lack of respect for the colonel and spent a great deal of his time in Fool Dog's tepee brothel. He was also twice accused of trying to rape Indian girls, and when off on a drunken spree, had to be carried to his bed by fellow officers. Another of Dimon's officers was accused of siding with the desires of the men to desert and with being drunk a great deal of the time. Colonel Dimon's reports are very full and detailed on these subjects.

The colonel, himself, was a moral man. No charges of tippling were entered against him and he refused an Indian girl concubine offered him by Chief Two-Bear as a gift. The Chief had not even asked the going price which, for a prime young squaw, was one blanket and a horse. The colonel was a much put-upon man, and perhaps his reports were more savage than his actions.

Not all frontier posts had such an uncongenial atmosphere though documents show dissipation was the rule, not the exception. What we do gather from journals, diaries, reports, and local news items is not the popular version of the hard, brave men in blue—standing tall in the saddle and holding the frontier to peace or setting the red man an example of the white man's discipline and firmness. The soldier, in rank and file and in the officers' mess, was human—often too, *too* human. Not habitually depraved, they were the victims of boredom, loneliness, the hard frontier life, and poor leadership.

It is possible to catch a glimpse of daily life at the average fort or trading post from one record kept by a trader, Charles Larpenteur: "Quiet times about the establishment . . . Weather extremely hot, musquitoes very bad for the first this season . . . Great row among the Squaws at night . . . having smuggled down a five-gallon keg of whiskey upon which they immediately commenced . . . a search was made but nothing was found. We turned them all out and making another search we found the five gallon and one bottle . . . very little while after been turned out they became sober and turned in again . . ."

If it all sounds like a small-scale buckskin Sodom and Gomorrah, much of it was a result of the agents' and traders' desire to mulct the Indian. The fort Poet, Enoch Adams, in a sober reappraisal, writes of the mercenary motives of the men by whose representations the season's operations have been controlled.

". . . We have long been convinced that the little knot of self-constituted guardians of this were animated by the sole desire of effecting the removal of the District Commander, and securing a successor less disposed to interfere with and to expose their nefarious Indian transactions . . ."

Chapter 18

THE FIGHT AT BEECHER'S ISLAND

Troops arrived in increasing numbers but moving more troops West was not enough to solve the problems. Events continued to be horrendous. It became clear that the Regular Army with its formal West Point ideas was not the sort of force to quell the Indians. General Phil Sheridan, Commander of the Department of Missouri, was dispatched in the crisis. Major George A. Forsyth suggested to Sheridan that what was needed was the implementation of a hard-hitting battalion of frontiersmen, scouts, trappers, and free-lance trail riders of the Plains who knew Indian ways and didn't know the rules and orders of white man's warfare to restrain them in killing Indians.

This plan was put into effect though it was officially decided to keep the number of these irregulars down to fifty. There was no trouble in recruiting restless Civil War veterans, burned-out settlers, Indian-haters, and buffalo and pelt hunters. They needed jobs and welcomed even the Army beans and coffee.

In September Major Forsyth was in the field with his polyglot shaggy crew to scout the Indian country. They were all mounted and carried carbines, Spencer six-shooters, Bowie knives, and whisky here and there in their deerskin packs. They were dressed in buckskin, old Army jackets, and a dozen different assortments of hats. One of them, as an afterthought, carried an American flag.

After a few days they picked up tracks of an Indian trail leading westward. The scouts figured from signs the aggregation was a big war party and they were right. They were trailing Chief Pawnee Killer's band and a guest committee of chiefs that included Roman Nose, White Horse, Tall Bull, and their warriors. These were shrewd, experienced fighters and they soon knew they were being trailed. It seemed a sound idea to lure the scouts down to the river.

The white adventurers reached and crossed the Arickaree which was not much of a river in September—yellow and sandy, a few yards of water trickling down a central channel. A shaggy island grown over with plum bush and cottonwood lay in midchannel. The frontiersmen decided to camp on the riverbank.

The day of September 17 broke with the loud, ominous cry of "Injuns!" as eight red raiders, flapping blankets and raising war cries, began to stampede the scouts' horses. The Indians got away with seven sorely needed mounts. Before the aroused camp could come fully to its sleepy senses, they saw the horizon was filled with mounted savages in war paint, waving lances, coupsticks, and rifles. Everybody hostile seemed to have on his best feathers and there were a lot of Indians coming down on the scouts, riding hard—enough Indians, it seemed, to completely fill the dry river bed.

With a wild rush the mass of whites made for the island in midchannel anchored in a few feet of tepid water. The scouts flung themselves into the brush and began to dig in with everything they had: frying pans, skinning knives, tin plates, even fingers.

The war party was a big one for fifty men to take on. A tall Indian in a magnificent headdress was roaring and riding back and forth on the riverbank. Major Forsyth and Sharp Grover, chief of the scouts, who was married to a Sioux squaw, figured out that the big Indian must be Roman Nose, himself. "Ain't another such Injun on the Plains." They were wrong. Roman Nose was taking his time dressing for battle and going through the ritual of putting on his magic headdress. He was facing that day an aggrieving theological problem.

A charge was mounted and coming, a cloud of Indians, speeding across the river sands, bent on overrunning the island. They were yipping and waving arms, and a blaze of colors—raw and savage—glowed in the sunny morning. Scouts skilled in Indian décor could pick out the various tribes represented in the war party. There were northern and southern Cheyennes, Arapahos, and the Brule Sioux. It was a battle with spectators, for squaws, children, dogs, and ponies were appearing on a hill overlooking the river—to witness the fight.

The scouts, on the first charge, grimly held their fire. They were not raw young soldier boys. They'd seen a deadly Indian rush before and bore scars to prove it.

At fifty yards' range, Major Forsyth yelled out: "Now!" White acid smoke and sharp red bursts of flame, shot from the plum bushes on the island, fired with deadly aim, hit the first rank of the charging riders. The repeating weapons kept up a steady fire. Horses screamed and tripped; riders fell from their backs. The squeals of tortured horses and outraged Indians could be heard over the rapid fire from the island. The charge divided to bracket the island with riders, who then drew off trailed by a few riderless ponies. Dead Indians lay within six feet of the plum bushes. The whites knew it was not over, coughed in the white smoke, panted in the white day, sweat under their hatbands. Many chewed on cuds of black-leaf tobacco and spit amber into the stream.

Horseless Indians began to creep into willow and brush to the south of the island. Rifle fire was exchanged and a few Indians died there before they moved out of range of the insidious repeaters.

The whites, once fifty-one men and officers, counted twenty-three dead and wounded. Among the dying was Lieutenant Beecher (the island was to be called Beecher's Island after him). Dr. Moorehead was also going into an agonizing lingering death in the heat. Major Forsyth had taken three wounds. Half the white force were casualties.

The Indians continued howling and reforming their ranks. Roman Nose was the man they needed but Roman Nose was having trouble with his gods.

The sacred war bonnet that rendered him immune was that day a defiled charm. He knew he was forbidden to eat food served him with an iron object but at a Sioux feast, a squaw slipped him a morsel of meat on an iron fork. When attention was called to this disrespect of the gods he rushed to make his purification rites. But he found there was no time. Major Forsyth and his men were on the riverbank and the rites needed calm contemplation and complete abasement of Roman Nose.

He refused to join the morning battle without his magic shield in full force. The Cheyennes were embarrassed by such a god-struck man because they were aware he might be called a coward (Sioux magic was not Cheyenne magic). They were troubled. But Roman Nose announced by midafternoon that he was ready for battle, no matter what his spiritual condition.

The giant Indian led the next charge. He rode ahead of the rush and it was now clear to the scout *this* was certainly Roman Nose—huge, his feathers tall, his headdress train fluttering behind him as wild war cries rose in pitch.

Roman Nose was almost on the island, his pony's hoofs flashing out of the stream to seek dry land. Two scouts standing to one side of the attack saw him and one, young Jack Stillwell, fired. The Indian chief fell hard, mortally wounded. He dragged himself into the brush, where several Indians came and carried him back to the waiting warriors. He died that night, his "magic" lost by the mundane use of an iron fork; died in the Cheyenne camp. The Indians fell back from the island lamenting their dead. Major Forsyth calculated that about one hundred Indians had died in the charges, though the Indians claimed they lost only seven men.

The night Beecher's Island eventually came into its own was an awful night—a time and place of dead, dying, and wounded. Fort Wallace was one hundred and fifty miles distant and the call for volunteers to make it out on foot and get help was announced. Every horse was dead and beginning to smell. The island was not too hospitable a place and every man who could move a limb—a phenomenon in the Army—volunteered.

The choice fell to Hank Trueau, an old and crafty trapper, and to nineteen-year-old Jack Stillwell, who presumably had fired the fatal shot which got Roman Nose.

The two men took off their boots, hung them around their necks, put on blankets in order to look like Indians from a distance and, after midnight, slipped off the island and away with curses and well-wishes for their luck whispered to them by the besieged scouts they left behind.

They made for downstream, aware the Indians were encamped someplace behind the river bluffs . . . Sounds of drumming and the cries of Indian women at their tasks (or dirges) came to their overalert ears. They left the river bed and crawled, taking five hours to cover two miles. At dawn, they hid in a dry gully. The strong sun beat down on them all day. They did not dare raise their heads to see if prowling Indians were about. Rifle fire from the direction of the island told them the desperate fight was still going on.

At the first cover of darkness, they were off at a quicker pace, still in danger from roving war parties. They hid once in the revolting carcass of a long-dead buffalo. Morning found them concealed under a riverbank and its tree roots. The next night they tried to make more speed and by morning they were on the great treeless Plains with no hiding place anywhere. The best they could find was a buffalo wallow, now dry, bearded with a few weeds among the bison chips. As they lay there, a small party of Cheyennes rode up and halted within sound range. Suddenly dime-novel melodrama was added to their agony. A rattlesnake in striking range lifted its head to eye the two paralyzed soldiers. They stared at it in frozen silence. A rattle from its buttons would attract the attention of the Indians. Any sound from the buffalo wallow would alert the Indians now resting their ponies.

Jack Stillwell had endured his parching journey by chewing tobacco, as most Westerners did in those days. He let fly a cheekful of acid amber tobacco juice, hitting the reptile in the head and eyes. The snake slithered away without making a sound.

The Cheyenne war party moved on soon after that and two very shaky soldiers looked at each other wondering why they were still alive. This would be a damn tall tale to tell around the campfires if they ever got out alive and kicking. After a night of relentless hiking, morning found Trudeau's strength failing, his steps beginning to falter. Stillwell supported him until Trudeau suddenly pointed and cried out: "Christ! there's the damn road!"

The road scarcely deserved the name but was well-grooved by stagecoach and wagon wheels and the hoofprints of shod horses—the Federal road to Fort Wallace. Soon Trudeau and Stillwell staggered into the fort area to deliver their dismal message of entrapment on the island.

Back there on the bush-covered island, things were no better. On the following night two more scouts were sent out to take the message to the fort in case the first two had failed in their objective. A 10th Cavalry, a Negro unit, finally arrived to find terrible scenes of suffering. The Indians had laid siege for six days, and when they rode away there were too many desperately wounded scouts to make up a party strong enough to break for freedom. Their only food was stinking horse meat, revolting in the heat. They had tried cooking it, mixed with gunpowder, but it was too far gone. They ate an unlucky coyote—a bit of a mouthful for those who were able to swallow. Major Forsyth, badly wounded, had decided that he and the wounded were to be abandoned. He had ordered all who could walk to start for the fort. The Negro troopers arrived in time to insist they stay where they were until a larger rescue force could reach the island.

On the ninth day after the first attack by Indians, a cloud of dust rolled up on the mainland. A scout warned of a new Indian attack but changed his cry.

"Hell, boys—it's a damn ambulance!"

Relief had come at last. The weakened men were fed and given whisky. The wounded received medical attention and slowly the rescued and the rescuers moved off to safety. En route, at the end of the valley, they saw a white teepee standing solitary and alone. Scouts rode forward to investigate. The body of a dead warrior chief lay in state, surrounded by his "medicine" and gear. The scouts assumed it was Roman Nose and robbed the corpse of weaponry, beadwork, and other war décor.

The body actually was that of the Cheyenne chief named Killed-by-a-Bull. He had been slain in one of the last charges at the island. The battle of Beecher's Island and the death of Roman Nose—because of his "lost magic"—has been romanticized by writers and raconteurs in Army camps, liars and tellers of tall tales. History in the Old West was no spectator sport.

Beecher's Island on the Arickaree River began to appear on the maps, and also many Indian names for places that still retain these early titles. For, if the Indian was in danger of losing his land, the land seemed in no danger of losing Indian identification in place names. (Lewis and Clark had been the first to use the label: *The Great Plains.*) The early migrants had no desire to use Indian names. The Spanish, the French, and the English found Indian dialects very difficult. Indians used several primitive sounds unknown to white people. The first white men put down what they *thought* they'd heard.

Scholars have industriously studied Indian names given to mountains, towns, and rivers of the West. The result is often confusing but there are obvious connections between original Indian names and place names we use today. *Yo-sem-i-ty* was the Indian name of a tribe, meaning Grizzly Bear. *Ouchage* became Osage after refinement of spelling, along with *Messouri* which became Missouri. Omaha originally meant *Up-River People; Oua-ouia* became Iowa; *Ouaeache* resulted in Wabash; *Ni-Bthaska* in Nebraska.

Some place names had curious derivations. In the Algonquin language the word *assin* meant stone. (The English called this tribe "Stonies.") The Indians called a great range of mountains in the west the *Mountains of Shiny Stones*. The French translated this to *Montaignes Rocheuses* and the English translated the French to *Rocky Mountains*.

The Minnatarie word for yellow stone was *mitsiadazi*. Probably the settlers couldn't pronounce it and translated it into English—Yellowstone. *Ouisconsink* became Wisconsin. Chippewa for valley crown, by the way, was *pa-sa-de-na*—which ought to surprise the population of that region today.

The Ute tribe named Utah; others gave titles to Kansas, Sioux City and Mount City; the Kiowa Apaches' name for the Comanche was *Idahi*, so Idaho was born. In the Choctaw tongue, *okla* means people, and *homa* red. Indian *M-chweaming* became Wyoming. (The city of Denver has no Indian roots. It was named for James Denver, a Commissioner of Indian Affairs, and not much more an Indian despoiler than most commissioners.) The tribal name Cheyenne may first have been recorded by a Frenchman as *chienne*—a female dog (a bitch). Sometimes the whites produced a pretty name where no pretty name existed in the Indian language. Minnesota is doubtful Indian for *Sky Blue Waters*.

The French also left their mark on place names in Indian country. From the Wolf tribe, they translated *Loup River*. In their Gaelic ardor, they saw female breasts in every mountain peak. *Mamelle* and *teton* became Nipple Butte and Tit Butte. *Cache* Creek and Powder River were named after locations of stores of gunpowder.

The white people didn't bother with too many fancy names in the beginning. Emigrant Gap and Battle Mountain explain themselves. Bull Rock was changed to Man Cow Rock. Civil War generals were honored by having forts and towns named for them —McClellan, Burnside, Sherman, and Hooker (the red-light district of Washington was called "Hooker's Division," as a tribute to the general's love of whores and the word *hooker,* east and west, to describe a prostitute, also honored "Fightin' Joe" Hooker). Sheridan, Logan, Rawlins, and Kearny also gave names to forts or stations. The sound of these names never had the music of the Indian sounds. Chili Gulch, Frying-Pan Slough, Slim Diggin's, Pancake, Hell-fer-Sartain, Whisky Crick, Hangtown, Gouge Eye, Chicken-Thief Flat, Brandy Gulch, Stud-Hoss Canyon, Red Dog (a card game), and Hardscrabble. All these have a rough-hewed male tone and are ruggedly descriptive. They had almost all disappeared. Hangtown, where somebody hung by the neck until dead, is now Placerville.

Some mapmakers made polite conversions of places: Guano Crick once had a more earthy four-letter name. Whore Creek became Putah Creek (Spanish translation made crude titles sound better to American ears). *La Panza* for the Paunch, *La Paleta,* for the Shoulder Blade. There are thirty-two Winchesters on the map, named after the popular shootin' iron, the reliable rifle of the Plains. *Cibola* is Spanish for Buffalo and there were once many Cibolas on the map.

The Indian names have remained the most popular and lasting. But truth is, not many bear much resemblance to the Indian originals. Experts often contradict one another's research.

Legend and myth are the bread of ordinary men. In time we want to believe it was as it should have been—not the way it really was. In tracking down history, it is necessary to add the grain of salt. Many great grandsons of the pioneers have been led to believe that their great-grandfathers were all giants who dropped the acorns to produce the forests and never made a false move. We accept attitudes toward our past that have little bearing on the facts. There is too much de Tocqueville in our bear-suet past, in the multiplicity of the alienations from our past.

Unfortunately there are no cities, towns, or states named after Sitting Bull or Crazy Horse, no rivers are called Geronimo, Black Kettle, Santana, or Cochise.

IV

Blue Soldiers and Redmen

How solemn and beautiful is the thought that the earliest pioneer of civilization, the van-leader of civilization, is never the steamboat, never the railroad, never the newspaper, never the Sabbath-school, never the missionary—but always whisky! . . . Westward the Jug of Empire takes its way . . .

—MARK TWAIN

The more Indians we can kill this year, the less will have to be killed the next war.

—GENERAL WILLIAM TECUMSEH SHERMAN

Chapter 19

CUSTER, THE MAN AND THE LEGEND SEPARATED

For all the vituperation visited on his name General George Armstrong Custer was a man of parts. He has been much maligned by historians, and his side of the story, the theoretic and the practical, has rarely been told. Custer was a better officer than his nay-sayers indicate. He fought remarkably well in the Civil War when he was just out of West Point. At twenty-six, he wore the insignia of a major general of Volunteers. He commanded the cavalry and his career as a leader was flamboyant and daring. He was able at that time. If he had lost too many actions he would have had his come-uppance then.

Custer was a forerunner of Patton-type leadership and in battle—firm and self-willed. He was dedicated to the Army and in trouble with his superior officers and high-placed civilians. Custer was his own worst enemy, next to the foe in the field. At Gettysburg, he was on the flank, battering southern horse when he should—serious historians think—have been better employed as the lookout for General Meade.

Custer was eccentric—perhaps to make up for his lack of height, his bandy legs, his sharp, hawklike face and absence of chin. A dandy, he designed his own uniforms; liked gold braid and velvet; shiny hip boots and flowing hair. The Indians called him "Long Hair" after the golden flood falling to his shoulders. (Most of the historic paintings of the Little Big Horn are wrong. He had had his locks shorn just before starting that last march.) His hats were wide—too wide. He took to frontier buckskin with all its fringes and even beadwork. He was a writer, producing vivid, blood-tingling magazine articles about the Western Indian wars and life at the Army posts (eventually collected as *My Life on the Plains*). His adoring wife, Elizabeth Barrett Custer, also wrote and left several volumes of memorabilia.

Custer came to the West seeking to renew his hopes for glory. He got into trouble interfering with Indian policy and made enemies in high places. Some military critics say he was a Captain Bligh to his troops, but we must give him credit for loving the Great Plains—for seeing the beauty, the crystal-sharp hardness of the West. He lived among stinging insect varmints and parching droughts. He knew, as the scouts put it, how often "the rain is all wind and the wind all sand." He was like an Indian at home among the mesquite scrub in weather that was often so blistering hot that "a wolf chasing a jackrabbit—why, they're both walkin'!" as the jest went. He ate sow-belly with his troopers when he had to, kept a clean camp, liked to set his dogs on the coyote or go into a quail covey and bring in a good meal. Custer liked style, ceremony, and the comradeship of his practical-joke-playing fellow officers. He drove his men, and he had no respect for Indians, except a liking for their women. He was a born soldier and that needs no psychological explanation.

Custer didn't mind the scouts talking of the Plains "so flat . . . you had to put up a sign 'rainy season' to tell the water which way to flow." Like General George S. Patton, Jr., whom he most resembled in everything but height, Custer was eager for fame, for public and official notice. There is nothing wrong in this in a soldier. One doesn't expect sensitive perception. War is an unnatural condition to most of mankind, and it must brutalize men and insist on their obeying any order merely because of the insignia worn by those in command.

Dedicated men like Custer kept the frontier in some degree of order—they had no easy time of it, and not much real help from the political powers who controlled the Army. The Army never had enough men; recruits were often the leavings, the dispossessed, the outlaws. Supplies for the Army made many men rich as contractors. These contractors sold supplies for exorbitant prices—often through bribery or patronage of the spoils system. Grant's administration was one of the most corrupt in American history. Rotten pork and beef, shoddy blankets, worn-out weapons, horses and mules not up to specifications were typical of Army supplies. Forts were dismal and functional at best—barracks hard to heat, hard to cool. Men like Custer gave the Army its reputation for quality and effectiveness. The Indian fighting armies of the West were good armies and many of the officers were splendid soldiers.

Custer faced the dilemma of how, on an indifferent frontier, he could regain the reputation and glory he had won during the Civil War—a little tarnished now that the country had had a glut of heroes and soldiers. The nation had made the gesture it often does of electing a popular general to the presidency, but the prevailing mood was no longer military.

Custer was settled in, writing gory, high-keyed prose for the Eastern magazines. His wife was accepting the worshipful, respectful glances of the young officers and the general's greyhounds were learning to chase the lean Plains fox and the fleeter deer.

General Phil Sheridan was upset by the failure to bring the Cheyennes to their knees and he decided the only thing to do was what General Sherman had done in his march through Ceorgia —destroy their bases, burn their homes (in this case, their winter camps), and leave those he didn't kill to starve and freeze to death in the snows of winter if they continued to reject reservation life.

This was a task cut out for the eager General Custer. The great blizzard of the 22nd of November, 1868, had left over a foot of snow underfoot when he headed the 7th Cavalry south out from Camp Supply, Indian Territory, to roust out Indians on the Washita River. On one flank was a column led by General Carr (seven troops of 5th Cavalry) and another column under Colonel Evans (six troops of horse-soldiers, two of footsloggers, four mountain howitzers). So flanked, Custer was protected on both sides.

On the 26th of November Custer picked up a raiding party's tracks—a band that had been killing mail-bearers, hunters, and even Army dispatch carriers. Hound-dog-eager, Custer followed the tracks coming upon the still-hot embers of the fires of Indian herd boys. Somewhere ahead was a Cheyenne village. An Osage Indian scout, Little Beaver, and the general himself went ahead, sniffing out the lay of the land from a nearby hill. The white surface of the snow stretched away, below dotted with a huge horse herd. From a distance came the sounds of songs and bells —signals confirmed Custer's opinion that he was almost within reach of a very big Indian encampment.

Truth was again stranger than fiction for the lodges were those of Black Kettle's own village—he who had been wiped out in another village, Sand Creek. Black Kettle had been trying to arrange a peace and he lay now with his tribe in plain sight of Custer. What Custer didn't know was that up and down the valley were other Indian camps filled with Arapaho, Kiowas, Comanche, more Cheyenne and even Apaches. In all, two thousand warriors could be mustered in these villages.

The Custer plan of the maneuver was simple: Four detachments under Major Elliott with three troops; Captain Thompson, two; Captain Meyers, two and the general to command four troops. He proposed the encirclement of the village he knew was there. (As yet, he was unaware of the other villages and he didn't do any scouting.) Custer was new to the Indian ways of doing things. Also, the Federation of the Tribes in force was not suspected of being so well organized. This could have accounted for his carelessness.

In position, the soldiers shivered, clicked teeth, cursed the land, the war, the Indians, and their officers. While waiting for dawn, the horses stood saddled, tails to the wind, heads down. Weapons gleamed as the first pale-pearl light of dawn came. The bugler set cold metal to chapped lips and blew a mighty charge. From four directions the soldiers in blue rode out. They rousted the Cheyennes from their sleeping robes by the clatter and hoofbeats and fired off one round of bullets before they hit the tepees.

Black Kettle, his wife, and many of the tribe died where they fell by their tepees. Men, women, and children were slain. Survivors, as was usual in a surprise raid, made for the river. The weather was mean—a record cold. The Indians were almost naked and the river was covered with an ice sheet. The Indians were razored by the breaking ice as they ran. Women made for the riverbank carrying or pulling their children. A number were ridden down by the smoking horses of the soldiers, with sabers and carbines taking toll. The icy water turned pink with Indian lifeblood. Some bucks managed to set up a small rear-guard action before being slaughtered. A squaw knifed a small white boy captive and was shot down. There was no mercy on either side in this brittle, biting cold, a world of white blotched by red stains.

At ten o'clock, Custer lifted his arm to signify the massacre was over. He saw, in shocked amazement, hundreds of armed warriors coming up the valley to attack. An Indian woman prisoner (Custer was sexually fond of Indian girls) cried out that there were villages full of Indians for ten miles along the river.

Custer didn't fluster. He was a genuinely brave man and experienced, if overbold. He set up a battle line of troopers and began to pull back to the hills. Score for the massacre: one officer, five men dead; one white woman captured and her child murdered; an unknown white boy murdered; Major Elliott and fourteen men missing in action. The Indian losses were far heavier: Two chiefs—Black Kettle and Little Rock—dead; over one hundred Cheyenne men, women, and children dead.

When it came to the animal kingdom, Custer shot seven hundred Indian horses. He burned a thousand buffalo robes, destroyed a thousand pounds of lead and powder and nearly five thousand arrows. This was war as General Sherman had made out, and it *was* hell.

Some historians point out we in the twentieth century are no longer shocked by military violence. We accept civilian bombing, napalm, atrocity as we do breathing. The people of the nineteenth century *were* shocked.

Custer took prisoners away with him—fifty-three squaws and children. There was still no sign of Elliott and his men, but it was too dangerous to hunt him now. A few days later, Custer was again on the trail out of Fort Supply, accompanying the 19th newly raised Kansas Cavalry. The detail was seeking two captured white girls—a bride—by the name of Mrs. Morgan, and an unmarried woman named White.

December 9th: Weather below zero ("freeze the balls off a brass monkey!" wrote one soldier). Direction: To the Washita. In the ruined village, which was quite empty, they discovered the fate of Major Elliott and his fourteen men. They had been surrounded by Indians (who were outraged at seeing the ruin of Black Kettle's camp) were overwhelmed and all the white men were killed. Now they lay frozen in death, each in exactly the position in which he had fallen. All were scalped, naked, multilated, with their white, dry teeth gleaming in the freezing air. Only the body of Sergeant Major Kennedy was missing. He had gone out to surround, fought his way out of the circle, then, instead, had sabered an Indian and was gang-killed. It was his form of suicide—quick and clean.

Of the women captives, there was no sign. Custer detailed a burial party to hack at the frozen earth and retrieve the bodies. It was too cold to fight, Custer contented himself with several Kiowa chiefs he found, arrested and held as hostages, to encourage their tribe to go back to the reservations. The war would have to wait until the spring thaws.

Chapter 20

WHITE WOMEN AND RED WOMEN

Custer wintered at Fort Cobb, aching for spring and action. There was certainly no glory in fretting in freezing, horse-smelling quarters. When spring finally came, Custer, guided by a Cheyenne girl, found the village where the two white women were being kept. He yearned to attack but he knew such a course would result in the quick murder of the captives. Days of strategy talk went on then Custer retaliated, seizing Cheyenne hostages for bargaining purposes. He also promised gifts in return for the white captives. The strategy succeeded and the two girls came riding out to him on one pony. Mrs. Morgan, the bride, didn't survive her Indian experience many years but Miss White married, reared a family, and lived to a ripe old age.

Custer had skillfully handled a very ticklish situation. He had been stern at the right time and recovered the women, but he was never popular and there was whispered talk that he had deserted Major Elliott and his men. By military rule Custer *had* acted properly to save his entire command from being wiped out. From now on, his luck was destined to go up and down; his striving for glory and action never achieved an immense peak and he moved toward the final tragedy at the Little Big Horn.

Private records mention Custer's fondness for Indian girls. One of the prisoners he brought back from Black Kettle's camp was the beautiful daughter of a minor chief who had been killed in that battle. She was called Monahseeteh. Custer talked General Sheridan into letting him keep her as "an interpreter," although she neither spoke nor understood one word of English. He lived with her as his concubine (mistress would be too respectful a word) for four months, leaving her behind only to rejoin his wife at Fort Hays.

The Indians by now had perfected a dedicated unit of fighting specialists—reminiscent of the S. S. Guards, or the Green Berets of the twentieth century. They were called the *ho-ta-min-tanio,* a Cheyenne word that could be translated as "The Dog Soldiers' Society"—a special fighting band of elite warriors; the best, the bravest, the most cruel of the Indians.

Eventually, the order spread to the Arapaho, Sioux, and other Plains tribes. The society had its own signs, omens, rituals, markings, music, songs, taboos, costumes, "medicine," and dances. Tall Bull (IV) was the leader. In the spring of 1869, the Dog Soldiers were camped near the source of the Republic River and from that base, they raided in all directions. They captured women, supplies and hundreds of mules and horses.

General Eugene Carr and five companies of the 5th Cavalry, together with fifty Pawnee scouts, sallied out in July, looking for Dog Soldiers. The Indians boldly tried to stampede the soldiers' horses but were driven off and a classic chase began. Somehow, the Cheyenne women, children, dogs, and baggage managed to keep ahead of the hot pursuit. The Indians scattered in all directions—an old trick to confuse with too many trails. The scouts suggested Carr follow the faintest trail as the well-marked one was a typical Indian ploy. When the faint trail was lost by the scouts Carr decided to go on anyway and, in stifling, dusty heat made sixty-five miles the next day. The heel mark of a white woman's shoe was discovered in the dust. On July 11, an Indian Army scout located the Indians' camp, the village of Tall Bull. The Platte River was running high and he couldn't get across it.

The soldiers spotted the enemy massed under a bluff in the valley below. Carr wasted no time and ordered a charge. The blue horsemen were in the village before many Indians were aware of them. A white woman captive running from a lodge trying to escape became a target for the Indians. A trooper cried out to her, "Lay down there!" The horsemen began to leap over her prone body as she lay in the dust. This hopeless creature was a Mrs. Weichell, a German woman taken prisoner in Kansas. She was wounded by an Indian bullet in her chest. She was not the only white captive in the village. An Indian warrior brained another white woman with a tomahawk in full sight of the troopers. The murderer, reputed to be Tall Bull himself, was killed. The white woman was said to be his concubine. Her child was strangled by other Indians. However, this was a case of mistaken identity. Tall Bull was still alive.

When the Indians finally broke and ran, fifty-two were dead and one hundred and seventeen prisoners were taken. The camp and its supplies and lodges were all burned. No casualties were listed by General Carr from among his contingent with the exception of one man wounded. The battle was soon to be called Summit Springs.

Tall Bull himself, his other wife (Indian) and his child were cornered in the shadow of a canyon where he stabbed his horse to death. (His horse was his most valued possession.) Tall Bull was shot down by an officer and his wife and child captured. Thirteen Indians died with Tall Bull in this melee. The chief's scalp was on exhibition for many years at *Pawnee Bill's Old Town* near Pawnee, Oklahoma.

The wounded Mrs. Weichell—so the records show—was presented with $1500 found in the Indian camp in reparation for her suffering. This engagement ended the war on the Colorado and Kansas plains for a long time.

In the south, the most deadly of the small Indian tribes, the Kiowa, had the war pipe smoking again. For their size and weight, the Kiowas, adding up figures in official records, killed more white men and women in proportion than any tribe on the Plains.

Their great leader was known to them as *Se-Tain-te,* White Bear; to the white he was Satanta. He had the usual Indian background (Indian history is banal and dull) almost a formula of any chief's beginnings. Great as a hunter, fighter, rider, horsebreaker, able to face all adversity, including starvation and privation, without succumbing to any vocal or emotional reaction. That is Indian tradition and Indian history of Satanta's life. He was probably far more human than his history admits. His later life certainly shows us a red Homer's Wily Ulysses—fond of the grape.

At twenty, Satanta was a blooded warrior and in partnership

with a chief called *Se-Tan-Gya* (Satank by the whites). When Satank died in 1871, Satanta had no rivals. He led war bands to raid clear to Durango, Mexico. His Kiowas and Cheyennes liked to wait in the shade of Pawnee Rock in Kansas, to come out, howling and shooting, against the wagon trains, freighters, stage-coaches. At times they dominated the Santa Fe Trail. They were like a dim hovering of bad dreams to the frontier.

Satanta, when not on the warpath, liked to get around. He even visited the forts and made speeches. He had the Indian weakness for long and fancy speeches. The U. S. Army officers felt he was a good fellow, when not a bloody bastard. He was welcome in peacetime, when sober.

The death of Tall Bull brought a kind of peace to the Plains unless a war party cut off a trader or trapper or carried off a white girl. Satanta was under honorable house arrest, held by Custer at Fort Dodge, but mostly he was rattling around the fort, drunk, continually cadging for whisky. A stage driver gave him some "mule-drench," an animal medicine, for booze and the chief gulped it down in one swallow and said he felt he needed something to take the bad taste away.

"It make my heart bad," he said.

An officer saw to it that the Indian got a bottle of the most sickening evil medicine; it was either done as a bad joke, or to punish Satanta. The second bottle jolted the Indian into a frenzy. Hopping on one foot then on the other in inner agony, he went howling through the fort, spitting foam, mouth gasping, eyes rolling in his head. Everybody thought his act very funny. They belly-laughed and slapped their thighs to see the God-damned drunken varmint get his comeuppance.

The next morning, Satanta burned the U. S. Army's hay supply, rallied his band and murdered three woodcutters. This was a heavy price to pay for a poor jest. Satanta then went on the war-path, killing and torturing. By May, the Kiowas were raiding in Texas in the Red River country. All the punishment for this was that Chiefs Satanta, Satank, and Big Tree were given jail terms in the Fort Richardson Penitentiary when they submitted to arrest.

Satank was in decline. He was old and eccentric—carrying the bones of his dead son with him, refusing to bury them. The whites took away the bones when they arrested him, and Satank became very depressed and no longer was accepted as a war chief.

In the Army wagon on the way to prison, Satank sent news of himself by a message to his tribe.

"Tell them I am dead. I died the first day out. My bones will by lying by the side of the road. It is my wish that my people gather them [the bones] up and take them home . . ."

Then he rolled his head and began to send out a death chant. Under the keening, he managed to remove his iron shackles from his hands, taking a great deal of his flesh away with them, then, seizing a hidden knife, he stabbed a trooper and grabbed up an Army carbine. But the gun's lever action defied him. Satank was shot down by the sergeant of the prison detail.

Satanta and Big Tree were peacefully incarcerated at Fort Richardson and the Indian world dissolved for them for two years.

There was still fighting on the periphery. Colonel Ronald McKenzie, with a section of the 4th Cavalry—two hundred and eighty men—found Chief Mo-wi and his Quahada Comanches camped on McClellan Creek in two hundred and fifty lodges with five hundred warriors.

The major cried out: "Right front, into line . . . *Charge!*"

Two-thirds of the troopers rode to attack; the rest went off to seize the pony herds. The Comanches broke and ran. The troops lost three dead; seven wounded; the Indians, twenty-three dead, and over a hundred prisoners.

Also, the huge pony herds were seized. The major burned the camp and the Comanches who had fled to the hills were on foot. For a Comanche, this was not only a disgrace but rendered him almost a basket case. A Comanche did nearly everything but mate on horseback.

The Indians attacked that night (a night attack was rare, but Indians would do it if desperate). They not only recovered all their ponies, but took along the horses of Major McKenzie's Tonkawa Indian scouts.

Naturally, a new Federal Commission soon was set up to create more treaties . . . The Indians' one demand was: "Give us back Satanta and Big Tree."

The two chiefs were released on parole. The agent at Fort Sill resigned at this turn of events.

"The effect," he said, "of the release of Satanta to the Kiowas—

he was a daring and treacherous chief—is like a dark, rolling cloud on the western horizon." They spoke that way in 1873.

Two years in a dusty, dirty prison cell had changed Satanta. Gone was the jolly, fun-making, drink-begging Indian. He was now, perhaps, stir-crazy, and while it had not crushed his spirit entirely, the prison term had made him inhuman: He was mean, defiant, full of the acid revenge—revenge on whites. At forty-three, he looked many years older, more morose than anyone could remember him.

He appeared to settle down on the reservation; then, suddenly, on a spring morning, he was gone. Kiowas, Cheyenne, Comanches were suddenly making bloody war again. This uprising covered five states and the general in command was the bitter, insane-eyed Satanta.

Of civilians, nearly two hundred died and many, many soldiers followed. Satanta ranged from New Mexico to Texas—from Camp Supply to the Washita and Fort Sill's agencies. At every place, a few dead whites were left, stripped, scalped, or carried away to be tortured in the most cruel way—torn, burned at leisure to fragments of living men, begging (if still able) for death.

As far back as 1864, there was brought to the attention of the Indians one sad truth. Something was happening to the buffalo herds. They were diminishing. Look where they would, the Comanche, Cheyenne, Kiowa, Arapaho hunters could find no herds. Indians who had been enemies for generations now banded together to seek the buffalo. They climbed buttes and canyon walls; they set up signals on promontories, keen eyes searching the vast void for the clouds of dust made by those thousands and thousands of bison. But there was nothing to be seen on the Plains, but high up a hungry hawk here and there, tirelessly circling on motionless wings.

Indian riders went out to the Staked Plains of Texas where a few scattered and small herds were still to be seen. But the spilling, churning, and almost endless passage of bison, those great migrations that had fed, housed, and clothed the Indians for so long, had dwindled and disappeared. "Medicine" was chanted to Great Lord Buffalo until the Indians dropped with exhaustion. No buffalo.

There was another factor of the Great Plains as important as the Indian and the buffalo. That was the grass. Grass had existed and evolved for thousands of years, and without it there would have been no great buffalo herds. Without the buffalo, no nations of Indians on the Plains would have developed. The white man first exterminated the buffalo, then got rid of the Indian, then proceeded to break the sod, to destroy the grass. Tragedy followed, for the grass roots, often six feet deep, held the soil together, kept the land fertile through great droughts, and helped control erosion when the mountain floods came and the rivers ran wild. With the grass destroyed the land became a ruin. The climax was reached in the huge Dust Bowl disasters of the twentieth century when much of the top soil blew away.

This continent was once the greatest grassland on earth, coming down from the Saskatchewan-Manitoba region, directly south, on the 98th meridian to the Mexican Gulf. The grassland ran westward to the foot of the Rockies, encompassing much of Wyoming, Montana, Colorado, New Mexico, the Dakotas, Kansas, Nebraska, Oklahoma, and what is still called the Texas Panhandle.

In 1837 an Englishman, James Silk Buckingham, was amazed at what he saw. "As far as the eye could reach, in every direction, there was neither tree, nor shrub, not house, nor shed visible; so that we were rolling on as it were on the bosom of a new Atlantic, but that the sea was of rich green grass and flowers, instead of the briny and bottomless deep."

In a mere fifty years the grass would be gone with the buffalo and the Indian. The homesteader, the rancher, the sheepman would have torn up the sod, the longhorn overgrazed the Plains, the sheep with their sharp faces and teeth and eating habits, devouring roots and all; these would make the land into a desert and encourage erosion turning the Plains to desolation.

The grass had been native to the Plains, conditioned to the environment, holding the moisture, lying dormant when it had to weather the dry periods. The buffalo had grazed and moved on before overcropping the grass. But the settler with his plow, the greedy rancher with his herds of cattle, the sheepman with his fleecy menaces were natural enemies of the grass that held the Plains, gave the buttes, the mesas, sandhills, badlands, and depressions protection in a land where the temperature could vary from 60 below in a blue norther to 115 above, when even the rattlesnakes went into hiding.

What kind of grass was it that covered the Plains? Blue grama, buffalo grass, three awns, partly mesquite, big blue stem. There were waving thickets of the tall grass in fertile areas and even on the worst land there was red ray, bottle brush, fool hay, jungle rice, pancake, panie grass. Millions of buffalo thrived on it and the grass grew a new crop in time for next year's herds.

Over thirty Indian tribes roamed and fed on this sea of green and umber grass; the Cheyenne, Sioux, Crow, Arapaho, Blackfeet, Apache, Comanche, Pawnee, and others. The homesteaders came on from 1862 with their plows. They could own the land for a small fee for their claims and five years homesteading on the land; the land was free by an Act of Congress. Fencing of the great open spaces began. In 1873 the first of the great droughts came to harass the settlers, followed by the Rocky Mountain grasshopper, which fed on stem and leaves of everything colored green, even tablecloths on the line. Overcrowding, overuse of grazing land, the sharp biting teeth of the sheep and their hoofs defaced the land. John Wesley Powell made a survey for Congress, in 1878, and reported: "Stock grazing is causing more injury to the grass lands than even the farmers."

By the 1890s the prehistoric sod was being torn away by the introduction of vast wheat farms into the Red River Valley. Farms comprising 65,000 acres became common. The grass was lost for good. Even the dry short grass lands, not really fit for crops, were put to the plow as the stock markets gambled in wheat and pigs and beef. The twentieth century paid the price for the destruction of the grass. Great dark clouds of dust rose from the windy Plains, reaching eastward to Washington, D.C. and the Eastern Shore of Maryland. Dust clouds were reported at sea, two hundred miles from shore, over a thousand miles from the Plains. By the time the damage was done, neither farmer nor cattleman could use big sections of the Plains. Russian thistle, tumbleweed, goosefoot, sunflowers took over. Then came the trash weeds: stickweed, little barley, peppergrass. In time and in some places nature tried again, with dropseed, wheat grass, the false buffalo grass. There was hope that the true buffalo grass, the grama types, the three awns would some day take hold.

The surviving Indians were locked away in barren reservations;

buffalo, even as zoo animals, were few and under protection in some areas. Vast armies of farmers and ranchers were ruined, drifting west in jalopies with the Okies; to be beaten back by the police of California, as unwanted as an Indian raid, or a stampeding herd of buffalo. Such was the tragedy of the end of the grass on the Great Plains, part of the final third act of the Indian's failure to survive.

Gone too was the careless fatalism of a Texas rancher bragging: "This ain't no country fer little two-by-four farmers. The big thing about the plains is that you don't have to feed stock. It can rustle fer itself. You can yoke it up with stepmaw Nature an' the pair, if they wants to, can make the dollars crawl into yer jeans."

Chapter 21

DEATH OF THE BUFFALO HERDS

The decline of the buffalo herds was the ultimate tragedy for the Indians of the Plains. Without buffalo, they starved. They had little else to hunt. Lost was the source for food, clothing, tepee covering, gear made of buffalo fur and hide. The buffalo was tasty eating: his hump a gourmet's delight and the gut, slightly singed, much prized. It was almost impossible for an Indian raised on buffalo meat to eat the stringy, tasteless steers the agency provided for him on the reservations and he got few enough of those from a dishonest agent. Most officials were indifferent to the Indian, except as a means of making a trader or agent rich. Bull boats, sleeping robes, saddles, belting, parfleche, pouches—all were best made from buffalo hide. Jerked buffalo meat, sun-dried or smoked, carried the red man over a hard winter. Buffalo chip—the dried dung—made fine fires on a treeless plain. Now the great herds were fading away.

The white men were not just thinning the herds; they were exterminating them in their greed for pelts. Buffalo hunters left hundreds of thousands, then millions, of carcasses to rot away unused, wasting vital food and abolishing all the other useful purposes the Indian might have realized.

A hide-hunter was interested only in cash value of hides; he didn't give a damn for the Indians' needs. A hide-hunting outfit with skinners could kill hundreds of buffalo in one day and the slaughter never let up. The hunters were armed with a deadly weapon—a Buffalo gun; actually, the Sharps .50-calibre, sending a 600-grain of lead shot backed by 125 grains of powder, for the kill. Heavy and long-bored, the Sharps rifle was deadly in the hands of an expert shot. Buffalo have poor eyesight and a hide-hunter on the right side of the wind could kill an entire herd while they grazed one by one without stampeding them. Thousands of buffalo hunters stalked the migrations.

The skinner was a skilled specialist. Two skinners with a team of horses—speedy workers—slit the skin of the bison belly and up the legs; then, hitching one end of the skin to the team, the horses were driven forward to peel off the hide. Bales of hides packed every railhead—40,000 accumulated some days at Dodge City. Prices fell as more hunters appeared—hides going from five dollars each to four bits (a half dollar). In two years (from 1872 to 1874) when some sort of company records were kept, the railroads shipped out a million and a half hides and nearly seven million pounds of buffalo tongues and hams.

Besides this, the railroad meat killers slaughtered thousands of buffalo to feed their workers. William Cody was such a meat hunter for the Goddard Brothers, who fed the construction crews of the Kansas-Pacific Railroad. In seven months he killed 4280 buffalo on the job. He was a feckless frontier drunkard but a handsome figure of a man with his fringed buckskins, long blond hair, and courtly goatee.

A journalist who called himself Ned Buntline labeled him Buffalo Bill and wrote a set of invented adventures about him. In this long series of dime novels, Cody was a great Indian killer, too. Actually, Army records show he was once a scout with the 5th Cavalry and that he had ridden for the Pony Express. Two quarts of whisky was his daily dosage if he could get it and mostly, he could. Of all the buffalo killers, Cody became the most famous.

For a truer picture of the buffalo slaughter, one can turn to the memories of Robert Wright who hunted, killed, and shipped buffalo pelts for fifteen years from the buffalo Plains country. He knew the buffalo when, as he says, it was impossible to count them. "I have traveled through a herd of them days and days, never out of sight of them; in fact, it might be correctly called one continuous gathering of the great shaggy monsters.

"I have been present at many a cattle roundup and have seen ten-thousand head in one herd and under complete control of their drivers; but I have seen herds of buffalo so immense in number that the vast aggregation of domestic cattle seemed as nothing at all compared with them. The southwestern plains, in early days, was the greatest country on earth and the buffalo was the noblest as well as the most plentiful of the game animals. I have, indeed, traveled through buffaloes along the Arkansas River for two-hundred miles, almost one continuous herd as close together as it is customary to herd cattle. You might go north or south as far as you pleased and there would seem no diminution of their numbers. When they were suddenly frightened and stampeded, they made a roar like thunder and the ground seemed to tremble. When, after nightfall, they came to the river, particularly when it was in flood, their immense numbers in their headlong plunge would make you think, by the thunderous noise, that they had dashed all the water from the river. They often went without water one and two days in summer and much longer in winter. No one had any idea of their numbers.

"General Sheridan and Major Inman were at Fort Dodge one night, having just made the trip from Fort Supply, and called me in to consult as to how many buffaloes there were between Dodge and Supply. Taking a strip fifty miles east and fifty miles west, they had first made it ten billion. General Sheridan said, 'That number don't do.' They figured it again, and made it one billion. Finally they reached the conclusion that there must be one-hundred billion; but said they were afraid to give out these figures; nevertheless, they believed them. This vast herd moved slowly toward the north when spring opened, and moved steadily back again from the far north when the days began to grow short and winter was settling in.

"Horace Greeley estimated the number of buffaloes at five million. I agree with him, only I think there were nearly five times that number. I lived in the heart of the buffalo range for nearly fifteen years.

"I am told that some recent writer who has studied the buffalo closely has placed their number at ninety million and I think that he is nearer right than I. Brick Bond, a resident of Dodge—an old, experienced hunter, a great shot, and a most reliable man as to . . . honesty says that he killed fifteen hundred buffaloes in seven days and his highest killing was two-hundred and fifty in one day, and he had to be on the lookout for hostile Indians all the time. He had fifteen skinners, and he was only one of many hunters.

"Charles Rath and I shipped over two-hundred thousand buffalo hides the first winter the Atchison, Topeka and Santa Fe. Railroad reached Dodge City and I think there were at least as many more shipped from there, besides two hundred cars of hind-quarters and two cars of buffalo tongues. Often have I shot them from the walls of my corral, for my hogs to feed upon. Several times, I have seen wagon-trains stop to let the immense herds pass; besides, many of them, wounded, would wander off, out of sight and reach, and were not found until they were unfit for market; and the Indians claimed that the noise of the hunters' guns and their mode of killing would soon drive the buffalo out of the country or annihilate them. Time has proved that the Indians were correct.

"A band of hunters cared no more for Indians than Indians did for foot-soldiers and, unless they greatly outnumbered the hunters—and then only under the most favorable circumstances—the Indians would not attack the hunters. They were afraid of the hunters' big guns, his cool bravery and, last but not least, of his unerring, deadly aim. Then, too, the hunter had but little plunder that was dear to the Indian, after the fight was won—only a team of work-horses and the redskin cared much more for riding ponies than for work animals . . .

"The buffalo-wallow is caused by the buffalo pawing and licking the salty alkali earth, and when the sod is once broken the dirt is wafted away by the action of the wind; then, year after year, by more pawing and licking and rolling or wallowing by the animals more wind wafts the loose dirt away, and soon there is a large hole in the prairie; and there are thousands of them—yes, millions.

"From the first of April and until the middle of May, was our wet season on the plains; this was always the case; you could depend upon it with almost the certainty of the sun and moon rising at the proper time. This was the calving season of the buffalo; the buffalo, not like the domestic cattle, only rutted one month—neither more nor less—then it was all over; no man I ever heard of or saw witnessed the act of copulation by the buffalo. It was all done after night. Then was the only time that the buffalo made any noise or fuss; but at this season they would keep up a low roaring sound all night and, as a consequence, the cows all calved in a month. At that time, there were a great many gray wolves in the country, as well as the little coyote. While the cows were in labor, the bulls kept guard to drive off the wolves and, in their beat, made the rings referred to.

"Buffaloes live to a great age. Some of them live to be seventy-five or eight years old and it is quite common for them to live thirty or forty years; in fact I think I have seen many a bull's head that I thought to be over thirty years old. After a storm, when we would go in search of our lost cattle, we could tell the buffalo tracks would be going against the storm every time, while our domestic cattle would invariably go with it. The buffalo is much more thinly clad behind than in front; nearly all of his coat is on his head, shoulders and hump and, when our cattle would turn tail, the buffalo would naturally face the storm.

"After a forced march in flight from Indians I was allowing my horse and cattle to rest and graze a few hours, before proceeding on our way to the ranch at Aubrey. While waiting for the animals, and for greater safety to myself away from them, I ascended a dry sand creek a couple of miles where the banks rose very steeply to the height of eighteen or twenty feet, and were sharply cut up by the narrow trails made by the buffalo.

"The whole face of the earth was covered with buffalo; they were grazing slowly toward the river. As it was a warm day and getting on in the afternoon, all at once they became frightened at something and stampeded pell-mell toward the very spot where I was. I quickly ran into one of the precipitous little paths and up on the prairie to see what had scared them. They were fairly making the ground tremble, as in their mighty multitude they came on running at full speed; the sound of their hoofs resembled thunder, only a continuous peal. It appeared to me that they must sweep everything in their path and for my own preservation, I ran under the banks; but on they came like a tornado, with one old bull in the lead. He held up a second to descend the deep, narrow trail, and when he got halfway down the bank, I let him have it—I was only a few steps from him—and over he tumbled. I don't know why I killed him—out of pure wantonness, I expect; or, perhaps, I though it would frighten the others back; not so, however; they only quickened their pace over the dead bull and others fell over them. The top of the bank was actually swarming with them; they leaped, pitched and rolled down. I crouched as close to the bank as possible, but numbers of them just grazed my head, knocking the sand and gravel in great streams down my neck; indeed, I was half buried before the last one had passed. The old bull was the last buffalo I ever shot wantonly, excepting once from an ambulance, to please a distinguished Englishman who had never seen one killed . . ."

Few hide hunters would use the word "wanton" about just killing buffalo. Then when the herds were devastated, the bone collectors came to pile up mountains of skulls and other bones of the dead bison, to ship them east to be ground into fertilizer.

By 1875, the hide business was almost finished and no one bothered to keep any records of the killings. Nearly every eastern family that could afford one had a buffalo robe or two and, for a little while, there were buffalo coats.

The loss of the herds, as much as the greed of land grabbers and gold hunters the continuous battles with the soldiers, signaled the coming of the end of the Indian way of life. The Indian treaties, pledged to leave some buffalo lands to the tribes, were not honored. As buffalo disappeared in the northern Plains, hide hunters invaded Indian lands in the Texas Panhandle. Teams of shooters and skinners, busy at their trade, were everywhere.

There was in 1874 an old, old adobe ruin in the Texas Panhandle on Bent Creek, of a Bent and St. Vrain trading post, called Adobe Walls. Hide men from Dodge City built a fort there: stores, saloon; hide buyers and dealers were housed. Some scouts reported seeing Indian signs, but the hide hunters and skinners went on hauling back great loads of hides to the Walls—predatory and destructive as ever. A hunter named Plummer, bringing hides to his lonely camp one day found his two partners killed and scalped, one with a stake driven through his heart. Plummer recognized the desolation and danger and rode hard for the fort. Two other hunters were killed at the Salt Fork of the Red River. The Indians were on the war path against the hide men. The hunters collected at Adobe Walls, shaking their heads at the situation. Night fell, heat lightning sawed the sky and, in the brush all around, desert owls hooted. The fort turned in to get some sleep: twenty-eight men and the wife of the owner of the eating place. Most of the hunters slept outside, on the ground, as the night was a scorcher. The horses were nervous in the heat and the lightning flashing on the horizon. In the Hanrahan Saloon at the fort—a building made up of piled-up sod held upon a cottonwood ridgepole—the pole suddenly broke, with a great crash. This woke everyone, to curses and laughter. Nobody slept any more. The roof was repaired at dawn.

A hunter named Billy Dixon went down to saddle his pony and went bug-eyed as he saw coming out of the woods a huge band of Indians, all in their war paint and feathers, whipping up their ponies. They saw Dixon and gave out their war cries. Dixon mounted and rode for the fort, shouting the alarm: "Injuns!"

The buffalo hunters and fort people grabbed rifles as the Indians charged right for the buildings, their howling growing more shrill in pitch. These were Cheyenne, horrifying to see, all garbed and smeared for war with lances, shields, and war bonnets. They came in a rush straight to the attack without dallying or prancing about. Two brothers, the Shadlers, sleeping in a wagon outside the fort, were killed at once. The charge came fast, overrunning the fort, massing between the buildings which were full of whites. The hunters were divided. Nine men were in the saloon among the whisky kegs. They were short of ammunition. Eleven men were in one store; six others with the woman, Mrs. Olds, were in the other. Windows were shattered, rifle and lance butts beat at the barred doors. The killing of Indians by skilled crack-shot hunters had begun. Wounded bucks scrambled for safety as the attackers suddenly withdrew.

The Indians tried a shooting match but the buffalo hunters' heavier guns outmatched them. The Indians were grumbling among themselves about their wizard medicine man, a Comanche named *I-sa-tai* whose miracle-working sacred objects and charms had failed. He had promised the charms would keep the white hunters' bullets from reaching them.

The medicine man *had* certainly failed if all those dead Indians proved anything. But I-sa-tai had a prepared excuse: Someone had defiled the magic by tarnishing a ritual detail and thus had destroyed the immunity. One of the white hunters was shot as he stepped outdoors for a better shot, and that encouraged the Indians to make another charge. The charge failed, but Indians began to pile up behind buffalo-robe bales in the stockade for close shooting.

The saloon full of hunters found they were out of ammunition. It was a hundred yards to a store for fresh supplies. Billy Dixon and another hunter made it on a wild run, zigging and zagging all the way as the Indians opened fire on them. Dixon stayed on to help defend Mrs. Olds, and his partner started back with the ammunition. He got through the storm of fire safely.

By four o'clock, the Indian fire died out and the survivors looked at one another with wonder. Some fool stepped out to see what was up and no one fired. The Cheyenne had pulled out, impressed by the deadly fire of the hide hunters. Nearby were thirteen dead Indians, but it was unsafe for their friends to go in to retrieve the bodies. There were fifty-six dead Indian ponies lying around. The hide hunters, in jubilation, claimed they'd killed nearly a hundred hostiles. The Indian official report was: nine Cheyenne and Comanche killed, which was fewer than the thirteen dead left beside the walls.

They did get the hunters' horses, but some strays were brought in. The hunters decided to stay under cover. Three days after the fight about a dozen Indians on horseback appeared on a high bluff a mile from the fort to look down on the late battlefield. Dixon's friends asked him to try a long shot. He was a remarkable marksman. He set his sights just right, took a few sample tests for aims, then he gently pressed the trigger. It looked like a miss, then one of the distant Indian riders twisted and fell from his saddle. A cheer went up and Dixon modestly said: "It was just a scratch shot . . ."

The excitement in the fort was not over. William Olds, whose wife had been the only woman in the fort, was killed by his own rifle while getting down from a ladder. Two days later, the dust column of a Dodge City relief company appeared on the horizon, and the battle and siege of Adobe Walls was over.

Chapter 22

BATTLE PICTURES

On August 11, three columns left Fort Dodge with General Nelson A. Miles in command. Water was low, the country dry and hostile. Scouts sent back for aid were waylaid and had bloody fights for survival. The Indians were more audacious than ever.

Lone Wolf, a Kiowa chief, had replaced Satanta while he was in prison. Lone Wolf was in camp at Palo Duro Canyon in north Texas with Cheyenne, Arapaho, and Comanche allies. They were all hidden in the deep-cut gash in the flat plain.

In September, Colonel McKenzie left Fort Concho with the 4th Cavalry and four companies of infantry along with Seminole and Tonkawa Indian scouts. The Seminoles had been brought on from Florida after their defeat there. Indians who served white men were loyal to them, for there was much bitterness between tribes. The scouts were cruel to their Indian brothers, were given to drink and half-dressed in Army gear, some with bare legs and some with leggings, some with wide hats stuck with feathers.

McKenzie, baffled after a long unsuccessful hunt for quarry, ditched his supply wagons and started north. He crossed the Tule and Palo Duro rivers, finding Indians' signs fresher as he went along. On the 28th of September, his scouts ran into rifle fire but the Indians were at long range and refused to close. In camp that night, double guards were set.

The moon was rising as the first attack by Indians came. They attempted to ride down the camp. The night sky was crossed by red-hot flashing of rifle fire; the Indians drew off, but hung around camp, howling. Spasmodic rifle fire was exchanged. No Indians were in sight as the sun rose. Then a lonely Comanche, sitting on a horse, was shot down by a Tonkawa scout, leaving the rider in the dust. The scout rode out to get the scalp. The Comanche, who was merely stunned, leaped up, tore the scout out of his saddle, grabbed his hair and began to flog him with his bow, giving the scout a merciless beating. The scout kept crying out: "Hey, you —why no shoot! Why you no shoot!" to the troopers who were riding up, roaring with laughter. As the blows became heavier, a shot killed the Comanche. The bruised, limping scout got his scalp— and a horselaugh.

McKenzie reckoned he was near the village. He sent out two scouts to locate it. They found the trails but no sign of any village on the plain, flat as a table, hot, dusty, and yet somewhere there must be hundreds of lodges as the horses' droppings and other Indian signs showed.

Then their own horses reared back on the rim of a huge fissure in the earth, Palo Duro Canyon. Far down below people were but specks on the canyon floor. The deep cut in the earth seemed to belong to another world.

McKenzie's scouts saw a meandering stream of water and the dark green of trees. Shadows cast by the high walls that hemmed in the village below partially concealed it. Off to one side, on the sparse grass, great herds of horses were grazing. The lodges of Lone Wolf's people lined the stream as far as eye could see.

It was twilight when the scouts reported back to McKenzie that they had found the Indian village. To reach it would be an all-night ride—twenty-five miles to the lip of the canyon. Orders were barked: *"Mount!"* Off went the riders to joggle along, already saddle-sore, when the sun rose they stood in mounted rows on the rim of the canyon. It was a marvelous sight. The smoke of morning fires drifted up through the cedars from the lodges below. Few noticed the mélange of colors, patterns, and silhouettes in the beauty of the morning. They were too preoccupied.

There was the game they hunted—but how to get to them.

Scouts dashed right and left, looking for the trail down. What they found was a mad dangerous crack in the rock wall, wriggling down the sheer cliff, certainly not made nor used by man but created by generations of deer and antelope thirsting for water.

It was this or nothing. McKenzie shrugged and gave the order. "Mr. Thompson, get your men down there and open the fight." "Yes, sir."

The scouts went first, clinging by handholds and shuffling for foot space. Then came the booted, spurred troopers, weapons hitched over shoulders, men moving slowly down the precipitous wall of stone. It was risky and they had to get to the bottom before the Indians discovered them. They would be live targets easy to pot-shot off the cliff if discovered.

Lieutenant Thompson moved with wary tautness. There came sections where he had to face the cliff and inch along on his toes. The hiss of feet on stone, the intake of hard breathing, a few grunts were the only sounds, except for the clink and rattle of war gear. A rock was displaced and started a slide of stone and earth. Men stiffened, rigid as death, then hurried their movements as more earth and stones fell away.

At that moment, a rich Indian named Red War Bonnet, who owned a herd of fine white horses, left his tepee to go look at his horses. Some sixth sense had warned him they were in danger. The falling boulder and its attendant earthfall was just above him. Red War Bonnet gave out a great war whoop. He was at once killed by scouts coming down upon him.

Indians alarmed by the war cry began to appear from all directions armed and whooping as they started to run up the gorge to meet the descending soldiers.

The scouts had reached bottom but the troopers were still up the cliff-side, inching along, many facing the cliff. The scouts and Kiowas began firing at each other. Some sharp-shooters hidden in a niche began to take pot-shots at the soldiers who were unable to fire back, pressed as they were to the stone cliff. The scouts seemed to panic as the Indian sharp-shooters kept up nicking hits from their niche. But soon the troopers were streaming into the canyon floor, arms ready and firing. The men cried out encouragement to each other as white gunsmoke in layers filled the bottom of the canyon.

The Indians bunched, retreated to pack up their lodges, fighting a rear-guard battle to permit the children and women to pull out with the camp gear and horse herds. There was a pass at the other end of the canyon and into this the squaws and children with camp gear and all their most-needed belongings were streaming. All that day the soldiers tried to halt the hegira but the Indians held them off.

The sun set and the troopers were still five miles from the escape pass the Indians were using to leave the canyon. It was a Herculean task against furious Indians. Darkness came before the last hostile and his brood vanished out of the place. Lone Wolf and his tribe had made good their escape.

For all the struggle and day-long shoot-out, the results were disappointing to the military. They found the bodies of four warriors but took care to mention no dead women and children in their reports. Indian sources speak of the killing of many women and children. McKenzie did capture fourteen hundred mules and horses, and a hundred lodges which he burned. In Blanco Canyon, he slaughtered all the mules and horses. (Today the piled-up white bones of these animals are pointed out to tourists, visible remains of the old Indian wars.)

The treeless Staked Plains provided no hiding place. The Kiowas eventually came in to surrender. Soldiers harassed those who continued to resist, driving them before them, rounding them up, pushing them back in big and small fights with much shooting. The Indians lost hope and stayed on the run only because they feared massacre if they gave up. In the end they could only commiserate and compromise.

Isolated whites were still in danger from armed red men. On the Smoky Hill River in Kansas, a family named German was attacked and most of them killed by an excessively irritable band. Four girls, seventeen, fifteen, ten, and five years of age, were carried off. A detachment went out to rescue the girls. Lieutenant Frank D. Baldwin tried with a troop of horse, a company of foot soldiers, a howitzer, and a wagon train. On November 8, he arrived at Chief Gray Beard's Cheyenne village. He sent his wagon-loaded infantry in on an insane charge of horse and wheels into the village, firing away. The Indians moved out so quickly that the two youngest German children were found in Gray Beard's lodge—alive, but very hungry, bruised, and scratched up. The two elder sisters were held by Chief Stone Calf, a Cheyenne roaming the Staked Plains. As one polite historian put it: "The girls lived lives of terror and ill-treatment."

General Miles sent Indian prisoners to Stone Calf carrying photographs of the rescued German sisters with a message:

To the Misses Germaine (sic): your little sisters are well and in the hands of friends. Do not be discouraged. Every effort is being made for your welfare.

Nelson A. Miles, Col., 5th Infantry

Stone Calf also received a message that he was to hand over the girls or be run into the ground with all the power of the Army. An offer of full amnesty for him was included *if* he capitulated. Stone Calf brought the girls to his own lodge and in January, they were turned over to the U. S. Army.

Later the girls pointed out seventy-five Indians who were, they said, involved in the massacre of their family "and other offenses." Those Indians were ordered arrested at once. When one tried to run for it he was shot down by a group of soldiers. Wild bullets strayed into a Cheyenne concentration camp close by. The Cheyennes broke out, a fight followed. On a hill, eleven Cheyenne—outgunned—died and nineteen troopers were wounded. Some of the Cheyenne, when found, were sent into exile at St. Augustine, Florida.

And the rescued German sisters?

They survived, married in time, reared families, and in the 1940s were still alive—two in California, one in Nebraska, and one in Kansas.

Tragic drama followed the fate of the Indian chief, Satanta: With no real proof of his guilt (nor proof that he was innocent, either) he was sentenced to life imprisonment in the Huntsville (Texas) Penitentiary. Satanta stood the confinement, the introspective loneliness, and the not-so-placid cruelty of his jailors for three years.

One day at the prison dispensary, he asked for medicine, saying: "My heart is bad." He was put into the second-story prison hospital ward. Soon there issued from the ward the spine-chilling death chant. Guards rushed in. Satanta stood on the window ledge. With no ostentation, he folded his arms, lifted his head to the sky where the Great Spirit waited, and plunged to his shattering death on the hard earth below.

He had, at last, escaped from his own disenchantment.

The image of the soldiers, trappers, and settlers who fought the Indians is blurred today by the overproduction of romantic material. The "facts" that exist are often only conflicting opinions.

Speaker of the House Champ Clark of Missouri wrote:

"All Missourians were natives of Virginia, North Carolina, Kentucky and Tennessee. They were the flowers of their respective stocks—the salt of the earth—courageous, hardy, intelligent, honest, industrious, honorable, patriotic and God-fearing . . . the finest specimens of manhood and womanhood betwixt the two oceans."

Senator John J. Ingalls of Kansas disagreed:

"Missouri is a place where climate, products, labor and tradition have conspired to develop a race of hard visaged and forbidding ruffians, exhibiting a grotesque medley of all the vices of civilization. To these fallen angels villainy is an amusement, crime a recreation, murder a pastime. To the ignorance of the Indian they add the ferocity of the wolf and the venom of the adder . . . Their continued existence is a standing reproach to the New Testament, to the doctrines of every apostle, to the creed of every church."

Somewhere between these two evaluations lies the truth; some people were good, some bad, some kind, some cruel—nowhere near as perfect as Speaker Clark claims and not all as bad as Senator Ingalls indicates.

The survivors were all tough. They had to be. Notes one eye-witness of a trek west:

"I find there is about 30 [abandoned] waggons to the mile for 40 miles of the road—1200. the dead animals will average about 100 to the mile for 40 miles—4000. water is being sold at $1.00 a gallon . . ."

They had little mercy for their fellow travelers—selling water at a dollar a gallon is no patriotic God-fearing act; the flag and Christianity they saved for the Fourth of July and Sunday.

And here is what they sounded like when chasing a bear:

"Then I jumped down into the sink and kicked him loose from the dogs, or he'd a-killed Coaly. Waal, sir, he wa'nt hur a bit—the ball had just glanced off his head. He riz up an' knocked me down with his left paw, an' walked right over me, an' lit up the ridge. The dogs treed him in a minute. I went to shoot up at him, but my new hulls [cartridges] fit loose in this old chamber and this one drap (dropped) out, so the gun stuck. Had to git my knife out and fix hit. Then the dad-burned gun wouldn't stand roostered [cocked]; the feather-spring had jumped out of place. But I held it back with my thumb *and killed him anyhow.*"

That sounds more like the boys we find in the folklore and the popular verse:

> And they fit for forty minutes
> And the crowd would whoop and cheer
> When Jack spit up a tooth or two
> Or when Bobby lost an ear.

An educated traveler, with a philosopher's touch, could sense the stamina of these Indian fighters. De Tocqueville wrote: "Nothing can offer a more miserable aspect than these isolated dwellings. The traveller who approaches one of them toward nightfall sees the flicker of the hearthflame through the chinks in the walls; and at night, if the wind rises, he hears the roof of boughs shake to and fro . . . Who would not suppose that this poor hut is the asylum of rudeness and ignorance? Yet no sort of comparison can be drawn between the pioneer and the dwelling which shelters him. Everything about him is primitive and wild, but he is himself the result of the labor and experience of eighteen centuries."

But it is hardly likely that the last line would have meant much to the people who were called Nutmegs, Jayhawkers, Badgers, Buckeyes, Sooners, Hoosiers, Sodders, Rawhiders, Mudsills, and other things.

Fantastic circumstances were given as to their reasons for going west. One of the most amazing is by a nineteenth-century director of the United States Weather Bureau: "I have not the data before me, but I am morally certain that if the mortality statistics of the various hospials were studied it would be found that more people die under the influence of the east than of the west winds. This may have a marked effect as one of the important environments that have to do with the character of the race that is now coming to be known as 'American.' He has fertility of thought and energy of body. May it not be that the climate has much to do with the development of the indomitable spirit that is now reaching out for the mastery of the world? . . . East winds either hug the earth or have an upward component of motion; they gather humidity, dust, disease; northwest winds come from above with a downward component of motion—from the region where the air is dry, pure and highly electrified, an invigorating air."

The frontiersman didn't find it at all like that. He was capable of descending to the savage level if very hungry. Listen as to how to prepare old rawhide when starving.

"The next day found us without food; and now came into use the long narrow strip of raw-hide which first bound together the old rotting logs of which the raft was made, then later to secure the mule of nights. It was now almost as hard as bone and nearly round, having been dragged through the hot sand while it was yet

12. Satanta, one of the most deadly raiders of settlers' ranches in his time, slashed his arteries and leaped to his death after spending years in prison.

13. Sitting Bull, the greatest of Indian statesmen, a spiritual leader, and a very great human being. There is evidence that he was assassinated at U.S. government orders, but full proof is lacking and would be.

14. Sioux Chief Rain-in-the-Face is supposed to have personally killed Custer, but two or three other "killers" of Custer have been "authenticated."

15. Sioux Chief Low Dog, hardly the kind of man to take lightly a thiefing Indian agent.

16. A horse—the only survivor of the Seventh Cavalry at the Little Big Horn.

17. Geronimo and members of his band going into exile in Florida. Geronimo (bottom row, third from right) has been called "the human tiger."

18. Chief Joseph of the Nez Perces, one of the greatest of all Indian generals, who defeated three U.S. forces sent against his few followers.

19. Sioux lodges at Fort Buford, 1881.

20. The deadly Modoc War Lava Beds — the most deadly Indian war for its size.

21. White River Utes of Colorado, participants in the Meeker Massacre. Their clothing is formal frontier — starch and broadcloth.

22. Officers of the Sixth Cavalry, Pine Ridge Agency, 1891. Here most of the Ghost Dance trouble came to a climax. Indians died here, exhausted from dancing.

green and wet, closed up like a hollow tube with sand inside. Two or three yards of it at a time was cut into pieces about five inches long, the hair singed off, the sand scratched out, and these pieces were dropped into our camp kettle and cooked until the whole formed one mass of gluten which was, to us, quite palatable. When the lasso had all been thus prepared and eaten, the broad girth which had served so well in holding the pack-saddle on the mule's back, was cleaned, cooked and eaten. These substitutes for jerk sustained us very well."

Or to put it on a practical level: a mountain man could say, "Iffen it didn't eat you, you et it . . ."

Chapter 23

THE ARMY OF THE WEST

The men who fought the Indians professionally were mostly Regular Army, either Civil War veterans or new recruits. They were usually mounted, for only cavalry could keep up with the Indian preference for warfare on horseback. Horseback warfare cost the Indian nothing for he had free grass and horses aplenty.

However, the maintenance of Federal forces in the West was costly to the government of the U.S. In 1865, some $300,000 a year was needed for supplies alone to keep a regiment in the field; $600,000 for a cavalry regiment. This does not include mounts or soldiers' pay. Only supplies, transport, and servicing—and that was real, old-fashioned money—not today's pallid dollar.

The figures rose when these troops were in the field of action; then a regiment might cost a million-and-a-half dollars a year. Such costs kept the Army to a small size at all times. Garrison duty cut down the number of men that could be put into battle. A company consisted of fifty men. Ten companies often composed a regiment. Seventy-five men to a company was desirable but not always available. The company had a captain and two lieutenants. A sergeant commanded each section and a sergeant and corporal each squad, usually numbering eight men. Usually is a word that means regulation requirement—but this could change on the frontier to what was there and ready to go.

Each regiment had a colonel, lieutenant colonel, two majors, an adjutant, and a subaltern who acted as quartermaster. The cavalry had buglers; infantry and artillery had drummers, fifers, and other bandsmen. Against Indians, who had no officer rank (just war chiefs), no supply problems, no music-makers (with the exception of their own voices), the Army organizations at first had trouble learning the game. Only about half the officers had ever been to

West Point for professional training and the territory was so vast few could learn the terrain or map it properly. Few actions ever involved more than six companies of a regiment at one time.

By today's standard this was a colorful Army on dress parade. Uniform facings on navy blue, called for yellow for the horse soldiers, orange for the dragoons, green for the mounted rifles, pale blue for the foot soldier, deep red for the artillery; shakos gave way to the wide-brimmed hat, necessary protection against the strong sun of the Plains. At one time, Jeff Davis as Secretary of War, included ostrich feathers for officers' hats. Polished brass, epaulets, starch, and polish gave way under war conditions on the Plains to hickory and flannel shirts, corduroy pants, slouch hats, pants legs inside field boots. This attire covered with grime, dust, and camp grease on an unshaven officer or rear-rank soldier was not very trim. Hunting shirts worn as jackets and felt hats of various designs were also seen at fort drills. Designs of muskets, rifles, and pistols actually changed slowly. General Crook trusted "in the unshakeable belief that the mounted sabre charge was the crowning event . . ."

The only effective artillery weapon in the West was the 12-pounder mountain howitzer, series 1840–41, which saw action until almost the end of the century. This cannon was built on pack principles, could be carried in parts, quickly reassembled and had several different carriages made for it. It was feared by the tribes for it could toss a 8.9 shell 900 yards to a mile at an elevation of 5°.

Living conditions for the Indian fighting army were comfortless, the food mean. The only escape of officers and men was drink. The records are depressing. A Major Hathaway is described as going through a series of delirium tremens seizures; and a Captain Judad, with a case of D.T.'s had to be left with the horse guard while his men attacked an Indian strong point.

Pay was poor. A colonel got $75 a month; a second lieutenant, $25. They received food and lodging allowances but it was poor lodging and poor food. The private, who usually served a five-year hitch at a time, was paid $5 per month in the infantry and $8 in the artillery as it was assumed more brains were needed to work a howitzer. A sergeant was a lord at $13 a month. A few dollars were added to this pay rate in time, but nothing significant. A re-enlisted man got $2 per month extra pay, because he was an expert. Uniforms, food, and shelter were furnished but none of these were worthy. They ate salt port or beef, if the stringy local meat was available, beans, peas and rice, bread and coffee, almost always substandard, as provided by some dishonest Army contractor. There was buffalo, elk, wild bird, and deer available on the frontier and a well-run mess offered these at table as a change from "the damn beans and salt-hoss (pork)" that came in barrels. Something called *desiccated vegetables* was also offered. Before the nineteenth century was over, the tin cans began to rust on the Plains.

When not carrying on a war the soldier was cutting timber, making planks, shoveling, doing heavy labor.

Court-martial hearings in forts were the local dramas: Such an occasion broke the monotony between the Indian raids. Solitary confinement on bread-and-water diets, forfeiture of pay were among the punishments, along with wearing a ball-and-chain, public whippings, iron collar with spikes, marching for days on parade, carrying a pack of bricks, being hung by the wrists. Officers might order these penances for an enlisted man with or without a court hearing.

Desertion called for a firing squad but was almost never ordered. Fifty rawhide lashings on the naked back was the substitute. The soldier's head was shaved, brand of a big "D" burned on the hip and the fort band played the *Rogue's March* while horse apples were flung at the deserter by the camp kids.

Ten percent of the soldiers were usually in the guardhouse for drunkenness or crimes committed while under the influence. Of 15,000 men, 3000 a year would desert; melt into the scenery as settlers, town dwellers; become outlaws; land agents; railroad workers; gun-runners, and whisky-peddlers to the Indians.

Yet for all this, the soldiers' record in the west for fighting power, bravery in action, and outlasting the Indians was excellent. For over seventy-five years the kind of soldiers described fought the Indians, became nearly as skilled as they were on horseback, and more dependable for all-around service.

The hierarchy of military and social position in the Western forts and garrisons was rigid. In photographs of the Custers in their rooms, we see them with wallpaper, their favorite pictures, ornate oil lamps and other comforts of home at an ordinary Army post.

Families of officers had a pecking order; there were many children, nurses, and—before the Civil War—slaves.

The enlisted soldier was low man in the Army caste system, but if he married, his wife could live in the fort or he could have the services of the laundresses, who were usually camp followers and whores. The specialists came from the rank-and-file. Blacksmith, saddler, farrier—each was an expert, as was the wheel-maker and arms-repairman. And there was always a band.

Scouting forays, fighting wars, surveying, road protecting, patrolling, hunting of deserters, outlaws or wild game, broke the daily grind of garrison life, as did horse-racing and the post dances, called "hops." The theater lovers staged plays and black-face minstrel shows, sang, read, or wrote books. Many officers' wives wrote books which give us a good picture of life on the frontier when it wasn't all war cries and wild horizons.

Drinking, gambling, and fornication were the main pleasure projects of frontier Army life for officers and enlisted men, when available. Adultery flourished among the officers' set and squaw-hunting was indulged in by rank and file.

Sutlers' stores, an early form of private PX systems, sold wines, beer, ales, and brandies which were often beyond the pay of the enlisted man. In any event he preferred the "hog ranch" where vile likker and doctored brews ate his gullet as "rotgut" and where there were the frontier whores who entered history as "dance-hall girls." The hog ranch became Americana when it came East as the "blind pig," the first name for a speakeasy which would one day provide illegal alcohol.

None of the frontier wars against the Indian was helped by the continual desk warfare in Washington, as to *who* really ran the Indian West. The Commander-in-Chief? Secretary of War? War Department? The General Staff? The General-in-Chief? The last —a strange title—was usually a rank with no power. Added to this was the dishonesty of the Indian section and scandals concerned with furnishing supplies to the Army and Indian reservations.

Yet good officers and brave men fought on. There are no records of major mutinies, no texts of disloyal officers, no reports of organized plotting. Stealing on the frontier was minor compared to what went on officially in Washington.

The Indian was a great horse soldier and a remarkably able guerrilla fighter. The Army never learned to cope with a native population in this kind of warfare and the only answer was destruction of the civilian population, their homes, and food supplies. A vast, wild, and inhospitable terrain in the West had to be fought in and the contempt for non-white enemies always existed, which made any moral balance in these wars impossible. As an officer's wife in this period states in a letter: "They are, after all, neither Christian nor white . . ."

A better picture of the Western Indian is that of Father Nicolas Point, French Jesuit. In 1835, he became a missionary and went where he found himself in a savage land. For the next six years he roamed with the Flatheads, Coeur d'Alênes and Blackfeet. In his diary, he wrote: "Among the Flatheads one finds the virtues of modesty, frankness, courage, goodness, and generosity. On the contrary, the Coeur d'Alênes are noted for dissimulation, egotism, and cruelty. The Blackfeet are notorious for being blood-thirsty and are well-known for their pillaging. Common to all three, with some exceptions among the Flatheads, is an unrelenting spirit of independence, laziness, a passion for gambling, cruelty to the vanquished, very little regard for women, forgetfulness of the past, and improvidence for the future . . . When they ate, foul sounds came from the nose, the throat, and the mouth.

"They called 'manitou'—that is 'spirit'—such apparently animated objects as the sun, thunder, and so forth and the cult they practiced they called 'medicine,' the object of which is the cure or removal of bodily ills.

"The instruments of the medicine are usually the hoof of a deer, a bear-claw, a feather, the cry of some animal, some strange sound, an exhalation, a menacing gesture, a grotesque dance, a ridiculous contortion . . . If, for example, the medicinal power is attributed to a bear's claw and is deemed applicable to the treatment of a wound, the medicine man hurls himself on the poor patient as a bear upon its prey, imitating as closely as possible the roaring and fury of the animal. Satanic power is finally established here; human dignity is degraded, divine majesty is eradicated. Such are the fruits of the perfidious work called 'medicine.'"

He never figured out that to the Indian, survival was more instinct than reason and that medicine and religion contain a certain palatable portion of superstition and cant.

Chapter 24

TO THE BIG HORN MOUNTAINS

When the Teton Sioux exploded in the war the Army stiffened. Thirty-five thousand of the Sioux nation—seven thousand of them warriors—sent fear shivering through the Dakotas.

By 1876 the Sioux knew all the treaties with the white man were worthless. The rights of the Sioux, as promised after the Red Cloud War, were not protected. The whites were bound by the treaty that "the country north of the North Platte, and east of the summits of the Big Horn Mountains shall be held and considered to be unceded Indian territory . . . No white person or persons shall be permitted to settle upon nor occupy any portion of the same; nor without consent of the Indians, first had and obtained, to pass through the same . . ."

The treaty now seemed so much paper. In 1874 official orders arrived to break the rules . . . "to make survey for military purposes." Custer went and came back to announce there was gold up there in those hills. The stampede of a gold rush was on—whites racing into sacred Indian ground.

The Army made some effort to keep out miners but local courts made judgments which ignored the treaty. Mining camps, vigorous, lawless, and crowded, sprang up—Custer City, Deadwood, and several others.

Red Cloud held off, making an issue. He couldn't locate enough buffalo to supply his war parties. In June 1875, Washington offered another treaty to buy the Black Hills' mining rights. The reservation Sioux pushed in a corner asked fifty million dollars. The commission offered six million. The non-reservation Indians offered battle and death. No deal was made and the miners dug.

Into the impasse moved celebrated Sitting Bull. He was a remarkable man and the legend we have of him as primitive, savage, cunning, and untrustworthy is open to question. He was a deeply religious, fractious, basic philosopher. Sitting Bull was an Unkpapa (or Hunkpapa—spellings differ) Sioux who was a valiant warrior but more than that. In his twenties he was already a noted fighter, having been on the warpath since his fourteenth birthday. He has left a deerskin autobiography recording that he took part in twenty-three attacks against Indians and whites and was on twelve horse-stealing raids. He was also a man of great moral courage. He never knuckled under to the white man and mistrusted him to the end, even when he made a peace treaty. Sitting Bull was a true states-man of the Plains, a diplomat and a dexterous politician. He was an Indian patriot. He brought the combined Sioux and Cheyenne nations into battle against the forces of the United States—a diffi-cult task among Indians who rarely could be contained in an or-ganized effort for any length of time. He probably knew the strug-gle was hopeless against "the white mouths wet with a taste for gold and land."

An Army report issued in 1875 that "Sitting Bull was not a chief, but a head-man whose immediate following did not exceed thirty to forty lodges," underestimated the man. He was not cruel in the traditional Indian sense. It is recorded that he had white women released from captivity and saved an enemy Assiniboin boy from death by torture, adopting him into his own family.

The Field Commander of the Sioux was *Tashunka Witko*—mistakenly translated into English as Crazy Horse. (The literal translation is Untamed Horse, but the frontier often mistranslated on purpose to mock the Indian.) Crazy Horse was born in 1844 and was a fighter as soon as he could shoot. At sixteen, he displayed valor against the Gros Ventres and at twenty he was a hero at the Fort Kearny affair. He was at Fort Kearny leading an attack in the Fetterman massacre and the Wagon Box battle. An Ogallala Sioux, he was allied to the Cheyenne. One overexcited commentator states that "Crazy Horse was to the Sioux what the great Robert E. Lee was to that other lost cause—the Confederacy." But it seems unlikely he could have handled or sustained an organized army.

The winter of 1875 was one of the worst for bitter weather. General Alfred H. Terry, in a foolish moment, sent a message to Sitting Bull that all Indians in that deadly winter must return at once to the reservations. It would have meant death to many to move in the below-zero temperatures through the great snow-drifts. The Indians did not—because they could not—move. General Terry set a deadline: January 1, 1876, for Sitting Bull and all his people to come out to the reservation, or "I'll come looking for you."

Sitting Bull sent back the answer: Let the general come. "You do not need to bring guides. You can find me easy. I will not run away."

Was it a plan to provoke the Indian to a war? Records are thin or missing. Most likely there was no official policy. General Terry probably acted on his own. The Army moved out on the day after the deadline and in early spring, three columns went forward to wipe out the Sioux. General George Crook—a splendid officer—was ordered to move north from Fort Fetterman. General George Custer was to press west to Fort Abraham Lincoln. General John Gibbon was to march east from Fort Ellis.

The weather prevented any Army force but General Joseph Reynolds' under Crook from going into action. It was 40° below zero and ten companies of horse soldiers were freezing to their saddles when Indian signs were finally found in Powder River Valley. A scout located the camp of Crazy Horse under the cliffs of Clear Creek.

The troopers went to the attack in three columns—one to take the horse herds, one to charge the lodges and the third to cut off the retreat of the Indians. An Indian horse boy gave the alarm and was promptly killed. The first soldier into the village met the first Indians springing up at the boy's outcry. The Sioux had no time to arm nor prepare for the sudden attack and they made for the bluffs. Firing began and men and horses went down. Indians died. The pony herd was captured and Sioux on foot felt lost.

But Crazy Horse did not panic. He rounded up Cheyenne and Sioux and they came loping up the valley in the freezing cold, vapor spurting from their screaming mouths. They picked out the high points and began to pour volleys of rifle fire on the troopers.

The soldiers in turn set fire to lodges and Indian stores. Powder kegs began to blow up and wild-fired slugs to travel in all directions. The troopers were beginning to suffer from cold, having been ordered to leave heavy clothes with their horse guards. Four were dead and the red warm blood of the wounded spurted in the snow where it froze shiny solid. Iron accouterments stuck to naked hands and the situation was full of anguish and danger.

Reynolds glimpsed a creeping attempt to cut him off, and had a retreat sounded. Not only were the dead abandoned, but one wounded soldier—whose fate in Indian hands must have been horrible—was also left behind. The retreat went on for half-a-dozen miles, Crazy Horse pushing hard, his savage warriors obeying doggedly. During the night the Indians recovered their horse herds. Nearly seventy soldiers sustained serious frostbite and many eventually lost toes and fingers. Reynolds was in a hell of a frozen spot but Crook came up in time to avoid disaster. Everyone was blamed for Crazy Horse's victory except Crazy Horse himself. There were military courts-martial and several officers resigned from the Army though the generals retained their commissions. Crook and Reynolds were considered at fault for mounting an attack in such killing weather. Both Generals Custer and Gibbon had called off the march of their columns at the start.

The Indians saw the invasion as a phenomenon. They did not at first understand that the white man had come to stay. And that the greedy whites saw merit in taking over the "empty" land. There was even a feeling among the more dedicated whites that the perfectibility of man and of society would take place in the West, unaware that whisky rather than civilization followed the flag, at least until the land was plowed and the rail tracks came. The Indian saw the first settlers unyoke their oxen, and it was the castrated ox rather than the pretty horse that was the muscle that made the West workable. No painter or writer of novels has done the oxen justice as the equal of the .45 or the Winchester in making a civilization. The settler wrote back home, "We are in the land of the living and in the place of hope." They were also on the sacred ground, guaranteed by treaty, of the Sioux, the Apache, the Comanche, and the Cheyenne.

The Indian had no need for seed or for the furniture brought along. As he saw the emigrant trains unhitch to set the sulky plow to break the sod, he did sense the determination of these daguerreotype faces in whiskers and sun bonnets that looked down so sternly on the Indians' lazy ways . . . "There is good land on the Massura for a poor man's home . . ."

It didn't seem to occur to them that it was the Indian's home, too, as the wagons went past Chimney Rock and the alkali deserts, or folk died of mountain fever. The Indians, watching from the shelter of buttes and cliffs, saw the dust of the overland stage roll past them from the Missouri to San Francisco in "twenty-four days of hell," as one shaken passenger wrote.

But the sod-busters picking up buffalo chips and settling in didn't take the stagecoach. They stayed. Even later when the Union Pacific would take a passenger from the Missouri to the West Coast for $45 and 150 pounds of baggage free, they stayed. The Indian world in its primal innocence was passing.

Chapter 25

WEAPONS THAT FOUGHT FOR THE PLAINS

My every thought was . . . not to be wealthy, not to be learned
—but to be great . . . to future generations . . .

Spring of 1876 in the West came late that year.

April was, indeed, the cruelest month—the snow lingered, and
it was not until the end of May that General Crook went north
headed for Montana Territory with twelve hundred troopers,
following new stratagems and with extra men to man his pack
trains and wagons. He had fought Apache in Arizona, and to
him, an Indian was an Indian. But the Sioux and their allies were
better organized under Sitting Bull and Crazy Horse than the
Apache had been.

Crazy Horse warned the general not to come to the Tongue
River. By June 9, Crook was camped on that very riverbank and
being fired on from the high bluffs across the stream. Crook took
action but the Indians, having fired their warnings, had left. A
few days later, Crook was joined by three hundred Indian scouts.
Crows under Chiefs Alligator and Stand-up, and Shoshones under
Chief Washakie.

Leaving his wagons behind, Crook mounted his infantry on
mules and pushed on, crossing the river with fourteen hundred
men—and carried his advance to the Rosebud River. He had a
high respect for the Indians' guerrilla tactics.

On the 17th he was in a wide valley with high walls of stone
all around. Scouts sallied out and ran into Crazy Horse's own
scouts and fire was exchanged.

The Crow scouts rode back, shouting: "Sioux! Heap Sioux!"

The bluffs were filled with Indians twanging arrows. Crook
sensed he had run into the main force of the enemy and he
rallied his men. A battalion under Captain Amos Mills charged

across a bluff full of Sioux. Major Royall on the left flank was also on the move. The simultaneous charges went on under heavy covering of fire of their comrades. Both charges pushed back the Indians but the going got harder. Indian reinforcements were pouring into the battle, making great noise and providing patches of color. Word was sent back to Crook for help.

Nothing the Army tried could force the Indians from the field. Crazy Horse was more than holding his own. After two hours of hard fighting, Little Hawk and American Horse and more Cheyennes came into the fray. Crazy Horse moved over to the offense. The left flank of the whites was badly exposed and Crazy Horse banged in with a charge of his best warriors. The howling was deafening and the troopers went down under the waving bonnets and weight of the excited Indian ponies. It was a rolling downhill tumble of men and horses—red and white—locked in hand-to-hand combat. In a milling circle, the company held off the warriors. They were pulled out of danger by reinforcements piling forward to aid them, just in time to keep them from being annihilated.

There was a pull-back to a better position. The Indians gave them no breather, but rushed in, rifle, lance, and club busy and finding targets. There was a mixture of bodies and red faces painted for war; ponies driven mad by the excitement; blue-clad soldiers wondering if this was the end for them; all mixed in nerve-shattering disorder. Captain Henry rallied his men. He was hit in the face, his features torn, raw flesh extruded. Blood poured down his mangled face and onto the ground. He swayed and fell from the saddle.

The Indians, seeing a white leader down, charged once again. The soldiers fell back, letting the Indians overrun the captain's body. It was time for a coup: to scalp the fallen officer.

The Shoshone and Crow military scouts saw the drama of this and rushed forward to prevent the coup and hair-removing. The countercharge they made was a dreadful mixup of rifle butts, knives, and tomahawks. It set the Sioux back on their deerskin heels. The Indians' scouts stood gallantly protecting Captain Henry. The soldiers came forward in fury and began to drive the Indians back . . . The limp body of Captain Henry was recovered and he was found to be alive. The position was again under attack, so carrying the wounded man, the soldiers and scouts fell back.

Casualties had been heavy. Henry recovered, and in time became a brigadier general.

The battle had become extravagant and wildly baroque. General Crook decided to try a diversionary measure. He suspected Crazy Horse's village lay in a gorge running northeast of the valley. He changed his position and sent Mills and his men into the canyon in columns of two. Before he could go far, Mills was recalled. He was desperately needed in the action. He actually was pulled back from an Indian ambush planned for the soldiers by Crazy Horse behind a great piling-up of brush and trees.

The whites were badly hurt and there was no real solution in sight as the Indians withdrew at dusk. Crook camped that night where he was, expecting an attack at dawn. In the morning, he sounded retreat and pulled back to his wagon train. Crazy Horse had beaten Crook. Sitting Bull was in the battle as a warrior, fighting beside the Indians. Only half of them had guns, the rest were bending bow to arrow. It was a great bravura victory for the Sioux chief. To keep their forces from breaking up, the Indians decided to consolidate. Crazy Horse and Sitting Bull moved their tribes into the Little Big Horn across the Big Divide. Squaws, children, dogs, ponies, travois (drag poles to carry loads) carried everything the Indians owned. In the Little Big Horn on a meadow six miles long, half-a-mile wide they set up their lodges. Sitting Bull's Unkpapas Sioux camped in a grove of trees in a bend of the river. On small creeks around him, the Minneconjo, San Arcs, Ogallalas, Brule, and Cheyenne set up their villages. United into one vast village made up of smaller villages, it was an amazing collection of Indians, geared for war—all in one place. Some estimates (all guesses) put them at twelve thousand people; three thousand of whom were warriors.

Game for food became scarce and the hunters wanted to go out far afield. Sitting Bull said no, they must stay where they were, and in force. They listened. He was waiting, unknown to himself, for the major actor of an about-to-be-enacted drama: General Custer, in command of the 7th Cavalry.

Let us, for a moment, look at the weapons of the coming action:
The Indian had become better armed. He had at first acquired his weaponry by trading for smoothbore muskets and flintlocks,

often in barter for beaver pelts. The traders would ask for a pile of tightly packed beaver skins, one on top of the other, until the pile was as high as a standing gun. Some of the traded firearms had unnecessarily long barrels and high stocks. They had also acquired the Model 1803, Harpers Ferry, rifles. A special American Indian carbine, Model 1807, was at one time government issue to some tribes.

The Indian decorated his rifle with brass tacks, leather binding, even with strips of human scalps. The old Leman Percussion rifles were treasured, as were the fine Kentucky rifles (usually made in Pennsylvania) and lucky was an Indian who could display a Hawkins octagonal-barreled weapon. Some French *Lebel* rifles from Canada were smuggled in, and by war or theft, a Remington-Hepburn single-shot could be in Indian hands. Another desirable weapon was the Winchester "Yellow Boy," so-called for its shiny brass band. The Indian used whatever he could get his hands on. His real problem was ammunition, to fit the various bores of the weapons he collected. Trading was usually under the counter, for traders soon saw the eagerness of the Indian for a weapon and what he'd give for it. At the Fort Bridger trading post, the ledger listed such items as "20 boxes Henry cartridges and 1008 Spencer cartridges." Any rifle was better than the 14-foot lance the warriors had previously carried on war parties.

Strange weapons turned up in tribal hands: a rare Dance Brothers' revolver (Texas-made), single-action Frontier Colts, Smith & Wesson Root of 1855—even the .31-caliber side-hammer pocket gun. If he couldn't get anything else, the Indian would use a 12-gauge double-barreled shotgun, a deadly weapon, and a forty-yard shot-scatterer, with scarcely a miss at close range.

The six-gauge shotgun carried a charge of an ounce-and-a-half of #3 shot, powered by coarse powder. The Kimball choke-bored barrel pleased the tribes, or a Winchester lever-action, five-shot pumpgun, easy to use on a running pony.

From a dead buffalo hunter came many a Sharps and gamblers, together with light ladies of the Frontier, gave up their Remington .41-caliber double-Derringers, or a vest-pocket .22 that fitted a dance-hall girl's stocking top. But those were "squaw guns" to the Indian and he preferred a heavy handgun if he had his choice.

The Indian also got the deadly Bowie knife from the white

man, which had been designed by the legendary James Bowie. This knife, broad and steel-tempered, with both a cutting edge and a stabbing point, was a fearsome weapon in hand-to-hand combat. The Army saber never impressed the Indian but he would carry one as a sign of victory and capture.

The American Indian of the Plains had almost no outside source for military hardware and he never went into battle armed with anything bigger or more deadly than a rifle—a weapon he decorated but could not repair, nor did he give it much care or cleaning. He adopted the weapons he fought with—besides his own lances, tomahawk, nail-studded club, bow and arrow, and the fighting and skinning knife from the white man. Everything made of hard metal he had to trade for, steal, smuggle in; he never improved a weapon nor added a major invention to guncraft.

With such weapons the Indians overwhelmed George A. Custer and the U.S. 7th Cavalry on the Little Big Horn, screaming their war cry "*Nakaha un ampetu owihanke!*" ("It's a great day for dying!")

And what weapons did the hoss soldiers carry as the 7th Cavalry piped out their regimental song "*Garryowen?*"

General Custer didn't have the two 45-70 Gatling repeating guns he could have carried—the forerunners of the modern machine gun. "The 7th Cavalry," he said, "is strong enough without them." Nor did the horse soldiers carry their sabers. These, too, were left behind in Fort Abraham Lincoln. They were considered noise-makers with their rattling they don't "permit surprise attacks . . ."

The soldiers had 1873 Model Springfield Carbines, .45-70-caliber, and Colt "Peacemakers," a .45-caliber ($12.50) revolver. Officers could bring their own weapons—a .50- .70 Springfield, or .50- .70 Sharps buffalo gun. The general, like a later hip-armed gun-toter, General Patton, wore two self-cocking, double-action Irish Constabulary pistols, pearl-handled, of course. Also his octagonal-barreled Remington sporting rifle.

The carbines had problems—even if good, up to 500-600-yard range. A 7th Cavalry trooper wrote that in rapid fire, the greasy cartridge often jammed in a foul breech—the extraction tool could not remove it and the discharged shell had to be forced free with a hunting knife blade. The Indians were actually better armed with captured Winchester and Henry repeaters among an assortment of odd muzzle-loaders and single shotguns.

Handguns in Indian hands were a grab bag of Remington, Colt, Smith & Wesson of various calibers from .31 to .45. Most effective was the Colt Navy handgun. A lack of ammunition harassed the Indians. They had little to spare for target practice—so were often poor shots. But Indian sharpshooters were as good as any. Two pistols *not* in the battle were General Custer's French-cased pair of Nimschke-engraved Colt Navy percussion revolvers, 1861 models, given him during the Civil War—a presentation set, they survive in a private collection.

As for Indian practices, Custer should have known them. The historian Turner defined the frontier as "the meeting-point between savagery and civilization." We now know this is true only in a political sense—the whites and Indians were both savage and each was encased in what he thought of as a culture, if not a civilization.

An unknown soldier at Fort Brown has left this description:

"The Indians, after scalping their victims and mutilating them beyond all power of recognition, tanned the scalp in much the same manner as any hide or skin. It was then stretched on a small frame or circular hoop of round tough ash, willow or reed with cross or diagonal pieces to keep it taut until in proper condition (dried) to attach to the scalp-pole (which is then their battle-flag) or on a rawhide shield or lance.

"The bows were made of the Osage orange or bois d'arc (wood of the bow), strung with twisted deer-sinews and strengthened on the back by strips of raw deer sinew, glued and allowed to shrink on hard until it is almost like steel.

"The arrows were made of mulberry or ash, tipped with wild turkey feathers glued to the shaft with bands of sinew.

"On the other end, was the spike 2 to 3 inches in length, made of ordinary hoop iron, sharpened on point and edges and afterwards hardened and tempered in both fire and water, making them like steel. The other end of the spike, after being roughed along its edges so that it would hold to the wood better, was entered into a cleft split in the end of the shaft and then carefully wound with fine deer-sinew along its entire length, then glued smooth. They could throw these arrows with the most deadly accuracy from 30 to 50 yards and at from 5 to 15 yards, they could send a plain, unspiked arrow shaft entirely through a buffalo, and hit a mark as large as a door-knob four times out of five.

Their saddles were generally made of the American elm, and were very tough and durable. They were made in three pieces, the bars or seat proper, the pommel and cantle, and they exhibited great ingenuity in making and putting them together.

"The pommels and cantles were made high with but slight pitch, the bars (open seat) of moderate length but comfortable. The holes for sewing were made with a rude red-hot awl; the joints were carefully and neatly brought together or sewed with deer-sinew and the seams made close, often with no other tools than their knives, an awl and a stone hammer, over these seams a pigment was smeared to keep the water out, over this a frame was stretched of raw deer-hide, first soaking it well and allowing it to shrink on snug and secure, a small soft bear skin was worn on the saddle as a pad.

"On the march they would live for days on sun-dried or jerked buffalo meat called by the Texas 'black strap' and by the Mexicans 'collops,' together with a little parched corn or an ash-cake made of pounded corn with salt if they could obtain it.

"When they shook hands, it was done in a hearty, good-natured but rather awkward or uncouth manner as though they were not used to it, accompanied always with a loud guttural 'How! How now! Cola!!!' repeated several times as if to make up for a lack of energy in the handshake. The left hand was used, the right hand scarcely ever, and the latter they would rarely ever take. This was explained thus: His early education taught him to distrust all such friendly approaches or manifestations; that all were enemies until they had proved their friendships, and the right hand must always be kept free to strike with knife or deadly weapon."

V

The Enigma of George Armstrong Custer

We kill plenty of game and an occasional Indian. We make it a rule to spare none of the bucks.

—One of Frémont's Party, 1847

Nothing lives long, except the earth and the mountains.

Cheyenne death chant at Sand Creek Massacre.

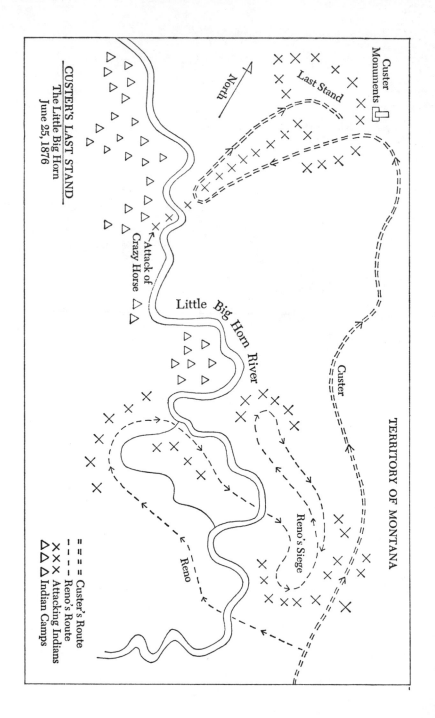

CUSTER'S LAST STAND
The Little Big Horn
June 25, 1876

TERRITORY OF MONTANA

North

Custer
Monuments

Last Stand

Attack of
Crazy Horse

Little Big Horn River

Custer

Reno's Siege

Reno

= = = = Custer's Route
– – – – Reno's Route
× × × Attacking Indians
△ △ △ Indian Camps

Chapter 26

THE TRUTH OF THE LITTLE BIG HORN

. . . by the time this reaches you, we will have MET AND FOUGHT the red devils, with what result remains to be seen. I go with Custer and will be at the death.

—MARK KELLOGG

There are many dissimilar opinions about the Battle of Little Big Horn and the various positions historians have taken, the mistakes and the final tragedy are often confusing. To most people, the Battle is best represented by a popular, colored beer-poster, which is wrong in almost every detail. They are various recent histories that point out what a fool Custer was and indicate he sacrificed himself and his men foolishly. To begin afresh from the original texts, and with the clearest kind of hindsight, the entire action and controversy can be seen in a new perspective, fairer to Custer as a force of assertion on the frontier, for all his boisterous arrogance, divergent moods and appetites.

Many of us are under the impression Custer commanded the action into the Little Big Horn. General Alfred Terry commanded that expedition and the 7th Cavalry and Custer was attached to it. Custer was already a man under a cloud. As always over-active, he had engaged in political meddling which would bring down a dour backhanded slap from President Grant himself.

The drama of the Little Big Horn is complex in its human elements. Of the three men most involved, Custer, the pushy soldier, appears the most direct and simple until one begins to investigate the vast amount of material available on him. A great deal of it is valueless, some of it prejudiced, and all of it fascinating. Folk heroes are an amazing genre.

Custer had been relieved of command because of his loud and vigorous criticism of the Western Indian agencies. Here he was right. Most of the agents were stealing, cheating, abusing, debauching the Indians. President Grant knew this, but he was the prisoner of his political party. He had willingly appointed greedy Indian agents as part of the political spoils system. George A. Custer's motive in exposing this system may have been honest. Most historians assume so. A few think he was a troublemaker who wanted to be seen and heard, acting out his role as a different kind of soldier. Custer was also in insubordination against his military superiors, disobeying orders in the field if he felt some idea of his own was better suited to the action. He had a crisp, crusty way of making reports on his expeditions, and his written statements were often in a heady prose. General Phil Sheridan demanded that President Grant remove Custer from his command and consequently Grant ordered Custer to return to the 7th Cavalry at Fort Abraham Lincoln, close to Bismarck, North Dakota.

Custer was in a taut angry mood. A proud, vain man, and a good soldier, he saw himself side-tracked. He needed one gallant deed, some headline-attracting incident to recapture acclaim by the public. Riding to the fort he told a Fargo telegraph operator: "I'm going to clear my name or leave my bones on the prairie." Only the intercession of Terry got Custer permission to join the planned expedition.

The second controversial figure of the Little Big Horn was Major Marcus A. Reno. From available evidence he seems to have been a book soldier, solid, duty-performing, unimaginative. From eyewitness accounts of his actions on the expedition and its tragic climax, he would appear to have been unable to make any fully committed judgment in a crisis. He turned away from the advice of his officers who demanded direct action. Today we would call him a neurotic who froze when a calculated risk was to be taken, one who delayed making a called-for decision, held back by inner fears and doubts. There are such men in position of power or command who go through their lives, carry on their careers, making the proper gestures, doing their duties, appearing on the surface as other men. But at the moment of truth, at the point of no return, they crack.

That, at least, was the verdict of a military court that sat and tried Major Reno after the expedition and condemned him for his actions, or rather lack of them, during the final tragedy at the Little Big Horn.

The year 1876 was to see a confrontation of forces that could no longer face each other in peace. General Alfred Terry was pressing the reservation Indians hard—too hard. It was clear to later historians that the policy taken by the commanders in the field was that the Indian was to be pressed hard enough for him to revolt. By spring General Terry had made a plan to drive the Indians into compact masses between his columns and destroy them.

The scene of the action was northern Wyoming, the southern Montana country. It was then and still is rough, harsh country. Cultivation and roads have improved, transportation has brought comforts of civilization, but in some ways the landscape remains as it was—beautiful but rugged, and craggy, too, weather-swept, primitive. One can imagine as one views it today the long columns of blue-clad troopers, the braying mules, the supply wagon trains and wheeled guns moving off along lonely trails and rough roads, toward a horizon where a lone mounted Indian showed himself.

From the safety of Fort Fetterman, Fort A. Lincoln, and Fort Ellis the Army columns were moving toward this area out of the security of solid walls and warm beds.

Of General Alfred Terry we have the usual, not-too-helpful Army records. He seems to have been a good soldier, a hard-fighting man when he had to be, an officer who saw his men were mounted as well as possible, fed, clothed, given the usual harsh Army punishments. Terry was well liked by his officers, but nothing suggests a brisk, daring, military genius. The frontier developed no Grants or Stonewall Jacksons. Terry was not a man to astonish Washington or to achieve unbelievable victories. Hunt and destroy were the tenets of his simple mission.

Of most of these frontier generals and their officers we have too little information. Many of them, as old men, wrote their memoirs, and although these provide information on frontier life, fighting, and the Indian wars, they are usually written in a stilted fashion and one suspects the publishers had a great deal too much to do with the final printed result. It is feasible to accept General Terry as history does—a good soldier doing his best in some sticky tight corners.

With officers like Custer and Reno in his command Terry may

have been aware that here were two men who might cause trouble. The first by his headstrong drive for action and glory, the second by doubt of his own abilities, doubts the general may, or may not, have suspected. Army ethics called for the covering-up of a fellow officer's weakness.

The expedition camped at the junction of the Powder and Yellowstone rivers, and Major Reno went out on a scouting tour and reported back on the Indians' trail found near the Rosebud River. The trail was so strongly marked that it was clear the migration was big. Actually, these were the markings of the tribes moving into the Little Big Horn Valley. Terry surmised the Indians were gathering for war talk and he moved in their direction. Custer and the 7th Cavalry was to lead the advance. It should be pointed out that General Terry who was in command of the column had no idea of the vast number of Indians Sitting Bull and Crazy Horse had brought together. The white men were under the routine impression that Indian allies soon drifted apart, and that no huge striking force of Indians could be maintained in the field.

On the Rosebud River at the head of Ash Creek the Indians held a Sun Dance during the sacred summer solstice. Sitting Bull was seeking a vision from the sun—an omen that would be a sign of victory, of strength against the white soldiers closing in. Sitting Bull bared his body. With an awl and razor-edged knife, one hundred bits of flesh were cut from his arms. Blood flowed from his limbs. He danced, leaned on the sacred pole, gazing into the sun from dawn to dusk, not stirring; waiting for a vision, a sign that would help his tribes. As twilight descended on the Sun Dancers, the limp body of Sitting Bull sank to the ground: silent, worn out, unconscious—in a deep astral "seance." The Indians drew closer to greet his awakening.

When he opened his eyes, he said: "I have had a vision . . . many soldiers come into camp . . . all *upside* down . . ."

This was interpreted as a sure sign of victory over the whites. There is no doubt that Sitting Bull was a true believer in his visions; like the man he most resembled—Brigham Young of Salt Lake City, leader of the Latter Day Saints, who also had definite and clear communication with the Lord—the disquieting irrelevance of their dogma did not obscure their skill as statesmen and leaders.

The dualism of matter and spirit were merged in them to strengthen their character and purpose.

That evening as a slashed, sun-dazed Sitting Bull was praying for a winning combination of visions, General Custer was also having visions. Talking to his Indian scouts, he announced that he, alone, was going to destroy the entire Sioux nation in one smashing battle and for his successes on the Plains, he would some day be rewarded by becoming the Great White Father in Washington. Unlike Sitting Bull, Custer was probably daydreaming to impress his Indians, but Freud had demonstrated that a man's dreams have something to do with his secret desires. Custer was quite capable of seeing himself in the White House, smoking nothing more drugging than his own ego and this at a time when he was most out of favor in Washington. Perhaps he was aware of the laconic irony of his situation and his remarks. Proud, violent, egotistical—he retained a rock-hard moral conceit of winning out in the end, *his* way.

The white soldiers had not learned to respect the Indian as a military unit, swift, cruel, brave, and able to cover ground in amazing short time. The Indian, in turn, never could comprehend the white man. He saw him as an explorer, thief, debaucher of women by his "wealth," and the warrior by the whisky. But the Indian also failed to respect the true abilities of the white man— his power to organize, to see the amusing side of his mean situation with a bawdy frontier humor that made him hard to stay beaten—"When you lose yer shirt, you cover yer ass with your hand . . ."

The frontier white man would travel on until the sun was twelve degrees from the horizon, dance all night (the hoe-down and pigeon-wing), take on fantastic dollops of rum, quicken to the *frou-frou* taffeta-rustle of an officer's wife's petticoats, and dream of his own "passel of land." Living among the scraggly mesquite and the drought-cracked clay, soldiers became plainsmen, eating out of grease-spitting spider skillets, fighting back when drygulched by a band of hostiles, they were able, once safe, to act as randy as boar coons. Where the frontier white differed most from the Indian was in that he could change, could grow with the country, stop chewing tobacco, poke around all day on a hard-scrabble ranch or homestead, see a future in the chinquapin scrub and sparkleberry brush.

General Terry ordered Custer to pick up the Indian trail where Reno had found it. General John Gibbon was to follow with troops equal in strength to Custer's. Custer was ordered, if the trail led to Little Big Horn, to move south and wait until Gibbon reached him, the two columns were to spread out then converge catching the Indians between them. Terry added verbal orders to Custer, personally: "Use your own judgment. Do what you think best if you strike the trail. Whatever you do, Custer, hold on to your wounded." You will find this quoted in General Nelson A. Miles' *Personal Recollections*, and Miles was a reliable, truth-telling soldier.

On the second day, Custer did find an Indian trail half-a-mile wide. He moved on twenty-eight miles up the Rosebud and decided to camp. Scouts saw Indian signs all around, and if he followed the trail it was clear it would go over the Divide. He held a meeting of his officers. He did not recklessly plunge ahead as is often claimed, taking no advice. He said it seemed best to cross over into the valley "to avoid detection by the Indians." Actually, he must have known the enemy was aware of his force.

At 2:00 A.M., he was at the Divide and he crossed it on the morning of June 25, 1876. He soon knew he was being stalked when soldiers sent back to pick up a dropped pack of hardtack killed one of a pair of Sioux warriors trailing them. Some sources say the surviving Indian ran on with the news of the Custer column to the village. Others insist Sitting Bull knew of Custer's arrival before the Indian brought the news.

Discovered, there seemed to Custer no sense in extra care. He decided to move on and attack whatever he found. From the heights of the Divide, Custer saw a big Indian village in the morning sun, partly shrouded in fog. He divided his command into four parts to take the Indians by surprise from all sides. Reynolds McKenzie, and Custer, himself, had used this plan in other villages for victory. It was an accepted military procedure. It is nonsense to claim he "foolishly divided his forces in the face of the enemy . . ."

Custer was a very good soldier, and a brave man. One might not admire his prickly pride, his ego, his glory-hunting, his desire for public acclaim—but one must see him here as a good soldier, acting in an approved manner. Custer did not have subconscious premonitions; he believed in the direct attack.

Major Benton, with three companies, was to turn left to circle the southern end of the valley. Captain McDougall, with one company, was set to protect the pack train. Custer and Reno marched on together until they reached the valley. Here, Custer slapped his leg with his hat and shouted, "Custer's luck! We've got them this time!" Here the two forces separated, appearing not to be worried about the intangibles ahead. Custer and the 7th Cavalry, five troops, went off to the northwest. Reno and three troops, the Arickaree scouts, moved directly ahead.

Only one white man ever saw Custer and his men alive again.

Let us first follow Reno down into the valley. Looking back, there was one last glimpse of Custer on a hill, snatching his hat from his cropped head, waving the hat, full of hope and happiness, approaching, he hoped, a complete victory.

"He rode on and away from the sight of his comrades forever."

Custer planned to attack the village from the high ground, while Reno accepted battle near the mouth of the creek. But Reno observed he was still two miles from his point of attack. Turning right, he led his men at a gallop into the valley. Mounted Indians began to appear, then the tops of the lodges were in sight. The scouts went after the Indian ponies and rifle fire began as mounted Indians came charging at Reno. Reno pulled up his troops. His men fired a volley in the dry, clear air. The landscape re-echoed the trenchant whine of bullets.

This was not a hostile scouting party; Reno was facing the main Indian force with Crazy Horse, Sitting Bull, Dull Knife, Two Moons, Little Wolf (it begins to sound like Who's Who of the Sioux and Cheyenne Nations), Pizi, American Horse, Hump, and White Bull who was Sitting Bull's nephew.

The war cries were fearful and the charging Indians seemed to cover the valley, rim to rim. Two troopers' horses went wild with fear and ran through the entire Indian force, never to be seen again. Most of Reno's Indian scouts fled in terror. Reno changed his position and set both of his flanks against a bend on the stream bed. The men dug in or hunkered close to the ground. Dismounted, they began to set up a fast and hot fire but the soldiers were taking too many wounds.

Reno, much too introspective that day, asked an officer: "What do you think of this?"

It seemed polite to answer: "I think we better get the hell out of here."

"*Mount!*" was the order, but it was too confused and noisy a time for everybody to hear it. By word of mouth, or following the mass action, the men mounted in disorder and started for a ford in the stream.

The Indians were on their heels, killing as they came. Troopers took up men who had lost horses or had been wounded behind their saddles. The chief scout, Charlie Reynolds, manned a rear-guard defense and died there. When they reached the other bank, they were a badly mauled group of survivors. Three officers and twenty-nine men were dead on the other side. Seven wounded were in serious condition. Lieutenant De Rudio and fifteen men were missing though some of these turned up later. Some had been skillfully tortured all day by the Indians. Fifty percent of Reno's command were casualties.

Where were the other attack columns? Benteen and his men appeared, coming from the east. His had been a fruitless errand. He had seen no Indians. With him was Bugler John Martini, the last white man to see Custer alive, and he had brought a message from Custer:

> Benteen, come on. Big Village. Be quick.
> Bring packs.
> P.S.: Bring packs.

This was a hasty, not-too-clear message. But it meant he was under attack and needed ammunition packs.

Benteen and Reno had no time for Custer. They were in mortal danger themselves. The Indians were keeping up a brisk fire. And the soldiers were exposed to firing from the bluffs. At three o'clock in the afternoon, the Indians, who had surrendered the two commands, broke off the action and, whipping their ponies wildly, rode off to the northwest, yipping war cries. Soon there was frantic firing from the direction they had taken. Custer was in trouble.

Reno, a bandanna handkerchief tied around his head, was sweating profusely. He appeared incoherent and made no move to go to Custer. His officers, speaking out of turn, begged him to move up to help the 7th. Reno refused. One captain without orders, went out to scout and a mile-and-a-half away he saw huge swarms of Indians milling about. Reno came up for a look and through his field glasses, he could see dust-clouds and Indians—but no soldiers. The heavy firing was over. His breather was over. The Sioux were soon moving in his direction. Reno decided to dig in deeper and hold his position. Historians indicate that if Reno had moved out at once to connect with Custer he might have averted the great tragedy. From all reports, Reno seemed distracted, apprehensive or numbed with fear. More likely it was indecision, not fear.

There was no eyewitness account of Custer's engagement from any white survivor nor was there a survivor. Indian recollections, often set down long after the event, are, in part, legend, distorted by the tribal rhetoric and as different manner of thinking and seeing. The Little Big Horn tragedy has to be put together from bits and shards, like a mosaic of a ruined painting in which patches, discolored and fallen are offered as a reconstruction that may or may not suggest the original.

While Custer and his men marched on alone, the bulk of the Indian force of the big village rushed out to engage Major Reno and his men, on the theory that this was the entire attacking force. Only Sitting Bull petulantly figured there might be another direction of attack from his experience in previous attacks. Word was sent back that soldiers might be advancing from a new direction although few warriors were left in the big village.

Custer's plans were to make a great circle, to strike the camp via a longer circuit of about ten miles. His force first appeared opposite the village across from a shallow stream-ford. This was at about the time that Reno was in retreat and moving across the stream to dig in. Standing on the bluff at the edge of the valley, Custer's five companies were in clear sight. There were so few warriors left in the village that if Custer had charged then and there, he could have captured it, burned it and been on his way. What did happen at a battle where no white eyewitness survived?

Chapter 27

OVERRUN

The squaws and children were in a panic and began to run from the village. Seeing Custer and his men, panic also seized the big camp. Custer began, confidently, to trot his men down to the ford to cross to the village.

From all Indian accounts, only four Cheyenne warriors were available to fight. They mounted their ponies and dashed across the stream to take on Custer's two hundred men. We know the name of three of these gallant defenders: Calf, Roan Horse, and Bobtail Horse. The fourth warrior remains nameless.

They were joined at the river by White Shield and Mad Wolf. Mad Wolf (not living up to his name) shouted: "No one is to charge the soldiers now. They are too many!" He and White Shield withdrew from the scene. The four Indians prepared to take on the horse soldiers. Custer and his men continued down the slope. A shot rang out and a trooper was killed in his saddle. Custer at once ordered the soldiers to dismount. Soldiers could handle an attack in force better on foot in firm, fighting positions. This was the proper military move, and shows Custer was not foolhardy here. Yet it was a tragedy, acting as a delaying tactic, for messengers were riding to reach Sitting Bull.

Crazy Horse was harassing Reno and his men up the valley. But the Indians moved away from Reno at once. One force went down the left bank to form a shield in front of the village; the other rode up a dry cut which was close to the hills where Custer was in position with his dismounted men. And still another group moved to gain a position behind the bluffs to cut off any retreat. It was a trap for the inevitable catastrophe.

There was one pinpoint in time where—if Custer had *not* dismounted his command—he might have slipped through the three Indians' groups moving to encircle him. But that moment passed, and he did not remount his companies immediately. His military behavior and thinking had always been that of a frontrunner—the qualification of a good leader of horseman.

While the escape hatch was still available, he did mount his men to start down for the ford. A swarm of Sioux, mad and eager, hove into sight—Crazy Horse, himself, out in front, screaming, weapons high, war feathers bent back in the wind of his movement. It was a remorseless charge, hideous to see and hear. Now the soldiers moved back in retreat *up* the hill.

Nobody knows whether Custer ordered a retreat. It is believed he did. He was certainly no man to panic. The Indians surrounded them and escape was impossible.

No imaginary painted scene could capture the terrible agony of that moment. Far from gallant or romantic, the scene encompassed a dusty two hundred men massed into a pack of screaming, dying horses and Indians dashing in and out and raining bullets, killing white men, the wounded crawling to a shadow of a rock or pack for a moment's hope of safety. Some killed their horses to huddle behind them. Custer, whose entire adult life had been spent in the Army in scenes of violent action, must have handled the situation as best he could, trying to order some line of resistance, attempting to survey the scene of action. No one knows whether he realized this was the end. Did he expect Reno and his men to come up the stream bed at any moment? Reno never came.

Custer moved his men across a deep gulch, and they climbed in an effort to escape their attackers and reach another hill. By the position of the bodies of his men when they were found, it is easy to follow Custer's retreat, up to his last desperate position. There was a knob on the top of the hill (a monument is wrongly in place there now), but he never reached that point. Custer had a slender chance of fighting off the Indians at the knob. The decision made sense; it was the only thing to do. But Custer, and no other commander in the field that day, had expected so many Indians.

Custer never reached the knob. He and the majority of his companies died about a hundred yards from the top of the hill. It is surmised that a detachment of Indians who had gone up behind him on the bluffs, came down on him, riding over the knob. The attack was swift, deadly, and the major part of his deployed command must have died there, quickly, as the savages pressed home the attack that could not be halted.

From the shaky evidence of Indian retellings, it is assumed that Custer and many of his officers died at the point where their stripped bodies were found. The surviving whites now tried to break out, or buy a little more life by moving southeast. This bloody route can be traced by the bodies. They fell as they headed over the ridge and along to the other side, back-tracking to their original line of march. How far they got can be marked by the location of the corpses of Lieutenant Calhoun and some of his soldiers.

Custer has been criticized for choosing the hill for his stand. The position was cut up by gullies which were good places for Indians to hide and pot-shot a deadly fire at his command. But it was the only hill he could reach. If there had been a better position and he could have reached it, he would indubitably have headed for it.

Much of the killing was done by the Indians with Sharps carbines captured from Reno's command, and with ammunition obtained from the saddle packs of dead or loose-running Army mounts. The Indians, some of them still armed with bows and arrows, were able to make use of weapons they took from Custer's dead. It is believed that the battle lasted, in all its phases, for an hour. But the main action must have required a much shorter time.

It is not hard to imagine the dust, confusion, powder smoke, war cries, the despair and the dark emotions of the doomed. The Indians closed in to scalp and yell over the dead and dying. They shot anything that seemed alive. A few moaning wounded were destroyed by clubbing. The stripped bodies appeared obscenely naked and white in the bright day.

Three Indians coup-touched Custer when he was dead. Some historians suggest that Custer saved his last shot for himself, but others claim Indians do not count coup on a suicide (which is nonsense, as an Indian in the heat of battle—or its aftermath—is not too aware of how a soldier died). Medicine Bear, who was still alive in the 1940s, said, long afterward, that two Cheyenne Indians—Two Moons and Harshay Horse—actually killed Custer. Foolish Elk, a Brule Indian, claimed that Spotted Calf, a Santee of Chief Inkpaduta's war party, killed Custer. Two Moons seems to be the man most

Indian specialists accept as the killer. Whoever it was, no one disputes the fact that it *was* an Indian.

There was a bullet hole in Custer's head from close range but the official burial party found he had been shot through the body and that the body wound was fatal. Some historians have accepted the idea that the head wound was a *coup-de-grace* given him by Indians after his death. It hardly fits Indian procedure, but we shall never know. There was no disgrace in saving the last bullet for oneself to escape the gruesome and dreadful Indian torture, and Custer was much hated by the Indians. He does not seem to have been scalped. Perhaps his hair was cropped too short.

Surmise is about all that can be offered about the actual battle of the Little Big Horn. What little is known does not show Custer to have been foolish, unmilitary, reckless, or disorganized. In attacking in columns from several directions, he followed the accepted method for overrunning Indian villages. He was unable to extradite himself from his position at the moment of attack, but even if he had, the battle would have been a close, hard thing. If fault can be assigned, the fault was Reno's for not moving toward Custer's fire when he heard it.

But who can say whether Reno was in a position to do it and survive? Reno was later tried and found in error by a military court. From court proceedings these facts are clear:

In that dreadful day long ago in the valley of the Little Big Horn, Reno, hearing the fire of Custer's men, felt pleased that Custer was attacking, but worried as the sound turned to the fury of a close and sinister action. Reno could see little to the northwest but dust. He could only hear the sounds of firing and the war cries that carried through the heated air. It was at this moment that officers expected Reno to move toward Custer's force to join action. Reno could not move. He seemed in panic, unable to make the gesture of mount-up or give the command. Then it was too late. The Sioux were back to the attack against him.

From the high bluffs the Indians poured deadly fire down on Reno's men and before dark eighteen troopers died and forty-three were wounded. In the night soldiers went down to the stream to fill their canteens and heard celebration in the Indian camp. Sniping continued in the dark and with the morning sun the Indians were back at the attack. Some of the Indians' rifles were better than the troopers' short carbines. At nine o'clock, the Indians massed a charge and nearly swept through the shallow trenches held by Reno's men. One warrior counted coup on a soldier and was killed in the act. The rest pulled back and, after some shooting, the Indians went back to the village, pulled down the lodges, gathered the pony herds and war booty and moved out of the valley.

That night Reno and his men waited for death, and there was not much talk of Custer's situation. Morning brought the plume of an advancing dust-cloud coming down the valley. The worn-down soldiers prepared for another Indian attack. But the dust was raised by Terry and Gibbon's men.

"Where's Custer?" was the first question.

Terry had expected to find Custer with Reno. Reno had assumed Custer was with Terry. Gibbon sent out scouts to see what was going on in what had been once an Indian village. Across the river, two miles to the east, Chief Scout Jim Bradley was carefully making his way in a landscape that still stank of gunpowder. He sighted a dead horse and some white shapes. Riding closer, he saw they were naked bodies—Custer's troopers, cut up and butchered.

The scout made a quick count: one hundred and nineteen dead soldiers. Nine more bodies were found later making a total of two hundred and six U.S. troopers who had died there. Custer had been stripped naked. He was not scalped nor mutilated.

There were no shovels for digging graves; just three pack-spades and with these, together with tin cups, spoons, and sticks, shallow graves were dug for the dead. Custer's brothers, T.W. and Boston, as well as his nephew, Reed, died with him; also a newspaperman, Isaiah Dorman.

The sorry expedition came away carrying its wounded, moved back to the Yellowstone, where the steamboat *Far West* took over the casualties.

Little Big Horn was the most successful battle the Indians ever fought against the white man. This slaughter entered folklore as the symbol of the savage Indians of the Plains fighting the U. S. Army. The bodies of the two lieutenants were never found, nor that of the company medical man, a Dr. Lord. They were presumed to have been captured and tortured. Reno's losses were fifty-seven killed, fifty-two wounded.

Custer, at first, was considered a hero, and his gallant stand at the Little Big Horn became the subject of oil paintings, posters, Western plays, and, later, films. With time and human inconsistency Custer became the victim. Historians elaborated on his non-military faults and vanities, his political interferring and his offenses of Washington dignitaries, including President Grant himself. This has clouded the issue.

The whole expedition may have been at fault. And it was not Custer's expedition. The complacency of the non-combatant in condemning Custer shows we can never fully understand men of action.

Chapter 28

CHIEF CRAZY HORSE'S THIRD ACT

The massacre at the Little Big Horn shocked the nation. But there appeared to have been no great interest for the Indian side of the story. White Americans were not yet self-critical. The drive and press westward took all the energies of the people seeking land and living room. One man had been worried over the settler's ability to push aside any opposition to his desires. "Indeed," wrote Thomas Jefferson, "I tremble for my country when I reflect that God is just and that his justice cannot sleep forever."

Abroad, there was critical comment on the Indian and his place in nature and history and the brutal pace of the Yankee drive. But would one really have expected the following angry entry in a famous nineteenth-century journal: "I dined yesterday at our Embassy and sat beside the wife of the United States minister to Brussels, an American woman . . . These men and women are destined to be the future Conquerors of the world. They will be the Barbarians of Civilization, who will devour the world . . ."*

The first serious historian to try to define the white frontiersman became famous: Frederick Jackson Turner, whose paper, *The Significance of the Frontier in American History,* created a furor when it was delivered before the American Historical Association near the end of the nineteenth century. Turner said: "The wilderness masters the colonist. It finds him a European in dress, industries, tools, modes of travel and thought. It strips off the garments of civilization and arrays him in the hunting shirt and the moccasin. It puts him in the log-cabin. In short, at the Frontier, the environment is, at first, too strong for the man.

"He must accept the conditions which it furnishes, or perish.

* *The Goncourt Journal,* 23 April 1867.

Little by little, he transforms the wilderness, but the outcome is not the old Europe . . . The fact is, that here is a new product that is American . . ."

"As has been indicated, the frontier is productive of individualism. Complex society is precipitated by the wilderness into a kind of primitive organization. The tendency is anti-social. It produced antipathy to control and particularly to any direct control. The tax gatherer is viewed as a representative of oppression . . .

"The result is that to the frontier, the American intellect owes its striking characteristics. That coarseness and strength combined with acuteness and inquisitiveness; that practical, inventive turn of mind, quick to find expedients; that masterful grasp of material things lacking in the artistic, but powerful to effect great ends; that restless, nervous energy; that dominant individualism, working for good and for evil and withal that buoyancy and exuberance which comes with freedom—these are traits of the Frontier . . ."

Turner does not show much interest in the rights of the Indian. The nineteenth-century mind involved in American history felt that the inevitable sequence of events would leave little place for the Indians' position over his rights.

One thing Custer's defeat did *not* accomplish was a re-evaluation of the Indians' situation, the withdrawal of the U. S. Army forces in the West, and the return of the Indian hunting grounds. The Indian land problem was to be a bitter fight, and a long one, rife with distrust on both sides.

Sitting Bull and Crazy Horse faced a problem after their victory. They lacked ammunition to carry on more such massings of Indian forces. They never again had the cartridges to engage in a major battle. The Indians were harassed by troops in the Badlands, but at first no important fights occurred.

Captain Anson Mills, acting as escort to a supply train to Deadwood, surprised the village of American Horse, one of Crazy Horse's followers, near Slim Buttes on Rabbit Creek. He rushed in in a quick attack, surprised the Indians, drove them up into the Buttes. He trapped American Horse, four men, fifteen women, and several children in a cave.

Mills sent back word to General Crook and attacked the cave-people. He was held off all day by the five men, and lost his scout, Buffalo Chips Charley, and a soldier to Indian fire. An officer's leg was shattered beyond repair.

Crook joined him with a detachment and the demand of "Surrender!" was sent out, the most abject humiliation to a chief.

"Come get us," replied American Horse. He was an old man now but always stood on his dignity.

Two hundred rifles began firing down the mouth of the cave but the five warriors kept replying to the volleys. A new offer to accept surrender brought out some of the women and children. American Horse cried out: "Crazy Horse, he come rub you out."

This could have happened. Indians were all around. The mass firing into the cave continued. Scouts again asked for surrender, and an Indian finally appeared, calling out: *"Waste helo"* ("Very good").

Two Indians came out supporting the figure of American Horse. He was suffering a cruel wound, shot through the lower entrails, and he was in agony. Sections of his gut were showing through a gaping tear in his body. Between his teeth he firmly clenched a stick to keep from crying out in pain as he handed his rifle over to Crook. Sitting Bull and Crazy Horse and some of their band appeared near the Buttes, but Crook was too formidable a force for them to take on. The old man died, not uttering a sound.

The winter of 1876–77 saw the Army active in weather that often ran to sixty-six below zero. General Miles wrote: "I equipped my command as if they were going to the Arctic regions."

He started to hunt down Sitting Bull in the Valley of the Big Dry, both forces moving for superior position. Sitting Bull attacked first. In a night raid he fired into the camp and two slugs missed General Miles by a couple of inches. Next morning, October 18, the column's supply train was rushed by a big war party and when Colonel Otis tried to outrun it with his wagons, the hostiles encircled him.

One Indian rode ahead and left a note on the road from Sitting Bull, transcribed by a half-breed named Big Leggins Brughiere, at the Chief's dictation:

Yellowstone:

I want to know what you are doing traveling on this road. You scare all the buffalo away. I want to hunt in this place. I want

you to turn back from here. If you don't I will fight you again.
I want you to leave what you have got here and turn back from
here,
    I am your friend,

SITTING BULL.

I mean, all the rations you have got and some powder. Wish you
would write as soon as you can.

One gets the feeling reading this letter—which still exists—that
the half-breed may have fumbled a bit the words that Sitting Bull
actually said.

Colonel Otis said he'd damn well go where he liked with his
wagons and after sporadic firing, the train got through. On October
21, Long Feather and a contingent of warriors approached General
Miles with a flag of truce. Long Feather came forward alone.
Would Sitting Bull be permitted to come through the soldiers'
lines? But Sitting Bull was too wary for that trick. He sent six
followers. Nothing of value was accomplished.

The next day, Sitting Bull agreed to a meeting *between* the
lines with six warriors and Chief White Bull. They met with Miles
and six soldiers. Both sides had their versions of this event. The
Indians claimed Miles raged at Sitting Bull, scolding him like a
shrewish squaw, saying the chief was an enemy of the whites. The
chief said he was no enemy so long as the whites let him be. Again,
nothing was settled.

The following day the meeting began with anger on both sides.
General Miles wrote: "Sitting Bull looked like a conqueror and
spoke like one." Sitting Bull said he wanted no war and he'd stop
fighting if the soldiers went away and abandoned their forts. Miles
replied that the only answer he'd accept was "unconditional surrender" of the Indians.

Sitting Bull went into a fantastic rage. "His eyes glistened with
the fire of savage hatred!" Miles wrote. Miles also wrote that
Sitting Bull cried out, "Almighty God made me an Indian—but
not an agency Indian." Indians who were there said he made no
such remark. But whatever he said, fifteen minutes later the war
was on again and the soldiers moved into a charge.

Fires were set by the Indians to dry grass but the charge went on through the smoke and flame. The Indians, short of firepower, fled and lost their lodges.

So passed the cruel, cold, derelict winter.

The Indians were chased and harassed throughout the Bad Lands. At last in desperation, Sitting Bull crossed into Canada. In the cold pine forests, the Indians with him lived in the dark moods of exile, loss of tribal followers, far from their old lands.

The Cheyennes were in Powder River Valley in a canyon of Crazy Woman Fork. An Indian captive gave information of where the Indians were hidden in their winter camps. On November 22, General McKenzie, commanding Crook's horsemen, took his eleven hundred troopers to the Crazy Woman Fork to "search and destroy!"—an Army term, still in use.

Snow was thick and heavy and the weather markings of freezing lower than ever. Arapaho scouts with McKenzie found a village. The soldiers surrounded the village and before sunrise on November 25, in brutal weather, the troopers moved to attack, horses and men breathing out vapors as they roared into the camp.

Most of the Cheyenne escaped, naked but armed. A few mounted Indians charged the soldiers as a diverting move to permit women and children to get away. Yellow Nose (it was *not* Crazy Horse's camp, after all) massed his warriors on a rocky rise which dominated the wintry scene. Lieutenant McKinney led the charge here and was shot down by the deadly fire of the cornered Indians. Three Indians ran forward to make coup on the dead officer.

Little Wolf was attempting to get the women and children out of the line of fire to safety. Two Army troops started to keep the women from the protection of Little Wolf but they were met by damaging return fire and a trooper died; the others pulled back. Dismounted in the chilling cold, the soldiers began peppering the landscape with rifle volleys. Nine Cheyenne died getting their women to safety. Small numbers of Indians were left trapped in the Valley. Yellow Nose on horseback with twenty Indian followers led a charge to relieve cornered warriors. Other hostiles joined and, shooting and howling, they rode forward. They were met by the strong fire of the troopers. Making two right turns, Yellow Nose led his band away from the firing. Many trapped Indians escaped during this action. Little Wolf and Dull Knife had meantime led their men up into the canyon ledges from where they began to fire down on the soldiers. Under this barrage, the troopers burned one hundred and seventy-five tepees, all the Indian supplies and ammunition. One hundred and fifty Indian horses were slaughtered. The troopers had lost five men; twenty-five were wounded and the Cheyenne left twenty-five bodies they could not carry off. Yellow Nose had been shot through the chest.

It was a cold, dismal victory in every sense. The temperature was still dropping. The Indians, nearly naked, were in desperate straits. Twelve babies died of the cold along with a few of the old and sick Indians. Body circulations were growing numb in the biting cold. So ponies were killed, the entrails pulled out and the Indian children pushed into the still-warm cavities to absorb the body heat of the creatures. Adults pushed frozen feet and hands into the gutted bony bodies. They were six miles up the valley, lacking winter clothing and without supplies.

The snow signs later showed the trail to be full of the bloody footprints of little children as they took the long march to the camp of Crazy Horse. The trek was a scene from a red man's Dante's Inferno. Not many found shelter with Crazy Horse. He was, himself, having a hard time. A large group of the dispossessed Cheyenne went off into the icy mountains, then gave themselves up later. They were devastated with cold and among them many had toes and fingers doomed by frostbite.

Crazy Horse was on the run; his warriors were melting away and his band short of ammunition and food. For two months, carrying the women and children, the chief kept just ahead of Miles' searching parties. On Tongue River on January 3, the troopers fought the Sioux; then, two days later, they fought again. Crazy Horse could no longer pull back and run. His people were worn out and the weather had not improved.

On January 7 (to keep up the fighting spirit) Crazy Horse tried to recover captured Cheyenne women and children during a night raid. This was a futile and grandiose gesture he could not afford.

Next morning by Wolf Mountain, Crazy Horse attacked in force in calculated desperation, taking the soldiers from their dismal breakfasts. From the heights, the Indians riddled the camp with rifle fire. Miles uncovered his two cannon and began to bang out shells onto the bluffs. Crazy Horse kept his men firing while the

shells burst all around them. They had great dislike and apprehension of the wagon guns.

At noon Major Casey charged a cliff where half a hundred
Sioux were firing down. He plowed through heavy snow. Big Crow
was in command, war feathers flapping, encouraging his men and
a prime target from below. At last he fell. The Indians moved out
as the troopers moved in. The canyon continued to inhibit the
Indians, who were now out of cartridges. A snowstorm, so thick
as to make almost everything invisible, began to fall and Crazy
Horse moved off with his Indians, vanishing like a cockcrow at
morning.

All that was left was the ghostly silence of snow falling.

In February offers of surrender and of peace found the Indians
nearly frozen and starving with their horses dead. Two Moons and
Little Chief gave up their people. About a week later Crazy Horse
brought in the two thousand followers who were with him and
surrendered them to the Red Cloud Agency.

Of all the people who had had a part in the Battle of Little
Big Horn, the only holdout was a Minneconjou Sioux chief named
Lame Deer. In May, Miles caught up with him and Lame Deer
came out to the general in person with a flag of truce. His son,
rendered unbalanced by the killing of his grandmother by the
the soldiers, refused to give up his rifle, crying out: "I am a
soldier on my own land." The rifle fired as soldiers tried to take
it from him.

Lame Deer, mistaking this contretemps for a white man's ambush,
seized his own rifle he had just surrendered and aimed directly at
General Miles, who put his horse into a wild rearing. The bullet
killed his orderly riding behind him, directly in the line of fire.

The soldiers began to fire wildly in all directions in retaliation.
Dead were Lame Deer, his son, twelve Sioux warriors, and four
soldiers. The remainder of the surviving Indians were moved, in
apprehension, in all their misery, to the reservation.

Crazy Horse, inert in illogical confinement, was not happy with
reservation life. The army feared he would break out again. Gossip
and spite kept him under a condition close to house-arrest on the
reservation. There was a ray of happiness when he fell in love
with the three-part-Sioux daughter of a half-breed named Louis
Richard, an interpreter at the Red Cloud Indian Agency. But the

sullen father felt the girl too good for a man with no white blood at all.

The two lovers had an Indian marriage in spite of her father and seemed to begin a good life together. But she sickened with a lung disease and there seemed little hope she'd recover. Rumor among his enemies was that Crazy Horse was so depressed at times that he planned to murder General Crook. The rumor was not true. He was in despair over his wife's coughing away of her life.

When a war against the Nez Percé hit the frontier Crook called a meeting to enlist the Sioux as Army scouts. Crazy Horse shook his head. "We tired of war. We come in for peace. Now Great Father ask help to go north and fight until no Nez Percé left . . ." An interpreter named Grouard, a Kanaka from the Sandwich Islands, who had deserted Crazy Horse to scout for Crook, mistranslated this as: "We will go north and fight until not a white man is left."

This version could hardly be called an honest translation. The Kanaka turncoat was probably out to get Crazy Horse shot. The general's attention was called to the lying translation, but Crook didn't trust anyone at that moment and decided in his own mind that Crazy Horse meant to go on the warpath against the whites. As a good general, he aspired to victory—not truth.

Crazy Horse's wife was clearly dying of tuberculosis. He knew the white man had medicine for the many illnesses they had brought the Indians. He asked permission to take her to Dr. McGillicuddy at the Spotted Trail Agency. Permission was refused.

Indian friends said to Crazy Horse he ought to appeal directly to the Great Father—the President, the patriarch chief of all the whites in whose name so many promises and threats were made.

Crazy Horse shook his head. "Me not hunting for any Great Father. My father with me . . . no Great Father stands between me and Great Spirit."

As his wife grew worse, on September 4 he called a few warriors together and rode out with his sick wife toward Spotted Trail without permission.

Chapter 29

THE CRIME AT SPOTTED TAIL

Panic reigned. Word went out on the telegraph that Crazy Horse of the Sioux had "broken away," which could only mean he was on the warpath. There was no mention of his sick wife nor his wish to visit Dr. McGillicuddy. Indian police ran Crazy Horse down with his party and his ailing wife. They ordered him to come back with them. Their predicament was real. The chief was a man to be feared.

Crazy Horse said, "I, Crazy Horse. Do not touch me. Not running away."

The Indian police—all renegades or enemies—did not press for his return. They followed Crazy Horse to Spotted Tail. The agent there panicked and insisted the Chief return to Red Cloud. Crazy Horse said: "I'm afraid something is to happen."

Asked to accompany some officers to another building, Crazy Horse suddenly found himself behind barred doors staring into a cell. He turned with a war cry, his long-bladed knife flashing high. There was no escape but they would never jail him. A captain stabbed at him with his sword. A pack of agency people who had followed leaped on the chief, howling: "Kill him! Kill him! !"

It was a close and dirty fight. Everybody was stabbing at Crazy Horse, kicking him, delivering blows any place they could land. Three Brule Indian renegades grabbed him at last, holding his arms so that he was powerless to defend himself. A soldier came lunging up behind him, out of sight, and drove a powerful bayonet thrust deep into Crazy Horse's side.

The body of Chief Crazy Horse slumped to the floor, while shouts, cries, and profanity echoed in the cell block. News of the murder spread among the Indians on the reservation—even among his enemies. A mob collected to protest the wanton betrayal and killing. An Indian battle seemed to be in the making but force and talk blunted the Indians' rage.

The dying man lay on top of a counter. Even the Indian agent tried to protest the military's tactics in jailing Crazy Horse and permitting murder while he was in their custody. The Indian took the man's hand and, choking, breath failing, he managed to gasp: "Friend—me do no blame you for this."

As he lay dying, Crazy Horse spoke again. "I was in hate of white man—we always want to go hunting with easy ways on our lands on reservation . . . but come time we no get enough to eat and we not allowed to go hunt for ourselves. All we want is peace to let us be by ourselves. Soldiers come in cold winter; destroy our village . . . Then Long Hair [Custer] come. They say we massacre him . . . but he do same to us if he can. At first we want to go away . . . but cannot . . . soldiers on all side . . . So then we live in peace, but government not let us be . . . I go to Red Cloud Agency . . . but they not let me be in peace. I tired of fighting . . . you try why to lock me up? Soldier stab me with rifle knife . . . I have spoken."

He started the Sioux death chant. His voice began to fail; his breathing grew more labored. Then he died.

There were many witnesses to all this. Was there a plot against Crazy Horse? Army records show that it was planned, by official orders, to take him in chains from the guardhouse in the dark of night and move him at all speed to the American Devil's Island, the Dry Tortugas in Florida, and keep him in a cell for life.

He was, one Westerner said, a lucky Indian to have been lynched instead.

On the morning of September 6, his white-haired old father and mother lashed their son's body to a travois and carried it to Wounded Knee Creek for burial. Crazy Horse was a man of stamina and courage, with an intuition for tragic endings.

Captain John Bourke, who had fought against the murdered Indian chief, wrote: "Crazy Horse was one of the great soldiers of his day and generation. As the grave of Custer marked the high-water mark of Sioux supremacy in the trans-Mississippi region, so the grave of Crazy Horse marked its ebb."

The Indian was unaware of the white man's philosophy: That all change in society is good, all permanence can be evil and lead to kings and tyrants. When the Indian realized the settler was in the West to stay, war was his only solution. He saw the sixteen-inch furrows cut into the sod that was buffalo grass, and the sod cut into sections became soddies—huts that in a generation would turn into cabins, then into two-story houses with ginger-bread decorations called "steamboat gothic," as affluence set in.

Were they happy, these white newcomers who saw the Indians watching them?

Sallie Long, whose father had been an early settler wrote: "If the public and private words and deeds of most of them [settlers] were published, it would prove a record alike discreditable of them and their descendants." But perhaps she was of that moody generation that wanted to go back to safety, taste the comforts of the east.

Ed Howe, the dour author of *The Story of a Country Town,* no smiling seer of goodness and light, wrote: "The most pioneers I have known seemed to feel they were better off than they had been before."

He doesn't mention how much worse off the Indians were. No one mentioned this as the march went on of men in butternut cloth, heavy clumsy boots of frayed leather, tobacco juice dripping over unshaven chins and "the old woman riding in the wagon, smoking a corncob pipe."

The trail forage of wagon trains diminished the grass the buffalo needed. Sweet Betsy from Pike and her lover, Ike, with their red rooster, replaced the summer camps of the Indian hunters. Where the Sun Dance had been held and the Indian ponies had bred and meat was jerked, ignorant randy preachers, gold hunters, hide-men and families with twelve to eighteen children settled down to farm. After the crops were planted, the Indians had opportunity to cheer the great clouds of grasshoppers that darkened the skies. Some of these clouds were a hundred and fifty miles long and a hundred miles wide and "ate anything from a set of harness to a hoe-handle."

What baffled the Indian was the perseverance of the white men urging their wagon trains on. They'd cross the same river nineteen times in six miles if it was crooked enough. They'd live in their badly made shacks, sleep on cornhusks on a bed named "the prairie rascal," with grease-paper windows and still be able to put up a good fight against a raiding party of Indians with six-year-old boys firing rifles. Their austerity was matched only by their drinking, if they were not church folk with psalms, hymns, and Christian Endeavor. They praised their God on a Sunday and went out to kill Indians on a Monday. They grew to like Indian fare, killed bear and elk and ate buffalo hump, beaver tail and catfish. They left less and less provender for the Indians who had no business sense, no supply wagons, no steamboats toting in goods from the east.

The white settlers prospered while the Indian remained nearly as he had been since he was a Dawn Man. All the Indian built up was an active aggression and a sense of the injustice the Great Spirit permitted.

Contrast John Bentley with any Indian when it came to making good; John had five children and more on the way. He was a carpenter, undertaker, sawmill owner, sheriff, U. S. Marshal. The settlers were like sands of the desert. They poured from Fort Benton, head of navigation on the Missouri, and spread like the grasshoppers but unlike the insects, they didn't go away. They stayed and bred.

"It was a hard time for women," wrote one frontier drudge. "They stayed at home and did the work. They were no better off than the squaws. Water was hard to get close by and a well cost twenty cents a foot to dig and you had to go down maybe a hundred feet, or two hundred.

"After buffalo chips gave out and the mesquite roots gave out, firewood had to be drug in from far places and there the Indians lurked. And a good prairie-fire, set by the hostiles, could burn out ten years of back-breaking, hard work."

No, the Indians couldn't understand how the whites stood it.

Chapter 30

CAPTURED BY INDIANS, A PERSONAL STORY

The Indians often took prisoners. The fate of the victims was not pleasant. From 1870 to 1879, a boy named Herman Lehmann, a captive at eleven, lived among the Apache Indians—first as a mistreated prisoner, then as an Indian warrior. Part of his story, as he told it himself, begins when he was out in a field with his brother and two sisters.

"We sat down in the field to play and the first thing we knew, we were surrounded by Indians. When we saw their hideously painted faces we were terribly frightened, and some of us pulled for the house. Willie was caught right where he was sitting. Caroline ran toward the house, leaving the baby, and the Indians shot at her several times, and she fell, fainted from fright. The Indians had no time to dally with her, so they passed on, thinking she was dead, and they often told me she was killed and I believed it until I came home several years later.

"They chased me for a distance and caught me. I yelled and fought manfully, when the chief, Carnoviste, laid hold upon me, and a real scrap was pulled off right there. The Indian slapped me, choked me, beat me, tore my clothes off, threw away my hat—the last one I had for more than eight years—and I thought he was going to kill me. I locked my fingers in his long black hair, and pulled as hard as I could. I kicked him in the stomach; I bit him with my teeth, and I had almost succeeded in besting him and getting loose, when another Indian, Chiwat, came up. Then Carnoviste caught me by the head and the other Indian took hold of my feet and they conveyed me to a rock face nearby, where they gave me a sling and my face and breast plowed up the rocks and sand on the other side. I was so completely stunned by the jolt that I could not scramble to my feet before the two Indians had cleared the fence and were upon me. They soon had me securely bound upon the back of a bucking bronco, stark naked. The Indians lost no time in getting away from there, and as we raced through the brush and undergrowth, my flesh was pricked and torn by mesquite thorns and catclaws and the sun blistered my naked back and limbs. Death just then would have been a great relief to me. My brother, Willie, was in the same distressing predicament as I but he murmured not.

"The Indians passed down near Loyal Valley and on to Moseley's Mountains where they located some horses in the valley. All of the Indians, except Carnoviste, who remained to guard us two boys, went for the horses and while they were gone, we heard some shots fired. Carnoviste went out to a point to ascertain the cause of the shots, and Willie and I tried to run away, but Willie was unable to run fast and Carnoviste soon caught us, bent us, gagged us so we could not scream, and threatened by his countenance and actions to torture us more if we made another attempt to get away . . .

"Willie and I were separated, he being taken with one party, and I with another. The Indians sent back scouts to see if we were followed and to cover up our tracks, if possible.

"Then they caught me, tied a rope around my neck and fastened the other end to a bush, strapped my arms behind me and tied my feet together. This done, they secured a pole, each end of which was placed in a forked stick driven into the ground, these forked sticks being about six feet apart. To this pole, I was suspended face down, my arms and feet being tied to the pole. I was so near the ground that my breast barely touched the sand and the least pressure would draw the cords deep into my flesh. Not content with placing me in this extremely painful position, those red devils placed a heavy stone on my back, pressing my face and nose into the sand; there I was compelled to stay all night long with no covering except that large rock on my back. I suffered all of the agonies of death, but when I would groan, one of the Indians would jump up and pull my hair and ears and beat me.

"How I lived through that awful night I do not know. About daybreak next morning, Pinero removed the rock, unbound the cords and then drew his gun on me. Chiwat strung his bow and fitted an arrow and they motioned for me to get up. I did not care if they killed me, for I was willing to die right there, but after several attempts I rose to my feet.

"I was so sore and stiff I could not stand at first. I was a perfect scab and a little moving about soon made the worst sores run, and the corruption and bloody water covered me. They put me on a horse and we started from there without breakfast. This was the fourth day without food. The water I drank the day before increased my fever, and I was so dry I could not expectorate . . .

"Yells, whoops and various sounds greeted our ears, as the Indians swarmed to meet us. This village must have contained 2500 savages. Chiwat jumped off and left me while Pinero led my horse on to Carnoviste's tent and halted. The squaws and children were yelling, hooting and making so much confusion I didn't know anything and was badly frightened. Several of them rushed toward me and I thought my time had come. One fat, squabby, heathenish, hellish wench grabbed me, pulled me from the horse, pinched me, slapped me, beat me, threw me down, walloped me while the others looked on in great glee. At last the old profligate let me up and the whole camp came marching around me, dancing and yelling. The old squaws were in the front group, the braves in the second squad and the young girls and boys brought up the rear. The women chanted their incantations, the warriors fired their guns and yelled, and they had a great jubilee. This storm passed over, and out came an old buck with a big knife and caught me by the hair. I thought he was scalping me, but he was only shingling my hair. Of course, he occasionally cut out a plug of the scalp and the blood trickled down my back, over my face and covered my shoulders, but I kept a stolid countenance and tried to conceal my fright.

"Another of the pesky barbarians, who had been heating a small iron, came up and stuck that hot rod through my ear, burning a hole as it went, while others held me. He took the iron out and inserted a buckskin string through the hole he had made. He then repeated the process in the other ear. And then, seeming determined to add to my misery, he turned the hot iron rod to my arms and burned great holes there. I have scars yet to show as proof of these assertions. I fought, kicked and raved, but they beat and burned me until I could stand it no longer, and I became exhausted."

In the next few years Herman became an Apache warrior, hated the whites, went on war parties and took scalps. He writes of his days as a savage:

"From our village we started on a raid upon the white settlements to get more horses, and to kill as many of the palefaces as we could. We Apaches never carried squaws or children along on a thieving raid, while the Comanches did. One of the braves, Tusciwhoski (Whitewood) and his squaw had fallen out. He had caught her in adultery with a Mexican trader. He killed the trader, and cut off his wife's nose—which was the penalty of a squaw for such offenses—and when we started on the raid, he said: 'I will never come back; I am going to die.'

"We knew he would make good his boast, even if he had to take his own life. We traveled on and rode for miles without Tusciwhoski saying a word. When we came in sight of Kickapoo Springs, we discovered a white man, nicely dressed. Tusciwhoski said, 'I will get that man!'

"It was the Indian custom to turn the painted side of the shield out, but he had the fur side out and when the chief called his attention to it and said the Great Spirit would not assist a warrior who would be so unreverential, Tusciwhoski said, 'The white man and I must both die.' And thus saying, he dashed toward the white man, who was about three hundred yards away. Silence reigned supreme while we watched the maneuvers of our companion.

"He dashed up to the white man and fired his Winchester, and the white man returned the salute with a 44-caliber Colt's revolver. Several shots were exchanged while the white man beat a slow and dogged retreat. We saw our companion reel and fall to the ground, and hurried to him, but he was dead. We hastened toward the white man, but he, too, tumbled from his horse and made an effort to rise but failed. He made several attempts to shoot us but was too far gone. He rolled over on his face and expired.

"We examined him closely and found four bullet-holes in his breast, made by Winchester balls. We did not scalp nor otherwise disfigure this man, because he was brave and fearless. He was riding a large gray horse, had a fine silver-mounted Mexican saddle, new red blanket, a stout heavy bridle, with shop-made bits, and in his saddle pockets we found a great quantity of silver and a roll of greenbacks.

"The bills we tore up, not knowing anything about their value. We took the sixshooter and other things and went back to the dead Indian. In his breast pocket, we found three holes where pistol-balls had entered and in his back, three torn places where the bullets had come out. These balls readily passed through the hairy side of the shield. We buried Tusciwhoski in a little cave after wrapping his body in buffalo robes and placing his weapons by his side. His horse we killed and left near him. There we left one of the bravest and best of the Apache tribe.

"We went down about Fort Territt and found some Rangers camped there. Their horses were loose, scattered around. We rounded up thirty or more and drove them away. Some were hobbled with chains and locked and we could not get these irons off, so we cut off the horses feet to keep the Rangers from using them any more. If we could not have them, the Rangers could not. One fine gray horse we carried along in hopes of being able to get his hobbles off by breaking the lock, but he, too, had to share the fate of the others.

"We came into a plain road and discovered a wagon in which there was a man and woman and three children. Before they were aware of our presence, we had them surrounded and it was but the work of a few seconds to kill and scalp the man, woman and a little baby; the two other children we carried with us—a little girl about eight, and a boy about six years old. The man was working an ox team. We killed the oxen and burned the wagon with its dead occupants. We went north and just as we were crossing a little ravine, four white men dashed in between us and our herd of horses. This was so sudden and so daring we were, for a moment, thrown into confusion. We rallied and turned on them, soon putting them to flight. One of the white men lost his pistol and Carnoviste got it.

"The whites outran us, driving our horses before them, but we held on to the captive children. The poor little things would not eat. We carried them four days and nights and they cried all the time. We could not slip up and steal anything for the noise they made, so two big buck Indians rode up—one on each side of the little girl. The one on the left took her left hand and foot and the Indian on the right side took her right hand and foot.

They raised her from the horse on which she sat and drove the horse away and swung her three times, the third time turning her loose. She cut a somersault in the air, and when she struck the ground she was dead, and every Indian rode over the mangled corpse. The boy was served the same way at the same time by two other warriors . . .

"I hesitate to recite these revolting crimes, but they were true instances of the savagery in which I was engulfed, through no choice of my own, and I tell of them in order to show the venomous hatred cherished by the Indian against the whites. We traveled on, and, just north of Beaver Lake, we came to a big clear hole of water. Here we killed a buffalo, built up a fire and roasted some of the buffalo's ribs.

"Some of the Indians were in bathing when suddenly the Rangers charged upon us. At the first fire two of our braves fell. We grabbed our weapons and went into a chaparral nearby and the Rangers got all of our horses and everything else except what we could pick up as we rushed away. We were pretty well scattered as we made our way from there, and we did not all get back to our village, which we reached—one, two, three and five together. Three more of our band were killed and one severely wounded, but he made his way to camp. When we brought in the news of our bad luck there was great mourning. Such hideous cries, such mournful howls! The squaws cut themselves all to pieces with knives. The squaw of the wounded warrior burned her own arm every morning that she might not forget her grief until her master's wound should heal. For several days, straggling warriors came in and the camp was a spectacle of grief, sorrow and despair.

"To add to the desolation of the scene, another defeated party came in carrying one wounded and reported one killed. A third party, who had gone on a raid, returned defeated, four dead and one taken captive. I learned he was brought down the old trail to San Antonio by the soldiers. We were sure we had offended the Great Spirit, so our medicine man began his incantations and howlings, went up the hill and waved cows' tails, and we all fasted. Then a fourth raiding party came in with horses and scalps and a better humor prevailed in camp."

A frontier woman and children often stood off an Indian attack. Mina Lehmann, sister of Herman, described a time when her mother and the other children, left alone, fought Indians.

"We thought papa was coming home with the cows and calves, and he always scolded if the gate was not opened, so I rushed toward the gate, and to my surprise and horror there came twelve big Indian warriors in a gallop holding their shields up before them moving to and fro like snakes, their long black hair dangling in the air. How hideous and frightful they looked! They never yelled nor made any more noise than was necessary. Silence is a trait characteristic of the Apaches, while their cousins, the Comanches, shouted, shrieked and made all the fuss possible. They rode around the house about fifty yards away the first round but kept circling, coming a little nearer each time. I fetched in the ax. We closed and barred the doors. The lesser children were terribly frightened. Some were screaming and others fainting. Mamma was nervous and excited. She had never shot a gun in her life and we little knew how we were to defend ourselves against such odds. We silently sent up our supplications to the Great Providence. I trembled and shook and it seemed that I would faint, but that sick spell passed off and I felt bold and determined—even furious.

"By this time, they had closed in on us and covered the floor with rocks, sticks and glass and still the missiles poured in and it seemed that we would be utterly buried in the great debris. The children, being barefooted, could not walk on the floor. I threw them under the bed—out they would crawl like the boy who tried to keep live beetles in his pockets. One little one made her escape from the bed-prison and unlatched the door and started out. I seized her, pushed her back under the bed. Sugar was a scarce article in those days but papa had just bought four bits worth. I grabbed that up, tore open the paper, and scattered sugar under the bed for the children, but they never licked any up that day. The Indians would dress up sticks and throw them in at the windows to get us to waste our ammunition.

"When the Indians first began to encircle the house, mamma wanted to shoot, but we only had one gun—a double-barrel shotgun, and none of us knew how to load it. So I advised her to wait until they came up and attempted an entrance. Finally one old chief ventured to poke his head in at the window. I held the gun up and told mamma to fire. She pulled the trigger. A loud report rang out. The room was filled with smoke, a scream of defiance was heard, then a heavy thud, then silence reigned supreme . . . Just at the crack of the gun the Indian raised his sheld and the full force of the charge struck that, glancing into his bowels. Soon the warriors summed up courage enough to remove their wounded chief and in the attempt to pay homage to their wounded leader, they came up in close range again. We fired our second shot, again striking a chief; this time, the shot scattered, wounding two or three. I forgot to tell you that they had already captured the horses. At first, they shot about twenty shots with short guns. [Herman says these were rim-fire Winchesters they had bartered from their friends, the Mexicans.] As they came more closely toward the house, ma looked out and whiz! came a lance, passing in close proximity to her temple and stuck in the table near, but after making a few more sallies, careful not to expose themselves to the deadly shotgun fire, they galloped away in despair.

"When Pa and Adolph came home, they became so excited and enraged that they wanted to follow, and mamma and I had to keep them from following.

"When we opened the door there stood the faithful old dog, Max. Several lance-wounds and the torn-up turf showed that he had done his part only too well, for his own physical good, but he proudly welcomed his mistress at the post he never forsook but, with an imploring look and a wag of his tail, he tumbled over, exhausted. All the other dogs, chickens, ducks, etc., sought a more calm, quiet and serene locality.

"This fight lasted about two hours; during a greater part of the time, I had stood on one window with a cane-knife or dagger that papa had sharpened the day before to use in the cane-fields, and mamma guarded the other window with the ax. Some Indians had gone into the other rooms, stole all the blankets, broke up the furniture, cut open the feather beds and made a total wreck of our once happy home.

"I have the dagger yet with which I fought Indians in that horrible battle, and I also have a wardrobe that has scars and indentations made by lances, rocks and missiles in that fight."

VI

The Great March of the Nez Percés

I think in his long career Chief Joseph cannot accuse the Government of the United States of one single act of justice.

—LIEUTENANT WOOD, *Aide to General Howard*, 1877

We were happy when the white man came. We first thought he came from the Light, but he comes from the Dark of the Evening now. He comes like a day that has passed and Night enters our future with him.

—*A Chief of the Plains*

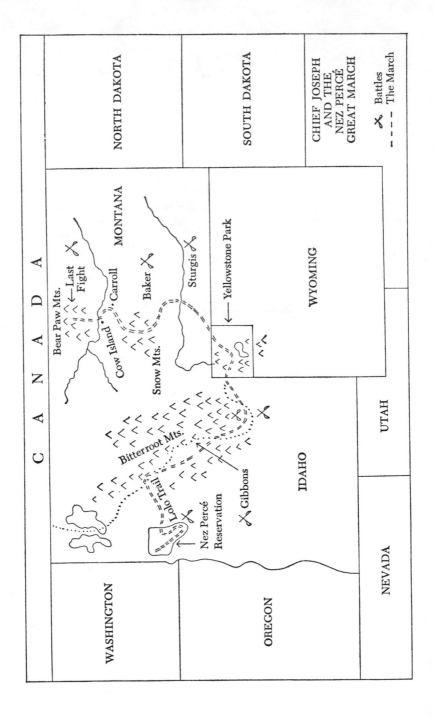

CANADA

WASHINGTON

NORTH DAKOTA

Bear Paw Mts.
←Last
Fight
Cow Island • Carroll
MONTANA
Baker
Snow Mts.
Sturgis
Yellowstone Park

SOUTH DAKOTA

Bitterroot Mts.
Lolo Trail
Nez Percé
Reservation
Gibbons

OREGON

IDAHO

WYOMING

CHIEF JOSEPH
AND THE
NEZ PERCÉ
GREAT MARCH

Battles
- - - The March

NEVADA

UTAH

Chapter 31

THE GENERALSHIP OF CHIEF JOSEPH

The Nez Percés tribe, in full assumption of their destiny, lived in the hills facing the Plains. In the Wallowa country lived a great chief called Old Joseph. He had a son, a remarkable man, who became Chief Joseph. His Indian name was *In-mut-too-yah-lat-la,* which freely translated means "Thunder Going Over the Mountains." When the old man lay dying he called for his son.

Chief Joseph the Younger related the story years later to a missionary, Bishop William Hare. His father, Old Joseph, could not resist a noble deathbed speech. "My son," he said, "this old body is returning to my mother, earth, and my spirit is going soon, very soon, to see the Great Spirit Chief. Give ear to me. When I am gone, think of your country. You are the chief of these people. They look to you to guide them. Always remember your father never sold his country. You must stop your ears whenever you are asked to sign a treaty selling your home. A few years more and the white men will be all around you. They have their eyes on this land. My son, never forget my dying words: This country holds your father's body. Never sell the bones of your father and mother."

The old man died and Chief Joseph led the Nez Percés. They were a tribe who had once pierced their nostrils to shove decorations and ornaments through them, so they came by their name honestly. Lewis and Clark encountered them in 1805 and admired their nostril art. They were magnificent fighters when they had to fight, but they preferred to hunt and fish. Unlike the other Plains Indians, they enjoyed a friendship with the white man. They even migrated when Oregon opened to white settlers, ceding their land there except for the Wallowa Valley and a portion of Idaho. The Gold Rush ruined their reservation life.

Miners swarmed in to push them aside and they were scheduled to be moved again to the Lapwai Reservation, where gold had not yet been discovered.

In 1877, the year the Sioux were beaten, young Chief Joseph had never fired a gun at a human being. He was a handsome man, with a clean, logical mind and a sense of duty that was almost Roman—more out of Plutarch than the West.

When General Oliver O. Howard received orders to see all the Nez Percés not yet on reservations must be placed there, he called a meeting with Chief Joseph and his subchiefs to come to talk it over. Joseph originally sent his brother, Ollicut, and five other chiefs, but the general applied pressure, and Chief Joseph came to the meeting at Fort Lapwai.

The Nez Percés differed from other Indians in their spiritual beliefs. Their religion was that of Smollalla, the Preacher. All the dogma was formulated by Smollalla himself, sharing God's dreams. This viewpoint gave Chief Joseph a Biblical tone when he rose to speak to General Howard and give him a lesson in common sense:

"If we ever owned the land, we own it still, for we never sold it. In treaty councils, the commissioners have claimed that our country has been sold to the government. Suppose a white man should come to me and say, 'Joseph, I like your horses, and I want to buy them.' I say to him: 'No, my horses suit me. I will not sell them.' Then he goes to my neighbor and says to him: 'Joseph has some good horses. I want to buy them but he refuses to sell.' My neighbor answers: 'Pay me the money, and I will sell you the horses.' The white man returns to me and says, 'Joseph, I have bought your horses and you must let me have them.' If we sold our lands to the government, that is the way they were bought."

General Howard's nose was out of joint and, to divert the talk, he got into an argument with the Smollalla high priest, *Too-hul-hul-sote*. The quarrel culminated in the arrest of the Smollalla who was locked up in the guardhouse. While his angry chiefs demanded justice and release of their holy priest, Chief Joseph decided, sadly but firmly, to move to the reservation picked for his people.

Three angry young men of his tribe, not without provocation, disagreed violently. One's father had been killed by a drunken white man; the other two had been tied off and flogged, without mercy, by the settlers.

On June 13, 1877, the three hot-heads staged a raid of their own on the Salmon River, where they murdered an old rancher named Devine. Riding on, they killed three more men, scalping them all. Waving the wet scalps as if they were recruiting posters, they enlisted seventeen more warriors to hunt out Harry Mason, who had flogged the two leaders. They killed him and, for good measure, seven more people.

In the next few days they rushed the Cottonwood House Ranch, leaving three whites dead and several wounded. In all, they dispatched eighteen white people.

Chief Joseph, when informed of these raids, at first tried to calm his warriors. But they were beyond listening to talks of being driven like cattle by soldiers to a new location. Chief Joseph knew the showdown had arrived. He was either for his people, who were determined to resist, or he was no longer chief. He decided to stay. The Indians needed him.

General Howard, when advised of the killings, rushed two companies of 1st Cavalry, under two captains, to guard the settlers and ranchers. This maneuver was an ordinary show of strength against the hostiles, who were expected to calm down and accept punishment.

Two days later, the soldiers, far from their base, were moving into the cut of earth made by White Bird Creek. The Nez Percés' lodges were located in the canyon. Captain Perry, with a hundred troopers, moved down valley looking for Indians. The Nez Percés sighted the soldiers before the soldiers became aware of them. Chief Joseph divided his two hundred men into two parts for the old Indian ambush game. One half were established in the brush on a canyon slope. The other half took position on the overlooking buttes. All were fine shots and purposeful.

The trap closed with a snap of rifle fire. Indians from both buttes and brush attacked troopers from all sides. Mounted warriors galloped up in a grand charge, head on at the outflanked soldiers. Captain Perry wheeled into position to face the attack and on the far left his own scouts, on a high cliff, opened fire on the enemy. A diabolical Indian fantasy engaged the soldiers.

The smoke of the rifle fire inside the canyon walls became a near-blinding fog and, as the Indians pulled back, Perry believed he had won the battle. But at that moment the brush-hidden Indians, under White Bird, charged on them from a flank, doing considerable damage. The scouts on the high cliff were driven off or killed. And a sergeant and six men were cut off. A rescue charge brought them out, just as the soldiers went into a quick, panicky retreat, which became a race for safety out from the deadly canyon and its brush. A rear guard of sixteen men and one officer tried to hold back the Indians who were in sight of victory. They were howling and attacking with the fury of those who know the foe is on the run and winded.

As the fear-stricken soldiers crossed the divide and rode out of the valley, the rear-guard fell back, firing their heated rifles. They never rejoined the main body. Every man of the rear-guard was run down and killed. The chase of the remainder of the company lasted until the remnant arrived at Grangeville. The soldiers lost thirty-six men out of a hundred. The old Indian ambush maneuver had worked again at a late date. Every officer in the West had heard reports of repeated successes the Indians had enjoyed with this simple strategy.

General Howard at once threw three hundred men into the fray—to catch and destroy Chief Joseph. But the chief had managed to put his entire tribe across the Salmon River and he was in a position to make trouble for any army attempt to cross the river. Chief Joseph was a military genius and his white counterparts were finding it out. As General Howard sat glumly staring across the Salmon, he had to admit: "No general could have chosen a safer position or one more likely to puzzle and obstruct a foe." General Howard at this point, had seven hundred men against Chief Joseph's two hundred.

General Howard made the mistake of sending Major Whipple with two companies to stop Chief Looking Glass's men from joining up with Chief Joseph. Chief Joseph pulled out in the dark, attacked the major's forces just as he met with Looking Glass's warriors. The major resorted to a protective circle on the Cottonwood River. Two scouting groups were mauled and an officer and eleven men died. By the time General Howard stumbled to the rescue on the Cottonwood, the survivors had to admit Chief Joseph was a mighty warrior. The chief's group augmented by Looking Glass's band, totaled two hundred and fifty men, but was weighed down with four hundred and fifty women, children, and aged folk. Indian wealth was not left behind. There was a horse herd numbering two thousand. The contingent was more a gypsy tribe than an army. The adventure had become an ordeal, exile would be bitter, but they were still free.

With General Howard driving hard on his rear, Chief Joseph looked ahead to choose the ground for battle himself. He entrenched on the banks of the Clearwater River, building up mounts of earth and breastworks of tree trunks. By the 10th of July, the scouts were firing at the entrenched Indians. Howard came up in full force, sending volleys into the earth works and tree-trunk breastworks. Chief Joseph moved out briskly to meet the attack, threatened the Army's supply wagons and managed to turn Howard's right flank with a brilliant move in force. Chief Joseph led several charges in person. The soldiers, sending out a deadly fire, held him off.

At nightfall, the battle simmered down and the soldier discovered first, that they were parched and thirsty and, second, that the Indians held the only spring and the riverbank. In the morning the dehydrated soldiers had to stand off new attacks. An officer subsequently wrote: "The Indian fire was terribly accurate, and very fatal, the proportion of wounded to killed being about two-to-one."

General Howard, a tough, no-nonsense soldier, had been waiting to bring up his howitzer and Gatling guns—early primitive machine guns with multiple barrels fired by rotating a crank. The combined fire of this heavy artillery drove the Indians back behind the tree-trunk breastworks. Major Miller led an attack through the left flank and took the Indians from the rear. Chief Joseph fought on two fronts. He drove off Miller and kept Howard at bay. Skillfully, expertly, he moved north, taking his time, and Howard was left holding the empty breastworks. Thirteen soldiers were dead, twenty-seven wounded. The big guns had killed twenty-three Indians, wounded forty-six.

Chief Joseph lacked the corruptibility of power. He called for a council of the chiefs at Kamiah Falls. The white pressure was dogged and persistent. They could stay and offer battle against great odds. They were fighting a war motivated by the upward mobility of a heterogeneous society full of ambition and ruthlessness with few scruples. An expanding power with the weapons and the men to claim its rights to tame the land. Chief Joseph recognized that his adversaries were remarkable people.

He could not face them head-on and hope to win. Could he now—he said later—pass on to the chiefs a plausible rationalization of his thinking? Joseph is one of the few Indians who left us his memoirs. Here are his own words, as taken down by Bishop Hare, in 1879:

"I said in my heart that I would give up my country. I would give up my father's grave. I would give up everything rather than have on my hands the blood of my people . . . I love that land more than all the world. A man who would not love his father's grave is worse than a wild animal."

Chief Joseph decided they would make a great trek, fighting all the way, to Canada as Sitting Bull had done. They would travel under attack a full two thousand miles. He called in his warriors. "Some of you tried to say once I was afraid of the whites. Stay with me now. You will have your bellies well-filled with fighting."

They responded with wild cries and the flinging into the air of their arms and weapons. Chief Joseph proposed to go north with no maps, and no true, detailed knowledge of the country. The Lo-lo trail would take them across the Montana Mountains. They would travel as a tribe with the women and children, the flocks and herds, all the animals.

Chief Joseph set up a rear-guard action that held Howard a day too long at Weippe while the tribe hustled for the Lo-lo Pass. It was an almost unreachable pass, a mere trail, over the mountains, with fallen timbers, a jungle of cruel, sharp rocks, abysses, wild roaring streams and waterfalls and a forest that threatened to bar all passage. The weather was bad. Cold torrents of rain fell and mud made the trail almost impassable underfoot. The soldiers with no heavy camp-gear, herds, children or women could barely make sixteen miles a day in the pursuit as the Indians outdistanced them.

Barring the Indians' way, down from the Coeur d'Alênes to the Plains was another fort. Captain C. C. Rawn with sixty men manned it.

Chief Joseph again showed his military skill. Refused free passage he made a loud, howling, fake attack in brisk frontal style, while the tribe slipped away through flanking trails around the fort. The Indians got to Bitter Root Valley, while Captain Rawn pulled out in haste for Fort Missoula.

Chief Joseph had told the soldiers he'd make no war, no raids. Wherever they came to a town, the Indians traded for food, rifles and ammunition. The Nez Percés were respected and liked by most settlers and the Army could not understand that.

General Howard had been outrun and was out of the game. From Helena General John Gibbon came to carry on the pursuit. Chief Joseph felt there would be no more fighting since the settlers had allowed him to pass in peace. He had deep psychic urges— almost traumatic—to avoid fighting.

The Nez Percés set up lodges in a meadow by the Big Hole River, among thick growths of brush with tall trees beyond. On the morning of August 9, Gibbon and two hundred troopers moved through the underbrush to surprise the Nez Percés.

A herd boy saw the soldiers coming across a shallow in the river. He sent up a wild war cry of warning. Gibbon ordered a rush attack that took the troops into the village. The Indians grabbed arms and babies and took to the brush, while the soldiers roamed the village. Chief Joseph at once took command, gave instructions to Ollicut (his brother), White Bird and Looking Glass, with that coolness a great strategist has. He deployed his people, and packed the woods and brush full of Indians ready for battle, the chiefs crying them on: "Since the world was made, brave men have fought for their women and children! Fight! Shoot them down!"

Captain Logan moved his men into the thickets where he was jumped by the Indians. The captain shot an Indian dead, and the Indian's sister grabbed her brother's pistol, and shot Logan from his saddle. Army losses were heavy in the eyeball-to-eyeball fight and the soldiers were pushed back. Two of the young warriors, whose flogging had started the war, died in the woods.

Chief Joseph set up sharpshooters overlooking the valley with orders to shoot down officers. Gibbon and two of his staff were wounded. Gibbon ordered charges, but they died out in the brush and trees. Lieutenant Bradley (who had found Custer's dead men after the Little Big Horn) was killed, and his detachment cut off. Few got out alive. Gibbon, badly wounded, ordered retreat to a nearby hill where sharpshooters from above fired on them. The Indians recaptured their village.

Gibbon tried to drive out the sharpshooters, killing one deadly marksman after he had done great damage. The Indians were attacking the hill from below. Gibbon, in pain, with wounded and dead all around, was facing a situation that could end in a massacre. He had the men dig in and pile up dirt before them. All officers took up rifles, even Gibbon, as losses continued. Gibbon called up his howitzer which had lagged behind coming out of the village. If the cannon could reach the hill it could do great damage. But Chief Joseph allowed only two shots before thirty Indian horsemen overran the detachment, put the crew to flight and pushed the howitzer off its wheels. The Indians captured two thousand rounds of ammunition in the same charge.

Near dusk, the Indians began to set fire to the dry grass, but a change in the wind saved the soldiers from a roasting. Night found the soldiers eating their dead horse (raw because fire would attract rifle fire) and sending sweating and frightened parties, heavily covered by guards, down to the river to fill canteens.

Leaving a small rear-guard, Chief Joseph struck his lodges, packed up, moved all of the Nez Percés—their herds and bundles—down the valley.

The soldiers had been defeated—with twenty-nine dead and forty wounded but at the cost of heavy casualties. The Indians had lost fifty women and children and thirty-nine warriors. Looking Glass was dead. Chief Joseph had lost two of his wives.

Gibbon still did not dare move. He remained dug in. It was not until after the 11th of August that he heard the sounds of General Howard and his men coming to his aid. Chief Joseph had had to turn southward, getting no closer to Canada but further away, like a sailing ship tacking away from its port at the mercy of forces it could not fully control.

Chief Joseph had to turn north again. His next move was unusually daring. Knowing a scouting party was established to hold the pass against him, Chief Joseph mounted forty warriors in regular columns of four, and after nightfall, they rode into Howard's camp as if they were the scouting detachment returning from the pass. They trotted into the camp past the pickets and began firing. They stampeded the horses and mules, shot down men who rushed from the tents. By the time the troopers realized the boldness of this ruse, the Indians were galloping away with the soldiers after them in a classic Indian and militia chase. The night still held more surprises. The troopers rode once more into a familiar ambush. The rocks were alive with Indian sharpshooters who began to shoot down their winded pursuers. The majority managed to get away, but Captain Norwood and his men were trapped until General Howard sent in force to bring them out. The soldiers then retreated to their gutted camp.

The Battle of Camus Meadows, as the place was called, stopped Howard in his tracks. Gibbon had lost his pack mules and there were many wounded. The nearest supply lines were in Virginia City. Gibbon was also out of the war.

Chief Joseph—free of pursuit—moved slowly to Tracher's Pass. The Army scouts had abandoned it at the first sound of firing. The Nez Percés trekked into Yellowstone Park surprising two pioneering parties of tourists. The men fought the Indians and were killed or wounded. Two women were made captives and then released untouched, causing one historian to express amazement. He recorded Chief Joseph's strange action as: "The only authentic case on record where white women, captured by Indians, escaped outrage." Rape, he indicated, was one of the rules of the game.

Moving across the park, at Clark Fork on the Yellowstone, Chief Joseph burned the bridge behind him and went on, straight north. All over Montana troops were on the move to find and destroy him and his tribe. He maneuvered around roadblocks, frightened off small detachments, and held the course true north. Always north, now. To freedom.

Chapter 32

END OF THE GREAT MARCH

On September 13 a Colonel Sturgis and the 7th Cavalry, mounted on fresh horses, caught up with Chief Joseph's Indians at Canyon Creek. Chief Joseph again proved he could design an action to fit the landscape. Reminiscent of the young Napoleon in Italy, he was able to force battles to fit his situation and use all that was on hand to serve his actions.

While the forces were far smaller on both sides, Chief Joseph and the United States Army fought a classic series of actions involving pursuit, withdrawal and side-stepping against a heavier enemy. These tactics had been used by Robert E. Lee against Grant in the Battle of the Wilderness, until Lee's forces were worn down by hunger and overwhelmed by superior numbers.

Chief Joseph at Canyon Creek set up a rear guard, while the women, children and herds were moved into the sheltering forest. The troopers charged the retreating Indians a mile downstream. The Indians retaliated with fire from the bluffs on both sides and two soldiers fell. The women, children, and herds moved on free of harassment. The troopers, numbering three hundred and fifty, dismounted to attack the hundred Indians on the ridges. The Indians pulled out and Sturgis, loaded with twelve wounded and three corpses, was out of the action at this point.

Again victory was costly for Chief Joseph. His losses were heavy. Over twenty Indians were killed or wounded and the Crow Indian scouts had dispersed nine hundred of the Nez Percés' ponies. Still, Joseph had defeated three skilled military forces, all greatly outnumbering his own warriors, and had left them behind, stranded, with their dead and wounded.

The Indians now turned northwest. The creeping telegraph lines and the railroad trains speeded up the Army's ability to throw soldiers quickly into an action. General Miles returned to the fray. Miles was loaded for bear. He proposed to stop this incomprehensible series of defeats by an untrained Indian. Miles had the 5th Infantry, two cannon, five troops of horses, a supply train that stretched back of his columns like a whiplash. His strategy was to march fast, at an angle, to cut into the Indian line of escape and come between the Nez Percés and Canada.

Chief Joseph had no telegraph wires and no railroad trains. He would not know of the new big push against him until his scouting system picked it up. The pace now was deadly. The Indians were wiry and hard, but they were beginning to tire. They slogged grimly past Snow Mountain. Chief Joseph hurried them along as if dreams and omens decreed: *"Hurry, hurry!"*

Fording the Missouri, Joseph found a fort on Cow Island with a dozen nervous soldiers defending it. He had no time to lay formal siege but he brushed against it, killing three men and burning the stores to draw attention away from the crossing of the women and children. He knocked aside local militia, backed by a troop of horses, and he saw in the distance Bear Paw Mountain. Beyond that rugged shape lay thirty miles of country, then Canada and safety.

A second-act finish was in the making—a ready-made motion-picture climax in real life. The Nez Percés' horses were dying on them from the driving pace and lack of fodder. Their trail was marked by the dead or dying animals. The human element was tougher but the warriors were worn down to emaciation. The tribe reached the mountain and sat down for breath. They were just a day's march from safety. Chief Joseph knew the delay for rest was dangerous. As a military leader he knew he should rally his people and march on. As a human being he could only pity the panting packages of bone and muscle, the staring eyes, the desperate physical state of his tribe.

He made the fatal decision: Like Napoleon holding back too long at Waterloo, Chief Joseph let his people rest at the wrong time.

Miles was riding hard to cut in ahead of the Indians. His troops were not tired, hungry nor worn down. Everything was fresh: men, horses and supplies. The Indians were on the north side of Bear

Paw and on the night of October 3, Miles, a truculent, disciplined soldier, rushed his men into position around the Indian camp.

Morning dawned cold with storm clouds quivering overhead. The wild honk of game birds fighting the wind was in the air. Rifle fire brought the Indians out into the brisk weather. They were at the bottom of a ravine surrounded by bluffs with Indian guards on duty. The troopers fanned out to encircle the camp. They outnumbered the red warriors four to one.

The soldiers rushed in from three sides, as if closing a pouch around the Indians, but deadly fire from the bluffs knocked half of Captain Hale's troops out of their saddles. Two supporting companies were sent in under Captains Godfrey and Moylan. Both officers went down under fire. It was a bloody sight.

Hale gave the order to dismount and charged on foot. Godfrey, badly wounded, managed to get on his feet but was shot down again. A lieutenant got "the deep six"—a fatal shot between the eyes. The soldiers struggled on over rocks and brush, under the heavy fire of the Indian sharpshooters. Soon the troopers were fifty feet from the top of the bluffs, then twenty, then ten, with bodies hurtling over their heads as their comrades died.

Hale was slain by a perfectly aimed bullet. The only officer remaining in the field was a Lieutenant Eckestrom. Under his orders, cursing and gripping tree roots and rocky handholds, twisting and climbing, the soldiers achieved the top of the bluff. It had been a costly climb. Of the hundred and fifty soldiers who had started at the bottom, fifty-three were dead or wounded.

Chief Joseph had calmly pulled his men out immediately before the capture of the bluff. He massed them on the ridge behind his camp and found himself completely surrounded. Bear Paw Mountain was fogged with gunsmoke as wounded men and animals screamed and moaned.

Miles moved in swiftly for the kill as if on drill parade. While he held the Indians at bay and unable to move, he mounted a brutal charge directly into the guns of the red men. The attack fell back, after a terrible toll, but Chief Joseph barely escaped capture. He had moved up to direct the defense in person.

The Indian camp was now cut into halves by the soldiers and the chief and seventy of his warriors were isolated in a pocket of resistance. Chief Joseph lifted his ten-year-old daughter onto a pony's back, gave the lead rope to White Bird and instructed him to get the child to safety. (Eventually the girl reached Sitting Bull's village.) He and the warriors then rode to assist in the fighting among the lodges.

"With a prayer in my mouth to the Great Spirit Chief who rules above," Joseph said later, "I dashed unarmed through the line of soldiers." His shirt was pock-marked with bullet holes and his pony expired under him. He rushed to his tepee and there one of his wives handed him his rifle. "Here is your gun! Fight!"

The soldiers pressed home hard attacks again and again. Nez Percé sharpshooters kept them from victory. Chief Joseph's brother, Ollicut, whom he dearly loved, was killed in the action. Ollicut's death was the turning point of the desperate defense. Chief Joseph seemed to sense the futility of all endeavor. With the death of this beloved brother, he seemed to experience a sense of alienation and withdrawal. In later interviews, this tragic mood comes through.

Night fell with the rebirth of hope that darkness often brings. The cries of the wounded persisted but blotted out was the sight of dead men and animals. The smell of gunsmoke lingered. Miles tightened his lines laying siege to the camp. He observed that frontal attacks on Chief Joseph's positions would be ineffective. By morning, Miles had his artillery in new positions. All day he dropped exploding shells among the Indians. By rights all of them should have been killed by the shattering barrage, but an attack by a company of troopers met with a strong rifle fire and fell back.

At twilight, General Howard and his staff rode into camp, hurrying to be in at the kill of the Nez Percé and Chief Joseph who had beaten three United States generals.

Miles was not too happy with the results of his actions to date, though he felt he could not lose if the game were played out as he planned it. He had lost a fifth of his men and he knew that just across the Canadian border, Sitting Bull might be massing his warriors to cross the border and ride to the aid of Chief Joseph.

Thought and worry prevailed in both camps. The generals no longer exhibited the incredible naïveté about "dirty savages, mere brute fighters." They had begun to respect Indian strategy. They had seen too many perfunctory, abortive attacks turned into bloody conflicts by fighters of stamina, competence and strength with military acumen.

On the Indian side, Chief Joseph also knew the score. He was up against keen professional soldiers who were remarkably brave.

The action on Bear Paw Mountain, trivial in the vast picture, set the pattern which was followed with the Indians: sweep them up, isolate them on reservations or wipe them out. Chief Joseph came to a bitter acceptance of events as they were and not as less thoughtful Indians saw them—a need for a suicidal battering of themselves in final annihilation.

At morning a white flag waved over the Indian lines. Chief Joseph did not come in to surrender himself until sunset. He rode in, head bent, a tremulous figure of defeat, followed by five of his best warriors, on foot. He clasped his hands over the saddle horn. General Miles and General Howard stood on a little hill, blue coats pulled into military order, boots dusted, faces stern. Joseph dismounted. He held his rifle out to General Miles, butt-first, a gesture of submission. The Battle of Bear Paw Mountain was over. The soldiers had lost twenty-four men and counted forty-two wounded.

Chief Joseph in his long march had never had more than three hundred Indians under his command. He had fought off five thousand troopers in the field, along with uncounted militia and civilians. He had confronted in battle more than two thousand soldiers at one time. He had killed or wounded two hundred and seventy of them. He had lost men, women, and children—two hundred and forty dead and wounded. He had marched two thousand miles, with no supply wagons nor pack trains, always burdened with women and children and herds.

This amazing military campaign, one of the most skillful in history on its own scale, had come within thirty miles of a victory. One moment of kindness, when he had permitted his exhausted people to rest, had defeated Chief Joseph.

Chief Joseph facing the generals and their officers and the victorious troopers began to speak.

"Tell General Howard that I know his heart. What he has told me before—I have in my heart. I am tired of fighting. Our chiefs are killed. Looking Glass is dead. *Too-hul-hul-sote* is dead. The old men are all dead. It is the young men who say yes or no [i.e.: decide in council]. He who led the young men is dead [Chief Joseph's brother]. Oh, it is cold and we have no blankets.

The little children are freezing to death. My people, some of them, have run away into the hills and have no blankets, no food. No one knows where they are. Perhaps they are freezing to death. I want to have time to look for my children, and see how many of them I can find . . . Maybe I shall find them all among the dead. Hear me, my chiefs, my heart is sick and sad. From where the sun now stands, I will fight no more, forever!"

So ends Chief Joseph's story—at least, that part of it which is history. He moved with eighty-seven of his warriors and two hundred and fifty women and children to a reservation. Moved from there, again, to another reservation, they eventually became "domesticated and peaceful." Chief Joseph no longer fought the white man's ways. He abandoned the unrealistic assumptions of the Indians and took on many of the conditions of life as the settlers led it.

The Indian remained a significant American problem. No matter what solutions were offered by the government, or enforced by the Army, the settlers and the hunters lived by a policy of survival and venal self-interest. Chief Joseph died in the autumn of 1904. If, as his friends claimed, he died of a broken heart at seeing his people dying in captivity, transported to malaria-infected land, hungry (one-fourth of them died in the winter of 1877-78), it was a delayed heartbreak. He lived long enough to see the defeated Indians rendered an alien people in alien places.

The white settlers persisted though they were soon badgered by land-grabbers, lawyers, bankers, moneylenders, and shady railroad dealings. Nothing could stop the big wheat spreads that rolled over thousands of acres. Fences and sheep cost money and the hard-pressed pioneer, often after a generation, with hungry children, could only look over his hard-scrabble acres and say of them, "A man could look farther and see less . . ."

Some pioneers became pick-and-shovel prospectors, easy prey to Indian bands. Others went to skidding logs. Some set up shop as merchants or joined the construction crews pushing the shining rails westward. The Indian, among all this activity on his erstwhile land, had nowhere to turn but to the warpath or the reservation, where he seemed likely to starve to death. In the towns, the Indian was prone to stand in a shabby blanket cadging drinks, listening to the hurdy-gurdy in the bawdy houses and watching transients passing through fighting dust, mud, "bedbugs and broad-gauge rats," suffering indigestion from grease-cooking. The Indian watched the change—the coming of the Peter Rife or Seth Thomas clocks, the four-poster, roped bed among the horn flies on the white caliche sands of the Pecos River. Fried rabbit gave way to canned oysters and other delicacies. Tow-linen shirts were replaced by broadcloth coats and the stovepipe hats. The towns grew into cities.

The Indian craved none of this and he was a poor customer lacking money even to satisfy his desires for whisky or a rifle. The Indian did not represent "progress" as touted by Horace Greeley, John D. Rockefeller, Emerson, or Jay Gould. And that, as the businessmen saw it, was nearly as unforgivable as a massacre.

The Indian had hoped the hegira of the white man would dwindle. How long could hordes of settlers trek west, come up the Great Valley of the Piedmont, out of Kentucky, cross the Appalachians, from their roots on the Rappahannock, to travail and jubilee on Indian land, held by treaties? The Indian saw the white man had courage—"more guts than you could hang on a fence." Where there had been Indian lodges there were cabins with smoke from chimneys twisting upward. Fox sparrows fed on wild strawberries in the new hedges and mud-daubers and wasps colonized on the new barn rafters. Nothing stopped the settlers. They brought trees to the Plains—poplars and cottonwood for shade, fruit trees for food—apple and pear and peach with hemlock and evergreen to hold off the wind. The women grew inedible things called roses.

The Indian could but wonder how many whites in slouch and beehive hats he would have to kill before the land was his again. The settler wondered how many "low down and ornery" Indians he would have to kill before he felt safe.

"Injuns make no sense no way," said the white man. Asked didn't he mind killing Indians, he added: "Warn't ashamed of it."

Chapter 33

WAR TRACKS OF THE COMANCHE

On the Staked Plains of the Texas Panhandle the white buffalo hunters were slaughtering the last of the bison. And the hunters, aware of their own strength, asked for no soldiers when they went to war against the Comanches in 1877. The Staked Plains War has had few historians. The few surviving herds of buffalo were the Comanches' only hope for survival. The buffalo roaming the Staked Plains were the survivors of millions wantonly destroyed. The Dodge City firm of Rath & Wright, Hide Shippers, set up an outpost to kill buffalo at Double Mountain Creek, a branch of the Brazos River. East of this post the Comanche lived on reservation. The Indian agents there kept them on starvation rations. Hungry, lied to and cheated by the government's agents, the Indians began to mutter and stir themselves to action.

The Comanches were cruel and remarkable fighters, fine paladins of the Plains as warriors. Two hundred years of war against Mexico had given them a military sense. From the Red River country they had raided again and again into Chihuahua. General Richard Dodge wrote that the Comanches were "the most cunning, the most mischievously artful, of all the United States' Indians." The Comanches had taken Parker's Fort in northern Texas under Chief *Peta Nokoni*—the Wanderer—who, after killing most of the defenders, captured the granddaughter of the man for whom the fort was named, Cynthia Ann Parker, thirteen years of age. She lived with the tribe until she became a woman, married the chief and bore him three children before she was rescued by soldiers. The eldest boy became Chief Quanah Parker, head of all the Comanches, and the town of Quanah, Texas, was named for him.

Black Horse, *Tu-ukumah*, in December 1876, led one and seventy warriors and their families out of Fort Sill, Oklahoma Territory, and headed, with horses, dogs, and children for the Staked Plains. It was winter weather, and the two troops of horse soldiers, fur-hatted, mustaches freezing, sent out to catch the Comanches got lost in a blinding snowstorm. The Comanche runaways camped in Thompson's Canyon where it opened onto the Staked Plains. It was a good hideout, sheltered from view, with enough game to fill the cooking pots, and far enough away from the disenchantment of the reservation.

Early in 1877 some of the young men of the tribe went raiding to see what was available. Two hunters attached to the Benson outfit exchanged shots with the young warriors. Warnings were sent that Comanches were lurking. A hide hunter named Soule was killed and his Sharps buffalo-gun stolen. Another camp had supplies of ammunition pilfered. A man named Pat Garrett went riding among the camps urging the hunters to gather at Rath's post, or store, at Double Mountain Creek. Garrett was one of the early Western types who lived up to motion-picture-star legends of frontier notables. He was the same Pat Garrett who, as Sheriff of Lincoln County, New Mexico, eventually entered folklore as the killer of Billy the Kid.

Three hundred hide-hunters, skinners and crews gathered at Rath's store. They sent scouts to find Soule's body which had been cut up and scalped. The hunters themselves decided to take care of the Indians. The obvious bully chosen to lead them was "a bartender, Limpy Jim Smith, an outlaw from Montana, who had escaped from jail, been hunted by the vigilantes and had got a bullet in his leg. He was called "Limpy Jim" from then on. His plan was simple—find the Indians and kill them. A hunter named Lumpkins objected to this approach.

"I ain't lost no Injuns and don't propose to hunt any," he declared.

This led to mean words between the two men and some time later, Limpy Jim and Lumpkins squared off to shoot it out. Lumpkins was killed and buried in Boot Hill. This was rather typical of frontier parliamentary procedure.

Limpy Jim persuaded forty-five men to go out with him to teach the Comanches a lesson. There were two other leaders—Big Hank Campbell, a Scot who had massacred Indians at Sappe Creek, and a man named Joe Freed.

The day after Washington's Birthday, the expedition was ready. It comprised thirty mounted men with fifteen on foot to escort the train which held supplies, food, and drink and two hundred and fifty rounds of ammunition for each man: powder, bar lead, primers, and reloading kits. On the frontier where ammunition was always short, empty cartridge shells were refilled. One of General McKenzie's Mexicans served as scout, a fellow named José, who knew the lay of the land. They had a quartermaster and a medical officer, not a doctor, but a druggist.

While this expedition is always described as being composed of hunters, nearly all of them were ex soldiers, for either the Union or the Confederacy, and they maintained military order. They not only were experienced in war, but were armed with the deadly long-range killer, heavy-caliber Sharps rifles. As buffalo hide-men they were dead shots.

They had news of an attack on old Godey's party of hunters by Chief Black Horse who ran off most of their horse herd. Against sixty hostiles, Godey's group did considerable damage to the Indians. Encircled for days, using captured guns, they fought back. Then old Godey, the hunter, said: "Well, this don't seem to be no place to be tonight. Let's go back." Under Indian fire they walked out of the circle, and came to Rath's store, bringing in three wounded men just as the expedition was about to move out. They joined up.

The wagons had hard going up onto the Plains but with double teams, whips and curses on the steep inclines, they managed it. An Indian trail was discovered and they followed it like hounds after a fox. At nightfall, they found a deserted camp with two lodges burned down, indicating that Godey's men had killed two Comanches.

Two members of the expedition found the Comanche camp the next afternoon and rode back to break the news. The hunters moved up and made camp two miles from the village, hiding in a gorge where they hoped the Indians would not discover them. This move was foolhardy and dangerous, but the hide hunters, with their heavy weapons, felt they could outshoot anybody.

When an Indian was spotted in a canyon near the hunters' camp, a half-breed Cherokee in the hunters' party put on red war paint and rode out after the lone Indian. Before he reached him, one of the hunters shot the Indian off his pony. The wounded Comanche got to his feet and tried to run for it. The hunters riddled him with bullets and put the body out of sight near a water hole to keep it from being discovered.

The wagons were left in their hiding place as three groups got set to attack the village. Hank Campbell was assigned to lead half the men with horses, Limpy Jim the other half. Joe Freed was chosen to handle the dismounted hunters. Old Godey and José joined the scouts. Limpy Jim's men were instructed to rush roaring through the village and stampede the Indian horse herd. Hank Campbell displayed a soft side to his tough Scot's hide: "Try not to kill no women and children if you kin help it."

At twilight, three scouts muffled the sound of their horses' hoofs in oat sacks and started for the village. They sought the trail by lighting matches shielded by a blanket. Before dawn, they were in position to advise the attacking parties on details of the camp.

It was March 18. Standing or mounted, the three groups of hunters were drawn up at the head of the pocket which led to the Comanche village. Horsemen were on the flanks, hunters on foot in the center.

"All right," said Hank Campbell.

Limpy Smith cried out, "Go after 'em!"

The men moved in. An ex-Johnny Reb named Squirrel-Eye, gave the rebel yell for God, for Robert E. Lee and for Jefferson Davis. Louie Keyes, the Cherokee, started his war chant. The rest cursed and laughed and broke into a charge. At two hundred yards the Comanches opened fire on the hunters from a low hill. Hank Campbell, cursing blue blazes like an inspired mule driver, yelled for the hunters to get back up into the canyon. Two were shot from their saddles. Several leaped forward to try to pull the wounded to safety and one of these got a shattered arm. The Comanches sent a sneak attack up the gorge to the right of the attackers. They remained undiscovered until the wounded men set up a cry on sighting the Indians. The hunters brought their heavy weapons into action and the Indians pulled back, dragging six bodies with them.

The attempt to stampede the Indian ponies had failed. The frustrated hunters were beginning to wonder what had made their plan of attack seem so foolproof. The Indians mounted up and began to circle the white men, letting out their war cries as they continued to rotate around the hunters, who were breaking up into groups to protect themselves and in order to fire in all directions.

The Indian war cries, as employed by all tribes, were not mere shouting or screaming. They were more like college cheers, having themes, sound groups harmony and noises that kept up a kind of throat-tearing, guttural grunting and crying out. They were psychological warfare, nerve-wracking to desperate people on the defense.

The hunters tried to close their ears to the war cries as they saw Indians cross a draw and disappear to reappear at the next one. The hunters were firing at everything in sight. Several horses had spun up on their front feet to turn a half-cartwheel before floundering with a thud into the hard earth. One Indian, dismounted, began to run for his life, to cover thirty yards to safety. The Sharps rifles began to rain death all around him. He fell.

Hank Campbell put it straight to Limpy Jim Smith: "Boys, we gotta leave this place. Jim, you take the hosses and the wounded down the side-ravine to the long waterhole. Rest of us will crawl up to that crest there and fire at the village till Joe Freed can pull his boys on foot out of the God-damn mess they're in."

The joy had gone out of the fight, since the Indians seemed to be on the point of annihilating their adversaries. The hunters Hank Campbell took up to the crest were four hundred yards from the Indian lodges. The horse herd was beyond that. In the camp, squaws were busy loading gear and poles for a getaway. An Indian signal made of red flannel hung on a tall pole, and a Comanche was sending out looking-glass flash signals for more red men. The hunters fired a few long-range shots and in return got a volley from the Indians. The hunters began to comb the crest with their rifle fire, hoping to scare off Indian shots from above them. Joe Freed's contingent was back. José, the Mexican guide, had a slug in his shoulder. José had to confess they hadn't encountered a handful of hostiles, they were facing three hundred Comanches. Moreover, there was a Lipan Apache band camped in a bend of the canyon.

Hank Campbell moved his cud of tobacco to the other cheek and said, "Maybe we bit offen more than we can chaw."

As the shooting died down, sooty plumes of smoke lifted into the air. The Indians had set fire to the grass. The prairie was ablaze in great sheets of flames. As the flames crept up, a warrior in fancy war bonnet riding a fine white horse, pressed forward almost into the flames. He seemed momentarily to escape all rifle fire, but at last a strong fusillade sent the white horse down and the rider hit the charred earth.

The rest of the Comanches charged, howling war cries and the hunters drew in quick breath and hoped for the best. They were tough and did not panic. The Indians stopped just short of rifle range, expecting the hunters to return the charge. But the buffalo hunters were too Plains-educated to be caught with that "ole Injun trick . . . why a Plainsman larned of that before he could suck an aig [egg]."

Where the smoke was thickest, a massed Indian charge came through the smoke and flame. It was like riding through a mist of gesturing shadows with flashing glints of metal and war regalia caught for a moment in the sun. The hunters put their heavy Sharps into action and that diminished the charge. The Indians withdrew with many warriors and ponies down.

Wounded hunters, in the smoke and fire, began to call out for water. Two men dashed to a puddle fifty yards away, licked at by fire all the way. They came back with their boots filled with water. The druggist gave the wounded a good belt of whisky, just in case the water wasn't too sanitary.

The hunters settled down for a siege, but as the firing dropped off and stopped, wary scouts crept out to find the whole Comanche tribe had escaped under the pall of smoke and the din of noise. They did not give chase. The hunters felt lucky to have come off as well as they had. They counted several wounded. One man was in such bad condition, shot with Soule's captured buffalo gun, he died of his wounds.

Indian losses totaled thirty-five dead, twenty-four badly wounded. The Soule gun was bad medicine for everyone who got his hands on it. The first Indian to handle it had been killed; the second, horribly wounded. Black Horse was shot down with the gun in his hands. Five Feathers picked it up and was killed. No Indian was willing to fire it after that. The gun was packed away in a blanket with the scalp they had taken from Soule, the original owner.

A few weeks later, Captain P. L. Lee, with a troop of the 10th Cavalry ran into the Comanche band at Lake Quemado, and in a hot, short fight killed four Indians, among them, Red Young Man, *Ek-a-wak-a-ne*, who had vowed he'd never give up and never live on a reservation. The soldiers mistook him for Black Horse. The rest of the Indians abandoned hope of freedom.

The Staked Plains War was a private confrontation which broke up the Comanche band. The hide hunters recognized that for all their skill and planning, Indian warfare continued to exact a heavy toll in lives.

The buffalo became rarer and rarer.

Chapter 34

WHEN THE BUFFALO GOD ROAMED THE PLAINS

In the 1870s, Captain Richard Carter not only fought but studied the Comanches, leaving a vivid and realistic assessment of their customs and life. He emphasizes their dependence on the buffalo. "The buffalo," wrote Captain Carter, "to most Indians, was almost a Deity: 'Through the corn, and the buffalo, we worship the Father,' say some tribes, while others ask, 'What one of the animals is most sacred?' and the reply given was 'The buffalo.' To the Indian, the buffalo was the staff of life. It was their food, clothing, dwelling, tools. The needs of a savage people are not many, perhaps, but whatever the Plains Indians had, the buffalo gave them. It is not strange, then that the animal was reverenced by them nor that it entered into their sacred ceremonies and was, in a sense, worshipped by them. The robe was the Indian's covering and his bed, while the skin—freed from the hair and dressed—was his sheet or blanket. The dressed hide was used for moccasins, leggings, shirts and squaws' clothes. The dressed cow-hides were used for their lodges or 'tee-pees,' the warmest and most comfortable portable houses or shelter ever devised. Braided strands of raw hide furnished them with lariats and lines, as was also the twisted hair. The green hide was sometimes used as a kettle in which to boil meat or, stretched over a frame of tough boughs, gave them their 'corracles' or 'bull-boats' with which to cross rivers. The tough, thick hide of the bull's neck, allowed to shrink smooth, made a shield which would turn a lance-thrust or an arrow or, sometimes, even a bullet. From the rawhide, the hair having been shaved off, were made their trunks or 'parfleches' which served the squaws to carry their small household belongings, gew-gaws and tools for scraping and dressing the hides, while the shoulder blades, lashed to sticks, made hoes and axes and the ribs runners for small sledges drawn by dogs. The hooves were boiled to make glue for fastening the feathers and heads on their arrows. This was 'lobbed' on sticks, and when cooled, carried in their bow cases. When used, it was heated in water or over a fire and applied to sinews lying along the back, backed their bows, the sinews also furnishing good thread and bow-strings.

"The hair stuffed cushions and the pads on their saddles and cinches for the same. The horns furnished spoons and ladles and ornamented their war-bonnets. Water-vessels were made of the lining of the paunch. The long black beard, in strands, was used to ornament articles of wearing apparel, and their shields and bow-and-arrow cases. Fly brushes were made from the skin of the tail dried on sticks. Knife-sheaths, bow-cases, gun-covers, sad-dle-cloths, awl and paint-pouches and many other very useful articles, such as 'travois' when moving; all were furnished by the buffalo.

"The saddle trees and bars were made of elm in several parts; each part was laboriously shaved down and fitted, the high pommel and cantle, to the bars, pierced by sharp tools heated red hot, and then carefully sewed with green deer sinew, a hair being used as a bristle instead of a needle, the several parts brought tightly together and the joints carefully glued with the 'lob' stick and rubbed down with their bone rubbers, and given a coat of Ochre paint. Their bridles were hair; no bits were used, a loop being formed just above the mouth so that free use could be made of it and the animal was guided by the pressure of the rein on either side of the neck or the legs from behind the cinch. So perfectly trained was the Indian pony that he could be stopped in his own length while running at full speed, or turned sharply in the arc of a circle without even the use of a rein, thus giving the warrior free use of both arms for his bow, lance or other weapon.

"A large lodge was generally used in common for all tribal ceremonies, although on one occasion, the writer saw a scalp-dance 'pulled off' in an ordinary 'teepee.' The visitors formed a circle, into which the young warriors, stripped to the breech-clout and adorned with feathers and painted for the occasion, came bounding in. The heat and steam from old rags, paint, ancient breech clouts, etc., would have driven an Eskimo crazy for fresh air out of his 'igloo.' Kettle drums, consisting of a dressed skin tightly stretched across a hollow log, kept up a most monotonous long-drawn-out noise of 'tom-tom-tom-tom,' which, with the low chanting or half-singing of the young bucks, and shrill screams and 'Yi Yi's' of the squaws, made a harsh, discordant noise which, had we not been determined to stay it out and see the entire ceremony, would have driven us almost frantic. With a slow, halting hop or dancing gait, the young warriors swept about the ring, occasionally stopping in the center to 'jabber' or talk an almost untranslateable jargon. This went on for some time; new and fresh dancers going into the ring, shortly, however, the squaws began taking their turn and then the fun began. At the termination of dancing of each set, they became furious—their rage (manufactured, of course, for the occasion) became so emotional, so intense that each squaw flung the scalp she carried upon the earth floor of the 'teepee' and sitting down upon it, ground it into the earth with so much vigor that I expected to see the trophy fairly torn to pieces."

The captain was no Indian lover. He respected their skill as fighters, but to their personal habits, he reacted as a white man whose social habits have been offended. "An Indian would rarely eat when on a raid or the warpath. This was not a human, but more of an animal instinct, to avoid the danger of wounds in the bowels or abdominal region, so that they would heal quicker when not distended with food. But, as soon as this emergency had passed, their animal instinct at once took another turn and, around the carcass of a freshly killed buffalo or deer, a small family would never cease eating, gorging themselves and displaying the most gluttonous appetites until nothing was left but the hide, hooves and horns; even the entrails being stripped through the mouth, breast, liver, lights and all parts devoured with the fierceness of wolves, and even the rich marrow dug out with their scalping knives and eaten on the liver as butter, the former cooked in the coals to the point of burning, and then all burnt parts cut off, leaving the balance to be sliced like bread, to accompany the roasted ribs, sprinkling with salt if they have it. A wild turkey was bled, dressed or 'drawn,' a few feathers plucked out and it is also flung into the fire of red coals.

"When one would suppose that there was nothing left of the

bird, the burnt, black mess was raked out, left to partially cool, then, with a dexterous movement of the knife, the skin is peeled or stripped from the neck downwards, taking the burned feathers, revealing a white and tempting morsel to a hungry man. It was then cut and torn apart and eaten with nature's weapons much as any wild animal would perform the same ceremony.

"In their habits, the Indians were filthy beyond all power of descriptions. While enjoying a swim for the sport it afforded them, or a temporary enjoyment, it never occurred to them to do it as a matter of personal cleanliness. The writer never saw an Indian wash his face; they rarely washed their clothes, and calico hunting shirt, leggings and breech clout, don't do full duty until, by decay and hard usage, they literally fall from them. They always wipe the grease from their mouths and hands upon these articles of wearing apparel instead of a cloth or napkin.

"Their hair, especially that of the 'bucks' or warriors, is a matter of great pride to them and daily about a village they could be seen carefully combing, greasing and braiding their scalp-locks, which are generally tied with red flannel, with otter or beaver fur braided in; the whole surmounted by one or more eagle feathers, and, in battle, by elaborate head-dresses or war-bonnets of the most unique and fantastical designs.

"They carefully plucked all hair from the face with a pair of tweezers made either of bone or metal. They could frequently be seen with their backs up against their lodges vigorously despoiling themselves of the hirsute growth and also busily engaged in the additional labor of relieving each other's heads of the super-abundant swarmers of insect growth which, strange to say, were not wasted but, in many cases, formed a part of their daily diet.

"They used paint for decorative purposes, in large quantities, and were very vain of the methods they employed in their art. Black is their war-paint, but olive green, red and yellow ochre predominate. With a head-dress of buffalo horns, or wolf-head with grinning teeth ingeniously combined with feathers, or even with the full war-bonnet of long feathers streaming down their backs and down their ponies' tails, they presented anything but a friendly or amiable appearance, especially when under a full run at their ponies' top speed they yell, whoop, circle about and launch clouds of arrows with deadly aim or fire their more modern breech-loaders at some enemy, supposed or real.

"Slinging his elaborately bead-worked bow-case over his shoulders, he grasped his weapons, lightly swung himself into the saddle and grimly proceeded to commit bloody deeds.

"This was the picture of the brave: the warrior, arrayed peacock-like for show and war; proud, conceited and vain as a city dandy or fop.

"He was the lord and master; arrogant and egotistic. He never worked but hunted and fought. How was it with the squaw? Maturing early, she was—by centuries of savage custom—his willing slave; with merely a significant look or nod from him she proceeded, lariat in hand, to catch his favorite pony, hobbled and grazing nearby the village; to saddle him or to pack the mule for the hunt or the war-path.

"Upon his return, with scarcely a word of greeting, the game was flung down before her; she proceeded to unsaddle, and lariat in hand again to hobble and 'turn him out.'"

The captain also explained Indian tactics in battle as he observed them, and their skilled use of the Plains' pony:

"One of the superstitions of the race was that a warrior who lost his scalp entered not the 'Happy Hunting Ground.' This explains also why they fought so desperately to carry off their dead and wounded. The matter then of bravery versus cowardice rested largely upon a matter of *scalps combined with personal safety.*

"The Plains' Indians rarely ever fought on foot, seldom except against lines of dismounted men. Their safety as to casualties urged them to always keep mounted, moving and circling like a swarm of bees and never 'bunching.'

"Their tactics under fire are difficult to describe; it was rather meagerly attempted in the action with Quanah Parker's band of Qua-ha-da Comanches in the mouth of Canon Blanco, October 10, 1871, when they assembled their entire force for an open field-fight with our command of the 4th Cavalry. Their rapid swing out or rush into a V-shape formation and then fanning out to the front from these two wings into an irregular line of swirling warriors, all rapidly moving in right and left hand-circles, no two Indians coming together, and their quick extensions, while advancing to the right or left, and as rapidly concentrating or assembling on the center, but without any close bunching and their falling back in the same manner, sometimes in a fan-shaped or wing formation, all was most puzzling to all of our Civil War veterans who had never witnessed such tactical maneuvers, or such a flexible line of skirmishers; all without any audible commands but with much screeching and loud yelling.

"The question has been frequently asked why Indians, mounted on small, undersized, bony, scrubby-looking ponies or 'cayuses' could out distance our cavalry troopers on the best thoroughbred or half-bred American horses which the Government could purchase.

"Every Indian's wealth consisted, not in squaws and household possessions, but in a large or small herd of ponies; his property consisting of many head of stock, so much cash. Many of these ponies were the finest short distance race animals ever bred in this country. These they generally rode when going into action. When raiding through the country he generally rode his poorest animals unless pursued and drove from five to ten along the flank, the half-grown boys herding them generally in one bunch or caviard. After depredating and murdering in the settlements, we will say within twenty miles of a Post or Fort, the settler would flee to the post and give the alarm often times afoot, especially if all his stock had been run off . . ."

Here is his picture of a chase:

"All was instant hustle. In an incredibly short time, a command had started for the ranch to find the trail. It had taken the rancher more than five hours, if afoot, and at least three hours, if mounted, to bring the news to the garrison. It took nearly one hour to 'saddle up,' pack the mules with rations and get underway. A ride of from three to four hours to cover the twenty miles; seven hours consumed at the lowest.

"No time was lost; the trail was fresh and off rode the command, not so very fresh after a 20-mile dash. The Indians had only stopped to scalp the dead, gather up the stock and head by the nearest route for their distant village. They went on the jump with experienced herders. They rode a pony 20 miles; took the saddle from his wet back; a fresh pony was brought up by a boy at a signal, the tired one joins the 'caviard' and, with a few moments' delay only, then went off again. All this, long before the command had come up.

"In this way they could cover in seven hours nearly 50 miles.

They never stopped for food or anything until they had covered at least 100 miles, or felt that they were safe from pursuit and capture.

"They went over rocky ledges, where the trail was completely lost, through streams where the trail was always obliterated, often crossing a river as many as twenty times a day; through timber and undergrowth where the hard and dry twigs gave little or no sign; over high prairies where the dry, sun-burnt wiry grass, springing back to its natural positions, as soon as the animal's hoof had left it, left no mark. And still, on they went."

The Indian was not safe from corruption from the white man's ways. Hundreds became scouts for the U. S. Army and helped murder their brothers. They took to palavering around the trading posts with the Indian agents, working for gewgaws, learning to play euchre and poker, aching to steal a 36-inch long-barrel Hawkins rifle made in St. Louis, willing to do anything for a drink called "strip-you-naked" whiskey.

Reservation life was dull and mean. Domestication only hastened the degradation. Wasn't it better to be wild and hungry and hunted, to roam the vistas of grassy swale the alluvial bottom-lands, the barrancas and chaparral and mesquite, even if chased by the horse soldiers?

No place was a safe retreat any more. The white muleteers and wagon bosses were along the Colorado and the Gila, all over expanses marked *terra incognito* on the old maps. They were on the Yellowstone and the Snake and down the San Joaquin Valley. Even the mountain man—shaggy friend of the Indian, often husband to a squaw—was fading out. The wedge press full of beaver pelts no longer went to market. There were no more wild rendezvous, visits to *presidios* and *pueblos*. The barbed-wire fences were appearing. There were sunshades for ranch women, and shoes every day for the kids. Like the Indian, the fiddle-footed, gristle-heeled white wanderer was soon to disappear. The wild whites were being tamed, married, shaved, all along the Seedskedee River, the Prova, and the Spanish Fork. A man once needed only a rifle, a spider skillet, a McClellan hull saddle with hickory stirrups. He began to acquire a roof, furniture, and responsibility.

The cowboy was about to materialize. There had been no cattle business until after the Civil War. The cowboy had little to do with the true settling and winning of the West. Folklore warped history and in the process, distorted the Indians.

In due time, on country porches and shady streets would be heard all the stale stories told by old folk bearing Indian war scars—the nostalgia for the hard past, the brevity of life, the transience of love, the failure of children to be the giants their grandfathers were. Indian survivors muttered worn-out, half-forgotten chants, repeated numb rituals, for old men are much alike.

Chapter 35

THE BATTLES OF THE LAVA BEDS

Emotions and prejudices have confused the basic facts of slavery in America. No advocate of Black Power ever admits that black chiefs and leaders sold their subjects and fellow Africans to traders with the price. Whole tribal cultures were wiped out by the greed of African chieftains to obtain captives for the slave trade, in collusion with white men who bought them and loaded them onto their ships. There was slavery among the American Indians too, and in the West and Northwest, this traffic reached the proportions of scandal.

Among the Tingrit Indians, one-third of the population were slaves. In Oregon, the Hudson's Bay Company encouraged slavery and recognized Indian slaves as property. A good redskin slave cost from six to fifteen blankets; women coming higher than men on the price list.

There were no cotton fields, rice swamps or tobacco plantations in the Northwest, but slaves cut wood, fished, dug camas root, and carried burdens. The Hudson's Bay Company owned slaves of its own. In the Klickitat tribe, a chief named Casino traveled with a retinue of over a hundred slaves. Dreadful ritual called for slaves to be killed and buried under the four corners of Tingrit houses. A Makah chief had his best slaves buried with him in his grave. Slaves could be murdered by their owners with no punishment for the killer.

While the wars against the Apache were in progress in the deserts, the Indians of the West Coast took a second look at the covered-wagon folk, the miners, the settlers. Oregon was green and fertile-looking to the settlers who came in over South Pass. There they met the slave-owning Modocs—cruel, hardy Indians who, in the rain forest and the winter cold, had devised a way of life. Fighting and raiding was their way of life with hunting and fishing following in the order named. They were notorious slave raiders, seeking human property as far away as California and Nevada.

Yet some Northwest Indians were among the most artistic people on the continent, approaching the Indian artists of the Aztec and Mayan civilizations.

The Tingrit and Haida carved argilite stone, ivory, wood and made fine masks inlaid with shell and ceremonial rattles of great beauty, which have influenced certain portions of the modern art world. Their surviving work rests in many collections. Ritual garments of goat hair on cedar back, decorated with complicated signs describing the wearer's genealogy. Their totem poles were amazing sculptures predicting much of the modern form so fashionable at present among the *avant garde*. They disliked blank surfaces, and they covered everything from their great canoes to their small rattles with interlocking, writhing patterns of excellent design. They wove the famous Chilkat blankets.

Aside from art, their peacetime efforts (Indians were loaded with free time) were devoted to ruining themselves in a social ritual called *Potlatch*. Chiefs showed off their wealth in carvings, food, guns, weapons, metals and in one grand gesture, gave away or destroyed entire accumulations of everything they owned. Rivals of a Potlatch-mad Indian would reciprocate with an even greater display and gathering of what he had and dispose of it. This game would ruin entire tribes. Potlatch was a variety of Wall Street plunging or Las Vegas madness—a compulsive gambling-away, at one throw, of worldly possessions.

White men, who valued material things, were shocked. As soon as they could they outlawed Potlatch, so that it had for a time to be a kind of bootleg game.

The Modocs, for achieving their states of elation, preferred to be slave-dealers. They created an abomination and desolation among less warlike tribes. Their special victims were the Digger Indians. These dismal and miserable people, low on the Indian pecking order, were dragged off to slavery among the Klickitat, Tingrit, and Haida.

The Modocs fought the white invaders as hard as they fought other Indian tribes. In a long series of attacks and raids, they killed and slaughtered, captured and tortured the settlers without mercy. The climax of early attempts to bring the Modocs to heel happened in 1852 after they had massacred a wagon train of thirty-three emigrants. California volunteers under Captain Ben Wright and Oregon settlers under Captain Ross moved with their weapons into the Northwest to settle accounts with the Modocs. Eighteen volunteers were killed saving a wagon train. For three months Wright tried and failed to find the Modocs, who avoided direct battle.

Wright primed a squaw with news he was giving a big peace feast and the Modoc were all invited to eat. The meat was sprinkled with a deadly poison, strychnine. But, as the Indians chewed and gorged, it soon became clear the Indians were either poisonproof or the strychnine was not strong enough to kill an Indian. Wright said later, in morose dissatisfaction, he had "been imposed upon by the druggist."

After the failure of this ugly scheme, Wright drew his "hog-leg" (revolver) and shot two of the guests dead. Every volunteer within sound of the shot opened fire on the Indians, who were staring at their hosts in amazement, their greasy mouths open at such shocking treatment. Thirty-six of them were killed.

Ben Wright became a frontier hero for his treachery. At Yreka he got a grand ovation. The California Legislature set up a special thank-you fund to pay the volunteers. Ben Wright, as a man who understood Indians, was made an Indian Agent. He was killed at his Agency four years later in a debacle when the Rogue River Indians sounded their war cries.

The Wright massacre turned the Modoc into a weak and hungry tribe, settled on a dismal reservation in southern Oregon, pushed around by their enemies, the Klamath Indians. But the Modoc survivors were smoldering and ready to take on a war. Shifted from reservation to reservation, unable even to harvest their miserable crops because of harassments, they waited for a savior, a leader.

He came in the shape of a powerful Modoc personality, *Kientpoos*, known to the white community as Captain Jack. Refusing to join the tribe on a forced move to a new reservation, he and a small group of rebels settled on the Lost River, near Tule Lake, to hold off disintegration. The settlers raised a hue and cry. The Indians, they claimed, were ruining the neighborhood, depressing land values and probably preparing to massacre everybody.

In the seventies General E. R. S. Canby was sent to settle this new Modoc dispute. He was friendly to the Indians, but Agent F. B. Odeneal demanded the Army put the Indians on the reservations and keep them there. General Canby's order was: "Do it peacefully if you can; forcibly if you must."

On November 28, 1872, Captain James Jackson, with twenty-eight soldiers and ten settlers, approached the runaway Modoc village on Lost River. A charge of murder was the excuse for this raid. Some time before, Captain Jack had called in a celebrated medicine man, a famous, high-howling shaman, to exercise his incantations on the chief's sick daughter. The girl died. Expressionless in the face of the loss, Captain Jack took up his rifle and shot and killed the shaman.

Jackson found the Indians camped on both sides of the river. Captain Jack remained in his tepee while the other chiefs listened to the arrest order. Chief Starface Charlie didn't approve of what was taking place. He had seen his own father lynched by the settlers. This could be the same trick. As the soldiers began to search the camp, Charlie fired his pistol. At the sound, Captain Jack forsook his mourning and came out to take over the Modoc War. That was how it began—with fourteen warriors.

Across the river, the settlers were attacking the other half of the village. In the process, three died and one was wounded. They retreated. Jackson's soldiers began rapid-fire volleys, hitting women and children. The Indians, returning their fire, killed a sergeant and wounded seven soldiers. Left with only eight men, Jackson also retreated and joined the defeated settlers at nearby Crawley's Ranch. He sent out a soldier to get help.

Captain Jack didn't wait. He led his people out to the Lava Beds. Eons before a volcanic explosion had spewed out hot lava covering fifty square miles of scarred, tormented landscape. An official survey report stated "the ridges form a perfect network of obstructions, admirably adopted to a defense by an active enemy; they seldom rise to a height of ten feet above the bed and, as a rule, split open at top thus giving continuous cover along their crest . . ."

Among these distorted natural structures, Captain Jack waited in a cave to be joined by the Indians from the camp across the river. (En route to the rendezvous they killed seventeen white men.) Camped in the Modoc Caves, Captain Jack now had fifty warriors. Colonel Frank Wheaton and four hundred soldiers with a battery of howitzers, moved to attack the Lava Beds. The Modocs mocked their adversaries, claiming they could hold off a thousand troopers.

In January it was wintry and there was fog. The colonel sent in three companies to attack. He wrote before the battle: "If the Modocs will make good their boast to whip a thousand soldiers, all will be satisfied."

The troops met strong killing rifle fire in the slag growths. A charge was almost impossible among the razor-edged crags. The fight went on in a deep fog which lasted all day. No soldier saw a Modoc all that day. The fog obliterated everything.

Bleeding, their shoes cut to ribbons, knees scarred with bloody wounds, the soldiers struggled grimly on. The colonel at last recalled his men due to concern over losses. There were nine dead, thirty wounded. Three officers were among the dead. The colonel sent for help. "In my opinion . . . one thousand men would be required . . . it must be done deliberately with a full use of mortars."

Against fifty Indians?

General Canby took charge of the situation. First he tried to talk sense to the Indians. The Indians refused to attend peace commission talks. Ben White's dangerous banquet was still on their minds.

Three months passed. Twelve hundred soldiers were kept on the edge of the Lava Beds. Another peace commission took the field. Captain Jack wrote to his sister: "I am very sad. I want peace quickly or let the soldiers come and make haste and fight . . . I want the soldiers to go away."

The whites, instead, insisted the Indians stand trial for murder. Captain Jack wanted to give up but the tribe voted to continue the fight. They put a squaw's shawl on the chief and said he was just a woman. He tossed off the shawl and said if they wanted war, they could have it. He would not be the one to ask for peace.

General Canby: He seems earnestly and honestly to have wanted to end this skirmish without a fight, accepted an offer to come unarmed with a peace mission into the Lava Beds. The group made up of the general, in person; a minister, who was the Indians' friend; two Indian agents; an interpreter, and his Modoc wife, and two of

Captain Jack's warriors who had gone out to guide the commission. They waited by a tent pitched at the edge of the Lava Beds.

Captain Jack and five warriors appeared, and all went into the tent. General Canby passed out cigars. The Indians carried pistols. Outside the tent out of sight, Captain Jack had placed twenty armed Indians. There was some talk with little meaning. The hidden Indians suddenly appeared. Captain Jack shouted: "At-we—all ready!" and shot General Canby through the head. The minister got a slug in his chest. He tried to escape and was picked off, to die in the lava dust. The General, a dreadful hole through his left cheek, rose, fell, rose, and he too was gunned down. Captain Jack leaned over him, making sure he was dead. The general moaned. Captain Jack drove his knife again and again into the general's back. All but two of the peace mission party were killed and those two escaped by running. The Indians yelled as the scalping began. The Modoc wife was beaten, but Captain Jack called off her attackers. Soldiers were coming on the run on hearing the shooting. Lieutenant Sherwood was shot. He died three days later. Macham, the friendly Indian agent, was found shot five times and partly scalped but against all bets, he recovered from his mutilations and wounds.

Colonel Alvin Gillem took over the command. Mortars began to fire, and a day's shelling took place. One shell did not explode and some curious Modocs tried to pull out the fuse with their teeth. The delayed explosion fragmented the group.

Three months after the first attack, the soldiers discovered the Modoc hideout caves, but they were empty. The soldiers had lost eight men, seventeen wounded. Three warriors and eight squaws were found dead. Six days later, Warm Spring Indian scouts came to hunt for the Modoc tracks.

Captain Evan Thomas, with eighty-five men, moved to a sandhill in the middle of the beds to observe the effects of the shelling. They were ambushed by Indians hidden in the lava peaks. Several soldiers made an effort to escape by running. Some dug in on the sandhill. Reinforcements tried to reach them. Captain Cranston and five men were wiped out. Lieutenant Bright and his squad were also cut off and aid sent to him was hit by a deadly volley of Modoc fire. Their own Indian scouts were mistaken by the panic-stricken soldiers for Modocs and came under rifle attack, but were not hit.

The utter futility of fighting the Modoc in the Lava Beds infected the soldiers. Spirit drained from them. Captain Thomas, who had first gone out to inspect the sandhill, saw disaster overwhelming his group.

"We're surrounded! But we can die like brave men!" he shouted. He did. Thomas and two other officers were killed.

Major Green rushed in all his troops not yet engaged, to try and save the survivors of Thomas' group. It was late afternoon when they arrived. The bloody sun was sinking over the ghastly black shapes of the moon-like landscape which composed the Lava Beds. All night, the survivors were under attack. The Modocs moved around in the inky dark, scalping and stripping the dead.

When morning came, the Indians had all moved away. The soldiers staggered out of the Lava Beds, carrying their dead and wounded. Eight men had been killed. Nineteen died of their wounds. Dr. Semig, the Army surgeon, sustained a shattered knee and his leg had to be amputated. The Modoc fighters had numbered only twenty-one and not one had been killed nor wounded.

General Jefferson C. Davis took over command at the Lava Beds at this point. Morale was low. The soldiers muttered they might refuse to attack again. There were minor skirmishes. Chief Hooker Jim of the Modocs, together with his band, decided to head for open country. Captain Jack also moved out. They wounded three guards and captured a supply train of four wagons near Tule Lake. Major H. C. Hasbruck, with two companies of horse soldiers and some Indian scouts, took off after Captain Jack.

The cavalry camped at Sorass Lake on the night of May 10. When the sun rose the following morning, Captain Jack, a macabre figure dressed in the bloody uniform coat of General Canby, followed by thirty-three Indians, attacked the camp. The mules and horses were stampeded. Major Hasbruck rallied his surprised men, and led a return charge. The Indians fell back abandoning their pack train of two dozen mules and nearly all their ammunition. One Indian died. There were three dead and seven wounded among the soldiers. The war was becoming a hideous nightmare. The bravery of the army officers—despite their losses—was amazing.

The Modoc War was cruel and bitter on both sides. The Indians, in defeat, began to bicker and fight among themselves. They were obtuse to the reality of their situation. Hooker Jim led away thirteen warriors, fifty-two women and children after a difference of opinion. The separation into two contingents showed the weakness of Indian discipline.

Hooker Jim's people were run down and scattered and, on May 22, they came in to surrender. Three of Hooker Jim's Indians who had murdered white settlers, offered to serve the Army and try to persuade Captain Jack into giving up. They found him at Willow Creek. Captain Jack had short shrift for the turncoats, who had once insisted he was a squaw not to fight on.

"*You* are cowards and squaws!" (women were maligned by all Indians at all times). "You got me into this war, and now you desert me. *Kientpoos* [Captain Jack] will never surrender. He will die with his gun in his hand."

The next day the Modoc traitor led the troops to Captain Jack's camp. The horse soldiers struck. Some Modocs got away, onto broken ground where the horses could not follow. One by one, the Indians were run down and captured. Cornered with two men and several squaws, Captain Jack sent out a warrior with a white rag. Would they accept Kientpoos' surrender?

They would.

Captain Jack stepped out from the brush. He held out his hands, expressionless, and the heavy irons were put on him.

He said only: "My legs have given out."

The Modoc War was over and a formal trial of war criminals now was in order.

General Davis wanted to hang them all, at once, on capture. But a Washington telegram stated that an official military trial would be necessary. From July 5 to July 19, the military court sat at Fort Klamath. Hooker Jim and his band turned State's evidence. Hooker Jim received immunity for helping to hang Captain Jack's Modocs.

Captain Jack and his cohorts were charged with "the killing of a civilian in violation of the rules of war" and with the murder of General Canby while on a peace mission. The verdict was a foregone conclusion. Captain Jack and his defendants offered little testimony. Unlike most Indians, he was no maker of impressive speeches. He said: "I have always lived like a white man and wanted to live like one. I have always tried to live peaceably and never asked any man for anything . . . have never gone begging.

What I have got I have always got with my own hands, honestly
. . . I don't know how white people talk in such a place as this."
(His army appointed defender seemed to have been cold and
hostile.) "But I will do the best I can."

He told of how the trouble had begun, by Captain Jack's attack
on his people. His Indians feared trouble, treachery, so they had
run away to the Lava Beds. He stated that he had wanted peace
and had been outvoted by Indians now testifying *against* him. He
broke down here and asked the court to continue the next day. He
had become inarticulate.

Overnight, Captain Jack was again an Indian leader—proud and
firm—staring down at the court which was trying him. He spoke
of the cowards who had forced the fighting to continue, those now
safe and condemning him. From white men, he expected no mercy.
He got none. The verdict was: *Prisoners all guilty and sentenced
to hang.*

At ten o'clock in the morning on Friday the 3rd, 1873, the troops
were drawn up at parade. The renegade Modoc, the surviving
women and children were penned in. The enemy Klamath Indians
all stood facing the gallows where Captain Jack and three of his
men were to be hanged. The Modocs faced their end stoically.
Captain Jack stood trussed up on the gallows floor, looking over the
crowd which was gathering and waiting in silence. He looked off to
the hill and wooded slopes and stared at the stockade where, like
steers his people were packed to watch him and his braves die. His
wives and children were there. He said nothing. Apparently, he had
nothing left to communicate.

The nooses were placed in position. Hoods were pulled over
heads. The trap fell away with a creak and a thud and the bodies
jerked in a swift, jarring fall. Modocs cried out in a great moaning
tribal sound joined by some of the Klamath. Captain Jack, after a
few moments of silent quivering, was on his way "to face the
great perhaps." A tent-show freak-collector got hold of the body of
Captain Jack. He had it crudely made into a mummy and went on
tour exhibiting it through the East. Admission: ten cents.

VII

Cheyenne Sunset and Apache Fury

No Indian has more virtues, and none has been more truly ferocious when aroused.

—CAPTAIN JOHN BOURKE
General Crook's adjutant on the Apache.

We took away their country . . . and it was for this . . . that they made war. Could anyone expect less?

—GENERAL PHIL SHERIDAN
Western Commander, 1878

Chapter 36

THE TIME AND GLORY OF LITTLE WOLF

By September of 1878, the northern Cheyennes were no longer *Tsi-tsis-tsa* "The People," as they had called themselves. They were located far to the south in unhealthy reservation in Texas, on the Canadian River—hungry, close to death in an American version of a German death camp, with no horses, few weapons, and many broken promises. In rags with the lodges rotting over their heads, Chief Little Wolf, his face pock-marked with the white man's disease, smallpox, pleaded that they be allowed to go north toward home. The answer was a short laugh. Little Wolf was no Johnny-Come-Lately chief. He had helped lure Fetterman to his death at Fort Kearny and had been in action at the Rosebud and the Little Big Horn. He had rescued the surviving women and children from the McKenzie massacre of Dull Knife's village.

His protests continued and eventually the Indian agent sent for Little Wolf with an idea of his own: "Three of your young bucks have run off. You give me ten of your young men to be held as prisoners, here, until I come back with the three who ran off."

"I will not do as you ask me," said the chief. "You'll follow the three men but you'll not find them. Traveling over the country, they can hide so they will not be found. You'll never get them and you will keep my young men in prison forever."

The agent had a simple way of putting on the pressure: "If you don't give me the men, Little Wolf, I'll cut off your rations!"

Little Wolf stood silent shaking his head. He shook hands with the agent and the officers in attendance remaining coolly expressionless. But his control of his pent-up emotions suddenly ceased. He shouted, according to the text of the interpreter, Guerrier: "I am going to my camp. I don't want the grounds of this agency to be made bloody. So listen to me. I'm going to leave here. I am going back to my north country. If you send soldiers after me, give me time to get some distance from the agency. I don't want blood spilled around it. If you want a fight, I will fight you and I will bloody the ground there."

It appears they thought he was play-acting. The tribe was camped twenty-five miles away on the Canadian River and there Little Wolf imparted his decision to move out. He had only seventy-nine warriors left and many women and children to protect.

The Indians pulled down their tattered lodges, rounded up their few starved ponies, loaded the travois and the sun rose on the Great March of Little Wolf. Emulating Chief Joseph he and his small band set out—not as well-armed, not as well-mounted, and weak from two years of reservation indignity and starvation. They were imbued with disgruntled truculence.

Little Wolf faced a greater enemy force than Chief Joseph. General Pope was established on the Santa Fe Trail. General Crook patrolled the Union Pacific. General Bradley occupied the banks of the Niobrara. Other forces held the Black Hills and General Gibbon straddled the Yellowstone. Thirteen thousand soldiers, posses of militia, miners, ranchers, and civilians with an itch to fire a gun. There were also the clicking telegraph lines, railroad trains, forts and the artillery as opposed to seventy-nine miserable men and their women and children without horses, arms, or supplies.

Scouts sent out by Little Wolf began to comb a thirty-mile area, seizing arms, horses, supplies. They moved across the Kansas, mounted and armed. Telegraph keys tapped out messages of their progress, their escape, and forecast war. Little Wolf had a run-in with cavalry at Little Medicine Lodge River but the troopers pulled back without forcing the issue. Two days later, Little Wolf approached the Cimarron, his force entrenched behind a barricade of logs and earth. The soldiers came to the attack on foot. Three died from Indian fire before they gave up the frontal attack. The Indians moved on, and the Cheyenne moved as no white horsemen could, at seventy miles a day. Dragging their women and children, with watchful and wary scouts on look-out seeking information from Indians they met, they moved on under two chiefs—Little Wolf and Dull Knife.

Turning west toward Dodge City, they began to confront the ranchers and the hunters, always trying to add to their meager stock of ponies, ammunition, and weapons. They slipped around Fort Dodge where two hundred and fifty troopers waited for them. On the night of the 19th of September, Cheyenne scouts were spotted four miles from Dodge City, Kansas. The wires hummed. The Cheyenne were trying for the Arkansas River, east of sleeping Pierceville. Little Wolf was at the river before sunrise, crossed over and pressed on. Colonel Lewis on a foray from Fort Dodge missed them. He rode ahead at an angle with his company, hoping to intercept their trail. His scouts found them at rest on the Punished Woman Fort at twilight of September 28. He expected the Cheyenne to be at the end of their tether.

The horse soldiers, outnumbering the Indians, charged. Little Wolf's rifle fire was deadly. Colonel Lewis fell from his saddle dead and three more men were killed. The Indians hurried away. The soldiers horse-packed the colonel's body back to the fort, lugubrious and morose at their setback.

Little Wolf moved on, guided by the North Star. He was still short of horses. They raided and seized what horses they could and killed anybody who resisted. They crossed the North Fork of the Solomon River, fighting off troops coming up from behind to harass them.

Three years before soldiers had raided Bull Hump's Cheyenne village at Soppa Creek, killing Bull Hump and twenty-one Indians in a senseless massacre. Little Wolf proposed to revenge this deed on the settlement of the whites at Sappa Creek. The Cheyennes burned buildings, killed eighteen settlers and raped a few women. Only one settler, a man named Colvin with his wife, stood off the attack, defending their cabin and lives.

The Cheyennes now faced the barrier of the Union Pacific railroad where General Crook and his men lay in wait. They split up into small units, widely scattered and moved across the raillines into Nebraska.

The pace was fearful and the Indians were human. Old people and little children died. The tribe lost ten warriors. The band was dwindling. Dull Knife was old and worn down. Little Wolf shouted in anger that they must go on. Dull Knife insisted: "This is our country. Nothing has ever happened to us here. Let us rest. The soldiers will not molest us, for we are on our own land."

This was not a reasonable argument. Little Wolf shrugged. "Go your own way if you want to. I will move up into the Powder River land. It is best we do not become divided."

But they were divided. In the night the people of Dull Knife moved away from Little Wolf's followers. In the morning, Little Wolf led his group north. Dull Knife asked Chief Red Cloud for protection, sending a runner. Red Cloud sadly replied that to resist the White Father's power was useless, but Dull Knife prepared to resist. Nearly horseless, with little ammunition and burdened with old men and women, he waited for the attack. On October 23, Colonel J. B. Johnson and two troops of 2nd Cavalry had a skirmish with the miserable, cold, hungry little band. There followed a parley with the officers.

Dull Knife insisted he would not go back to Indian Territory. For two days the talks went on but the only answer was: *Go back to Fort Robinson*. Dull Knife asked permission to go on to the Sioux Agency. A great snow storm came up and the Indians dug in along Chadron Creek. But by morning, two big guns and the Army artillery were in position. Dull Knife gave in and the march to Fort Robinson began.

His son, Buffalo Hump, and his daughter "The Princess" were with him. Although they were searched, they managed to conceal eleven revolvers and five rifles. The weapons taken apart were divided among the band. In chilly barracks the Indians put together their weapons and buried them under the floors. Outside the winter storms raged and far away the Interior Department officially ordered them to go back to the Indian Territory at once. Dull Knife refused to move and was put under guard. Red Cloud and American Horse were brought over, as "friendlies" to persuade them.

"Listen to Red Cloud," the chief said, "your old friend, and do without complaint what the Great Father tells you."

Dull Knife, old, tired, dressed in cast-off rags, answered: "All we ask is to be allowed to live and live in peace. We bowed to the will of the Great Father and went south. There we found a Cheyenne cannot live. So we came home. Better it was, we thought to die fighting than to perish of sickness."

To the officers, he added: "Tell the Great Father that if he tries to send us back we will butcher each other with our knives rather than go."

Captain Wessells, who seems to have been a kindly man, said he'd pass that message on "to the Great Father." But he, too, experienced disenchantment with the Interior Department. January brought a great blizzard with deep snow. The temperature fell ten to twenty degrees below zero. The word from Washington was: March them back the way they came.

Captain Wessells pitied the Indians but he was a soldier. He had never refused an order in his life. Though he did not understand the bureaucrats in Washington, he called in Dull Knife and told him the bad news.

Dull Knife said: "It is death to us. If the Great Father wishes us to die, very well. We will die where we are. If necessary, by our own hands."

Reading the yellowed reports today is a chilling experience. The stupid official position as opposed to the desperate words of the old chief give the reader pause. Dull Knife was deep in his sixties, very old for a Plains' Indian. Wessells was trapped by his orders. He announced he would cut off all food, water and fuel for the Indians in the arctic winter. This truculent minority of tribal tramps must be forced to give in.

The Cheyenne lived in the freezing barracks for days without supplies or fuel. They sang their death chants and the starving, dying children joined in. On January 9, Wessells brought back the "friendly" chiefs for another talk. But this time, Dull Knife did not appear. Left Hand went with two others who were seized and clapped in irons. Left Hand knifed a guard and rushed back to tell his people all was hopeless. He was overpowered as he gave his cry of warning and despair and led off to a cell.

The barracks took up the cry of despair and rage. Bundles and tables were piled up to barricade the place. The hidden weapons were pulled from their hiding places. Clubs were made from stove legs. Benches were broken up into bludgeons. The Cheyennes waited in the cold all that night of January 10, hungry, without water, fire, or warm clothing, bereaved but still ready to fight.

The soldiers did not attack them so they took the offensive. Quick mass suicide could be accomplished that way.

Taps sounded in the fort. Shots suddenly killed three sentries. The Indians came pouring out into the snow and seized the arms of the dead soldiers. They rushed out of the fort untrammeled. Nobody had expected an attack. The little band, mostly women, children and old men, began to trek across the snowy plain. The shots had alerted the troopers and they came running out (half-dressed) to pursue the fugitives, shooting and killing as they went. The main group of Cheyenne sacrificed their rear guard. Half the warriors were dead. The remnant reached a high ridge dividing Soldier Creek from White River. It was a melancholy scene. Women were shot down as well as men. Weapons were snatched from dead hands and fired. The soldiers, half-dressed and a mile from the fort, were freezing. They gave up the chase.

Soon they were back, dressed in winter gear, mounted and armed. They followed the Indians across the frozen river. At the foot of the bluffs, the last stand was made.

The troopers charged once and fell back. Dull Knife's daughter, The Princess, fighting with the men, was killed, along with others. The survivors climbed the cliff. The attack waited for morning. The Indians froze in the open. Dull Knife's son, Buffalo Hump, was among those left crumpled in the snow. In his book, *Reminiscences of a Rancher,* E. B. Bronson writes of Buffalo Hump on that day:

"He lay on his back with his arms extended and his face upturned. In his right hand, he held a small knife worn by years and years of use . . . As I sat believing him dead . . . he rose to a sitting position and aimed a fierce blow at my leg . . . I jerked my pistol out . . . But he fell back and lay still . . . dead.

"So died Buffalo Hump—a warrior capable, with half a chance, of making martial history worthy even of his doughty old father."

The soldiers waited out the night in the fort. The Indians decided to move on to keep from freezing to death. They managed seventeen miles; a remarkable accomplishment for people, young and old, who had not eaten for five days. Camped on a knoll they waited, first setting up an Indian ambush.

In the morning, Captain Vroom led his troopers into the trap and five of his men perished. Dismounted, the troop surrounded the knoll and battled for it all day. They left decoy fires that night and went back to the fort. The Indians came down to the fires to warm themselves, then marched on. The story of their journey, not a war party, but tribal remnants is astonishing. Records bear out their fortitude and magnificent defiance. They proved Emerson's text: "The world is nothing; the man is all—in yourself is the law of all nature."

Thirty-seven Indians were dead and fifty-two wounded were cap-

tured. The remainder held out far up Soldier Creek in a dangerous position to attack. The Cheyennes ate the remains of a
trooper's dead horse, their first food in seven days. Stripping the
carcass to the bone, they moved on again—six miles to the bluffs
—prepared to fight on. The soldiers were deterred by an old Indian unable to march with his frozen feet and tired limbs. He remained behind to hold off the troopers with a worn-down carbine.
Sixty troopers tried to gun him down but he managed to keep on
firing. His right arm was shattered and he fired on with his left. At
last he rolled over, dead.

There were five bullet wounds in his body. He had killed a
captain and wounded a private in his rear guard action. This old
man's name is unknown.

Now a twelve-pounder was brought up from the fort and at
noon, the cannon began shelling the Indians, dropping forty rounds
into the Indian position. No sound came but they were there,
lying prone against the freezing ground, as shards of steel and
ice broke among them. A suggestion for surrender almost resulted
in the death of the messenger, who cried out the demand. A cordon
of troops surrounded the position but by morning, the Indians
had managed to escape. They had gone up Hat Creek dragging
half-gnawed horse bones with them.

Six more days of this cat-and-mouse game continued, savage
and without mercy. The band was smaller every night they pushed
on to take up new positions.

On the morning of January 21, 1879, the last stand was made
on the Hat Creek Bluffs. Wounded, with legs and arms frozen
and nearly dead, the Cheyenne waited.

At a new call to surrender, they fired their last six shots. Unarmed,
they huddled together. The soldiers charged and poured a huge
volley down on the grounded people. As the troopers pulled
back to reload, across and up from the wash where the Indians
were dug in emerged three ghostly figures, thin and weak with
hunger, limbs blue with freezing, their bodies bloody from wounds.
Two had knives. One flourished an empty pistol. Their war cries
were weak but they moved on, not men any more but pure spirit
and will. They threw themselves into the rifle fire of three hundred troopers.

The long trek was over. Behind them lay twenty-two dead,

nine badly wounded. No one could tell which bodies were men and which were women. Only the children, because of their size, were identifiable. A body count showed all the Indians had been accounted for except for six. Dull Knife was missing. In the fearful last days he had been separated from the main party while scouting positions. He and five others were still on the move. Dull Knife was never captured. In the end the old man was given shelter by the Sioux.

Little Wolf did not come to such an heroic end. Moving north, raiding and killing, he reached the wilds of Montana. There he was persuaded by Lieutenant W. P. Clark to join the troopers as a scout for the Army. He "aided and did valuable work for the government in helping run down the few outlaw bands of hostile Sioux." Some ordinary men become heroes and others begin as heroes but save their own skins when hope is gone.

The recovery of white captives held by the Indians was also a pressing problem of the Army. A firsthand account of an attempt to recover a white woman held by Indians is given by Robert Wright.

"The guard learned from the Indians that they were Kiowas—old chief Satanta's tribe. Fred Jones, who was Indian interpreter at Fort Dodge, was requested to come down and ascertain what was wanted. The Indians informed Jones that they had two paleface squaws who they wished to trade for guns, ammunition, coffee, sugar, flour—really, they wanted about all there was in the fort, as they set a very high value on the two girls.

"The Indians wanted everything in sight, but a trade or swap was finally consummated by promising the Indians some guns, powder and lead, some coffee, sugar, flour and a few trinkets consisting mainly of block tin which has quite a bright, glittering tint. This was used to make finger rings, earrings, and bracelets for the squaws.

"The bracelets were worn on both ankles and arms of the squaws and, when fitted out with their buckskin leggings and short dresses, covered with bead, they made a very attractive appearance.

"The Indians knew they had the advantage and drove a sharp bargain—at least, they thought they did. They insisted on the goods being delivered to their camp near the Wichita mountains which was quite an undertaking, considering that a white man had never been in that section except as a prisoner, a renegade or possibly an interpreter.

"The night we arrived at the Kiowa camp we were located on the banks of a creek. The young warriors commenced to annoy us in all manner of ways, trying to exasperate us to resent their annoyances so they could have an excuse to make an attack on us. At this time, Fred Jones and Lieutenant Heselberger, who had been up to Satanta's lodge, came to our camp and, seeing the taunts and annoyances to which we were being subjected, admonished us not to resent them for, if we did, the whole party would be massacred or made prisoners and burned at the stake. Jones, the interpreter, immediately went back to Satanta and reported the situation. Satanta, at once, had a guard of old warriors thrown around us and thus saved us from further annoyances. Not that Satanta was any too good or had any love for us that he should protect us but, at that immediate period, it was not policy for him to make any rash movements.

"All night long the Indian drums were continually thumping and the Indians were having a big dance in their council chamber, which was always a custom, among the wild Indian tribes, when any unusual event was taking place. The next morning, we were up bright and early and teams were hitched to the wagons and proceeded to the center of the Indian camp in front of the council chamber where the goods were unloaded. The two young girls were then turned over to us by one of the chiefs. They were a pitiful looking sight. They had been traded from one chief to another for nearly a year and had been subjected to the most cruel and degrading treatment. The eldest girl gave birth to a half-breed a short time after their rescue. One of the girls was seventeen and the other fourteen years old. They had been captured near the Texas border and had been with the Indians some time, according to the story told us. Their father, a man by the name of Box; the mother, and their four children were returning to their home when they were overtaken by a band of Indians. The Indians killed Mr. Box because he refused to surrender. The youngest child was taken by the heels and its brain beaten out against a tree; the mother and three children were taken back to the main camp. The mother and youngest child were taken to the Apache camp—an Apache chief purchasing them from the Kiowas. We felt confident that, later on, we would get possession of the mother and youngest child for the Apaches would want to trade, too, when they learned how the Kiowas had succeeded.

"As we expected, a few days after our return to Fort Dodge, the sentry reported a party approaching from east of the fort. All that could be seen was the glittering, bright ornaments—dazzling in the sunlight; but shortly, the party approached closely enough for it to be seen that they were Indians.

"The Indians proved to be Apaches and the whole tribe came in, numbering about two thousand. They had brought along the white woman, Mrs. Box, and her young daughter, expecting to make a big 'swap.' There was no intention of giving anything for them but there was a plot to get the Indians in, gain possession of the chiefs and head men of the Apache tribe and hold them as hostages until they would consent to surrender the woman and child. It was a desperate and dangerous experiment for the Indians outnumbered us greatly. I don't think, at this time, there were over one hundred and seventy-five men, altogether, at Fort Dodge, including civilians, and against these was one of the most desperate tribes of the plains.

"When the time arrived for the council, about a hundred of the chiefs, medicine men and leading men of the Indians were let in through the big gate at the east side of the fort. As soon as they were inside, the gate was closed. When they were all ready for the big talk and the customary pipe had been passed around, Major Sheridan instructed the interpreter to inform the Indians that they were prisoners, and that they would be held as hostages, until Mrs. Box and her daughter were brought in and turned over to him.

"The Indians jumped to their feet in an instant, threw aside their blankets and prepared to fight. Prior to the time the Indians were admitted to the fort enclosure, the mountain howitzers had been double-shotted with grape and canister, the guns being depressed so as to sweep the ground where the Indians were located. Some of the soldiers were marching back and forth with guns loaded and bayonets fixed, while a number of others—with revolvers concealed under their blouses—were sitting around watching the proceedings. The main portion of the garrison was concealed in the dugouts and the men all armed and provided with one hundred rounds of ammunition per man. The Indians were all armed with tomahawks which they had carefully concealed under their blankets.

"When they were informed that they were prisoners, they made a dash for the soldiers in sight as they were but few, the majority, as has been said, being hid in the dugouts; but when the men came pouring out of the dugouts and opened fire, the Indians fell back and surrendered. One of the old chiefs was taken up on the palisades of the fort and compelled to signal to his warriors in their camp. In less than thirty minutes Mrs. Box and her child were brought to the big east gate, and one of the most affecting sights I ever witnessed was that of the mother and girls as they met and embraced each other. It was a sign once seen, never to be forgotten. Major Sheridan then told the interpreter to inform the Indians that they could go, warning them not to steal any more women or children."

Chapter 37

THE LAST DAYS OF MR. MEEKER

The Utes, with inexhaustible energy, made their homes in the mountains that faced the Plains. They loved to sweep down to raid and do battle and kill the Plains Indians in a centuries-old primitive tradition. They traveled far distances molesting white settlers close to Denver and Pueblo. The raids the Cheyenne and Arapaho made in retaliation against the Utes, caught the settlers in between. Like most Indians, the Utes signed a peace treaty with the Great Father early, and, as usual, were pushed aside when the white settlers wanted their land. Chief *Ouray,* the Arrow, was a wise man. He carefully measured the white striking power and ordered his followers to keep the peace all along the White River, Uncomphagre, the Cimarron, and the Uintah.

The southern Utes, under Chief Ignacio, had different ideas. It was bad enough to have the white-gold hunters invading their land but the discovery of rich silver veins added insult to injury. Silver was easier than gold to find and miners came in hordes. The Utes' valleys and gullies, streams and canyons, were filled with wild prospectors who didn't respect treaties.

Another villain was Horace Greeley, the editor and publisher of the New York *Tribune,* who supported a town called after him, Greeley, Colorado. Greeley secured an appointment for an egotistical reformer, do-gooder, and fanatic named N. C. Meeker, as Indian Agent of the White River Utes in the year 1878.

"For their own good," Meeker transferred the Utes to a new reservation that pleased him better, the Powell Valley on the White River. This was only winter hunting camp and turning it into a reservation drove off the game the Indians lived on. As an Indian who knew Meeker put it: "He was always mad.

I think he was sick in the head . . . We never knew what to do. He was mad all the time."

Meeker's answer to every protest was simple: "I shall cut every Indian down to the bare starvation point if he will not work." Instead of farming, the Utes built a race track. They were wild for horse racing and this sport kept them peaceful. They could not comprehend the Christian virtue of hard work.

Meeker built a schoolhouse across the race track, destroying it. Meeker also insisted these mountain hunters become educated like white men, and he insisted the children attend his school. He was unable to explain the importance of education or to make it attractive. The Indians felt it was a way of depriving them of their children and destroying the tradition of Indian lore they wanted passed on to their broods. Meeker, earnest and humorless, was also impetuous and petulant. Indian sensibilities were superstitions to him.

By September 1, 1879, Meeker was threatening to have soldiers move in to drive the Indian children to school. Soldiers did insist the Indians, for their own good, should send their children to the school. Meeker ordered the whole valley plowed up for crop-growing.

The Utes, accustomed to bows and rifles and living off the game, could not consent to so much progress all at once. Civilization was forced on a primitive people, not yet ready for it. White men came with their plows and shooting followed.

In the end a half-breed named Johnson beat up Meeker in his own house and threw him out the door. The telegraph disseminated calls for help to Fort Fred Steele. The commander of this fort, just north of the Wyoming border, dispatched Major T. T. Thornburgh with a hundred and fifty infantry and three cavalry troops. Moving south he was stopped at the reservation line by a party of five Utes—chiefs who advised him that he had no right to move forces on to their land. The major replied that he had orders and that he'd camp where he pleased. The chiefs returned to the tribes and held a council, not waiting for their leader, Chief Ouray, who was away, hunting. They agreed that the soldiers must not be permitted to go on. Basically, the difficulty was a land problem. The Indian held his land sacred. The game was his food and he saw the game being depleted. The swales, bogs, banks of alders and red osiers held ducks and wild rice and patches grew gourds, maize and beans. Muskrats and coot skins were made into clothing.

Crow Wing Lake, Red-Eye River, Mantrap Valley—all these were not suitable for farming. Indian lands were beautiful under the sky and smoothed out by ancient glacier retreats. The white man cared little for the millions of monarch butterflies, the sunflowers that the Indian used for fodder, yellow dye, textile fabrics and a "cure" for rheumatism or ground up as a coffee and planted to "prevent" malaria. Fat squirrels were a sign of snow and a cold winter. Starry nights meant mild weather. Brittle leaves prophesied a cold spell.

The Indian determined that the land must remain as it was, for the redwing in the canebrakes, for the Canada and Blue geese, the green-winged teal, the night hawk, the kingbird, even the woolly bear caterpillar. He accepted a balance of nature; he was *part* of nature.

The white man didn't understand these things. Everything was at the cruel mercy of the plow and the miners' blasting powder. Men were ruining the gorges of the upper Snake, Jackson Hole below the Grand Tetons, the ebony, volcanic earth of the Blackfeet. Game hunters for Eastern tables, pressing West, were killing and shipping mallard at a price of $1.50 the dozen; $1 a dozen for teal. On the Utes, the shadows of Meeker's plows darkened hope.

Major Thornburgh decided to camp just above the Agency and wait. He led his command through a deep cut called Red Canyon. The scrub oak was thick around the old game trail he followed, and here Chiefs Colorow and Jack arranged an ambush for him behind rock and scrub. They were armed mostly on arrows.

The soldiers marched in, wagons in the rear, falling behind by half a mile. Indians were sighted and scouts were sent forward to investigate. The Indians began to fire their few rifles and winged a host of arrows. The major sent in his horse soldiers, ordering the wagons to form a protective corral in the rear.

The Utes kept up a brisk attack and one group set out to seize the wagon train. The military order was "Fall back!" In a slow, but dangerous, retreat, the troopers began to move back down the canyon. Major Thornburgh never reached the wagons. He dropped from his horse, shot dead in the saddle.

The Utes had only about seventy-five warriors at the start and were outnumbered two-to-one. They drove the troopers back to the wagons near the White River, a train already under attack. The Indians held two high ridges that rained fire on the wagon corral. The Utes were great hunters, could aim as well as any white sharpshooter. They set fire to the brush and followed in its flames, but did not charge. They took their time in the killing of the Army horses. As darkness fell, only five steeds were left alive. A trooper named Murphy volunteered to ride out for help and he carried the hopes of a confused and trapped command.

The Agency was twenty-five miles from the Red Canyon fight and Meeker was unaware of the battle in progress. Meeker wrote a letter to the dead Major Thornburgh: "Things are peaceable," he cheerfully set down. Sealing the letter, he sent a white man and two Utes to deliver the mail to the major. Two miles down-trail, the messenger was murdered by two Indians named Antelope and Ebenezer. The Meekers, after family prayer, sat down to supper. Afterward, Mrs. Meeker and their daughter, Josie, washed up. Insects buzzed around the oil lamp and the wife of the post-trader, a Mrs. Price, did her washing outside. Men were weather-tightening a sod roof by patting earth into place. Meeker and his carpenter went to take an inventory in the warehouse. Meeker was a careful bookkeeper.

When the killers of the messenger came back to the Agency, the attack on the whites was begun. Shooting and yelling, the Indians came out of their dwellings, howling war cries, according to Agency reports. The Indians claimed the whites became worried at the Indians' change of mood and began firing at them. It seems possible that the Indians attacked on a signal, taking Meeker by surprise.

Whatever happened, it was certainly a massacre. Meeker was murdered. Two other white men were killed. Another man was shot in the leg. The laundry woman, Mrs. Price, rushed to the Agency building and gave a rifle to the wounded man, Frank Dresser. He broke a window pane with this rifle and fired, killing the half-breed Johnson's brother.

Mrs. Meeker and her daughter, Josie, joined Mrs. Price and the wounded man in the building but decided that the fireproof adobe milkhouse would be safer. They made a rush for it and reached it as the last Agency white man died, firing his rifle. They were now the sole survivors.

The Indians were burning everything in sight. They piled up loot and danced around the rising fire columns. The milkhouse filled with smoke and the three women and the wounded man ran for the woods. The Utes, with a fearful cry, took up the chase. The wounded man was killed. Mrs. Meeker was injured. The Indians divided up the women. Mrs. Price was won by a horror called *Ahu-un-tu-pu-wit,* who kept grinning and threatening: "No burn white squaw. Heap like-'em." Josie, the daughter, was claimed by an ardent young buck, Persume, but another Indian, named Douglas, tried to grab her and there was another fight. Douglas settled for the slighted and wounded Mrs. Meeker already in agony from fear, wounds and worry about the fate of her husband. During this massacre and women lottery, the Red Canyon fight was in progress.

The night was dark and warm and the wounded cried out in terrible thirst. Twice, soldiers tried to reach the river bank where their dead major lay to fill their canteens. Morning brought out the Indian sharpshooters stationed on their heights. The wounded were put into a protective pit. A wounded horse, mad from its injuries, fell into the pit and would have crushed the wounded with its thrashing hoofs, but it was killed before the wounded men were mangled. The soldiers' ammunition was low and as the heat of the day rose, Lieutenant Paddock and Dr. Grimes were killed.

The horses were all dead and no one could ride out for help. Thirteen troopers were dead, their bodies lying among the wounded. Nearly half of the expedition was out of action. The troopers grimly waited their fate. They were good soldiers, trained in a tough school.

October 2 was sharp and airy but sunny. As the sun began to climb, horse sounds came from downvalley; then shouts and shots, and into action came a troop of the Negro 9th Cavalry. Murphy had gotten through with the news, and aid was coming. The Utes were not much impressed by one troop of soldiers and kept up their fire killing off all the Negroes' horses.

From Fort Russell, General Wesley Merritt was moving up in the heat and dust with a company of infantry in wagons with four troops of horses. At Rawlins he got four more companies of wagon-riding soldiers. They pressed forward all day and all night. On the 3rd, they passed a settler's wagon train, all the people dead and mutilated. Merritt went into the canyon and moved into position by the besieged soldiers. An Indian cried out with pleasure at the sight. "More horses! More shoot-um!" Merritt sent out a little advance, but it failed and he pulled his men back to rest them after the long ride. He planned to attack in force in the morning.

Chief Ouray had come up to the battle scene, riding all day to reach the Utes in their attack. According to official Army records, a white flag of truce appeared on the Indian side the following morning and a white man, a miller from Los Piños named Brady, accompanied by an Indian, came forward under the flag. Brady claimed to have a letter from Chief Ouray ordering the Utes to stop the battle. The soldiers accepted the chief's wise ruling for both sides. Meanwhile, the Indians slipped away, not waiting to see how the white men would take this order from their chief. They had much to be elated about.

The wagon corral was a revolting, stinking place with rotting horses and unburied dead men. The Indian losses were said to be six. Merritt reorganized his forces and went on to the Agency. The sights he found were terrifying. On the way, they stumbled over bodies of four white men scalped and in horrifying condition.

The White River Agency was a prime horror. Ash and charred timber mixed with the muck and looted supplies, fixtures and furnishing were all that remained. Meeker had taken fearful punishment. His head was mashed in. A barrel stave had been driven down into his throat through his mouth while he was still alive. His body was whittled and slashed. He wore a steel chain around his neck, by which he had been dragged alive over the ground. Dogs and wolves had fed on the dead. The remains were gathered up and hastily buried. A scout moving on to follow the Utes fired on some friendly Indians and he and a lieutenant were killed.

The work of trying to free the women began. Persume, the young warrior, had fallen madly in love with Josie Meeker. He promised her an easy life if she stayed with him, and even did the non-Indian thing of weeping and lamenting his love in front of his fellow Indians as they decided the fate of the women.

On October 23, the white women were turned over to Merritt. There is no factual record of the reactions of newly-made widows and a molested maiden after the obtained freedom; Persume, the

Indian Romeo, inspired scandal as he carried on, claiming Josie Meeker was his wife, his squaw. He became a sad, brooding Indian.

Josie went on to work in the Treasury Department in Washington, D.C., where she died a few years later. When news of her death came to the Utes, the Indians insisted sarcastically that Persume should have painted his face black and gone into ritual mourning for his late wife.

Suddenly news arrived that Chief Ouray, the peacemaker, was dead. This brought the end of talks and meetings as to the Utes' fate. Official orders arrived from Washington and the northern Utes were sent to the Uintah reservation up in Utah. The southern Utes were moved to valleys in southern Colorado. Leavenworth Federal prison swallowed up the most guilty of the Meeker massacre party; Douglas, Johnson, *Ahu-un-tu-pu-wit*, Colorow, Matagoras and the lover, Persume. Matagoras went insane in prison and had to be killed by the Utes when released.

The Utes lost the freedom to move over what once had been their land. They subsisted on government rations and, as for wild game, not too many shoveler and cinnamon teal appeared in season. Perhaps they dried buffalo-gnat-larvae and ate it as *kootsbe* (a treat). But the old days when Clark of Lewis and Clark, wrote in his simple spelling: "The gees continue to pass in gangues . . . these people gave us to eat a large Been" (bean) "which they rob the mice of the prairie . . ."—those times were gone. The Utes were no longer to roam the ravines, ridges, buttes, mesas, gullies where they had found a way of living among the salmon-pink and powder-blue rocks, nor own the red, oxidized iron bluffa.

Also gone are the "huge gangues of buffalow" swimming the river. Wolves, antelope, pigeon-hawk, and chickadee had to adopt or perish as the figwart, nightshade, cinguefoil were turned under by the cotter-plowshare that cut furrows in what had been the Ute hunting grounds. *Leaf Fall Moon,* as the Indian had called autumn, and the omniverous bear that shared the berries with the squaws saw the Utes no more.

As yet the small animal life persisted. The Cheyenne River magpie, the porcupine who was hunted for his quills to make decorations for Indian buckskin, the Rushmore golden eagle whose feather had filled so many war bonnets. The Indian missed this small animal life when it began to disappear, as he had missed the bugling bull elk, the lobo wolf of Currumpaw County, the gray-green sagebush, the rimrock country around Corpse Draw.

In time the small game followed the big game away from the settlements and the reservations. The redtail and rough-leg hawk of the Plains preened on the buttes watching the Indians go into exile. Hardy survivors are the black and white magpies. You find them today at the grave of Sitting Bull, at Fort Yates, begging peanuts from tourists.

Today, the weed called Russian thistle and the unkillable pest, the tumbleweed, which drops 180,000 seeds from a single rolling plant, and can wait forty years to germinate, covers much of this land. Some say the ghostly rolling tumbleweeds are the sighs of the lover, Persume, come back to hunt the shade of Josie Meeker.

Why did the Indian go on fighting when he sensed it was no longer a matter of survival? Perhaps the philosopher, Kenneth Boulding, suggests an answer:

"Survival is not the highest human value. One doubts, indeed, whether it is even the highest value in the biological world. One suspects that survival is frequently a by-product of the play of genetic forces. It is by the willingness to risk death that both men and animals gain life. For most people, there can be little doubt that the value-image is mainly a product of a transcript. Education in most societies is a matter of harnessing the biological drives in the interests of establishing the value-system of a society. By constant reiteration these acquired values become internalized and acquire the same status in the image as the biological values—or perhaps even a superior status."

Chapter 38

THE INDIAN MESSIAH COMETH

The great Indian wars of the northern Plains were over. Towns were going up, even if small Sioux bands were still moving about and being chased by troopers. The action had moved to the deserts against the Apache, who had made problems since the war with Mexico.

But that grand old man of the Plains, Sitting Bull, was still alive. The Red Coats in Canada had no problems with him living there in exile with several hundred members of his tribe. Sitting Bull was there from 1877 to 1881. Some of his young bucks were accused of stealing horses from some other Indians, but aside from that his people were well-behaved. The horses were returned by Sitting Bull and the bucks punished.

Both the United States and Canada recognized that Sitting Bull was a power even old and in exile. The Sioux continued to raid in small bands and, while they were not his people, his influence was suspected. The Canadians hinted that the guests were outstaying their welcome. After much talk, the French trader, Louie La Gare convinced Sitting Bull that he should return to the United States. With infallible instinct, the chief recognized the pressures of diplomatic exchanges and life in Canada became for him a slow leaking-away of existence.

On June 19, 1881, he rode into Fort Buford, Montana, to give himself up. He was kept a prisoner at Fort Randall for two bitter years, then permitted to move on to the Standing Rock Agency, where he was little better off. To tame him, attempts were made by the agents to have him replaced as head of the Sioux by other chiefs and strip him of his power. At one meeting when Indians were being pressured into taking up the plow, he rose to talk but was brushed off as a rank-and-file Indian with no chief's rights.

Sitting Bull, expressionless, made a small hand signal at this news and every Indian left the meeting room. A new meeting was called and Sitting Bull was permitted to speak freely. The Sioux never accepted any other chief. They ignored his advice when they signed away a great block of their land, through General Crook, for a ridiculously low price. All their dealings with the whites were naïve and sad.

The Indians indubitably felt Sitting Bull belonged to the past of defeats and exile. As they sat in a cold chinook wind and listened to the prairie dogs bark with the rime of heavy frost on their lodge poles, they dreamed of a new leader—a Messiah. Let the white men dig for gold in the sand and silt; let the savanna sparrows gorge on pigweed seed. It was the time, the old men said, for Indian visions to change things. Land-stealers were not punished. Thieving Indian agents were starving them. The winter of 1889 was hard and the settlers were more greedy than ever.

The Ogallala Sioux heard of a Messiah far to the west. Not only the Sioux but all the tribes of the Plains on their reservations were whispering about this thing.

The Messiah had come before, they knew, as the priests had told them, but the whites were cruel to Him and they tortured him on two sticks and he died. He no longer loved the whites but would come to save his red children. The Indians had always believed that the spirit should have superiority over the body.

Early in 1889, two events took place. First, a thirty-five-year-old Paiute Indian called Wovoka was sick of some obscure misery that no medical man diagnosed. On New Year's Day, near Walker Lake in Nevada, the moon was suddenly blotted out, moving in front of the sun and erasing it in a total eclipse.

At that moment, Wovoka was in a trance. He died in his vision and was carried up to the great sky. There was the Great Spirit on all sides were "all those people who had died long ago, busy in the old-time sports and activities, all so happy and always young."

But Wovoka was not yet dead he discovered. The Great Spirit ordered him back to earth to talk to the living so "that they may be good and love each one the other; have no quarrels, and live in peace with the white men. They were to put away the old tribal practices that led to war. And if they obeyed faithfully the Great

Spirit's orders, they would in time themselves be united again with their friends waiting for them in the other world."

There was to be a dance, Wovoka was told, and he was to teach the Indians how to perform this dance. So Wovoka came back to life—reborn—ready to tell of his vision.

Wovoka spread the new gospel. From Walker Lake it traveled to the Plains, and as the honored Messiah of the tribes, Wovoka was received with respect and awe, the one chosen to lead the tribes from misery to joy eternal. As the tribes waited, they danced the Wovoka's Ghost Dance, the sign of their conversion to the new faith.

There had been other Indian visionaries, but Wovoka came at the right time. Reservation life was mean and miserable, disease was killing hundreds, the buffalo herds were gone for good. And working the land had proven for them a snare and a delusion. Drought killed their plantings and wind and dust carried off their hopes of harvest. The new gospel spread over an area two thousand miles wide. Wovoka's village became a shrine and delegates arrived to visit with the Holy One. The Plains Indians rode up in droves. Sixteen tribes were present at one session with the new Messiah.

The Ghost Dance was an unpleasant tribal ritual to the officials, comprising a five-day program to test the believers and their physical endurance, as well as their ability to come closer to the new vision. Food and water were not permitted, and these fasting holidays killed off many Indians. A good Ghost Dance produced four to five hundred Indians in an exalted frenzy. The ground was littered with fallen figures while fresh dancers crowded in. The true believer worked himself toward ecstasy of the moment when he, too, might have a vision and produce a trance.

Like most dogma, this faith had been modified to ignore the call of peace. The Sioux, the Cheyenne, the Arapaho, Iowa, and Apaches, as they whirled and fasted, glimpsed powerful images. Journalists, in their reports East to their newspapers, spoke of the "savage nature of the spreading Ghost Dance," and the "cries of the dancers which could mean bloody war and a more desperate Indian uprising."

At first, Wovoka was unknown even to the army men and the old Indian fighters, who continued to blame everything on Sitting Bull: He *was* a great leader; he was a man high among the Indian elders. So Sitting Bull and the Ghost Dances merged in the rumors that predicted war. There is no evidence that Sitting Bull was involved in the Ghost Dance crusade. He had not hurried forward, as so many chiefs had, to be anointed as a follower of Wovoka. But to the Indian-hater, rumors and speculation turned into facts. The whites chose Sitting Bull as the focal point of attention as the Ghost Dance hysteria spread. As rumors of war increased an exodus began. Settlers from farms and ranches rushed to the safety of towns and villages or to forts for protection.

By fall, 1890, Indian agents in South Dakota were calling for more troops to patrol the reservations and to be on hand if trouble should begin. Troops were sent and the Indians decamped. Two thousand Sioux trekked to the Dakota Badlands. Actualities and certainties faded as the Ghost Dances increased.

On the reservations the Indians, morose and taciturn, were showing old sparks of temper. Their visions now had a grip on them. Impulses not to be resisted were boiling up. They waited for some sign or omen.

Henry James said: "Money is the great American sedative." The frontier settler was tied to this philosophy whether he wanted to be or not. He *had* to produce a cash-crop. He became involved in business interests, in trusts and combines which marketed his cattle, grain, furs and timber.

The Indians merely aspired to a nobility in nature, not to cleanliness nor goodness nor industry, but to a continuous affirmation of primitive life. Sitting Bull, wrongly blamed for the Ghost Dance problems, had a dignity, a grace, that few white leaders could arrive at. As a patriarch-chief, he was the voice of authority who could calm with counsel, or castigate with scorn.

The whites were basically a water people, sea-derived, moving inland, and the primordial Plain was, to them, a sea of grass, a grain land. They had no respect for the original owners. The Ghost Dance was not, to them, the desperate ritual of a people close to the breaking-point, seeking in the supernatural a pure relationship between themselves and a living, mysterious universe. In their condition, the Indians were in the mood of Franz Kafka's line: "What does it matter as long as the wounds fit the arrows?"

The Ghost Dances continued. One session is noted where five hundred Indians at Pine Ridge marathoned for three days with not one of the dancers eating or drinking. At the end of the session over two hundred were unconscious or in trances. Another Ghost Dance at Wounded Knee resulted in eight deaths.

It was at Pine Ridge, where the dancers died, that the real trouble began. R. F. Royer was a new and untried Indian agent who listened to every rumor. He was told the tribe was about to go into "a big outbreak." War cries would come, and Indian massacres. Royer telegraphed for soldiers. In October 1890, soldiers were swarming over the Agency. The newspapers moved in, making a sensational series of features out of the Ghost Dance cult building the event into a much greater crisis than it was. Sitting Bull remained the one well-known Sioux chief to blame for all this turmoil. He was living simply with his followers on the Grand River, after a year's tour with Buffalo Bill's Wild West Show.

On Thanksgiving Day, Royer at South Dakota, was giving out gifts of stringy beef to the Indians. Agent Royer, called by the tribe *Lakota Kokipa-Koshla*, or Young Man Afraid of Indians, was nervous. He exploded when rumor persisted that hundreds of lodges and thousands of Indians were camped on the Cheyenne River, and growing in number.

Chief Short Bull made a speech:

"My friends and relations I will soon start this thing in running order. I have told you that this would come to pass in two seasons, but, since the whites are interfering so much, I will advance the time from what my father above told me to do, so the time will be shorter. Therefore, you must not be afraid of anything. Some of my relations have no ears, so I will have them blown away.

"Now, there will be a tree sprout up and there all the members of our religion and the tribe just gather together. That will be the place where we will see our dead relations. But before this time, we must dance the balance of this moon, at the end of which time the earth will shiver very hard. Whenever this thing occurs, I will start the wind to blow. We are the ones who will then see our fathers, mothers and everybody. We, the tribe of Indians, are the ones who are living a sacred life. God, our father himself, has told and commanded and shown me to do these things.

"Our father in heaven has placed a mark at each point of the four winds. First: a clay pipe, which lies at the setting of the sun and represents the Cheyenne tribe. Second, there is a holy arrow lying at the north, which represents the Cheyenne tribe. Third, at the rising of the sun there lies hail, representing the Arapaho tribe. Fourth, there lies a pipe and nice feather at the south, which represents the Crow tribe. My father has shown me these things, therefore we must continue this dance. If the soldiers surround you four deep, three of you, on whom I have put holy shirts, will sing a song which I have taught you, around them, when some of them will drop dead. Then the rest will start to run, but their horses will sink into the earth. The riders will jump from their horses, but they will sink into the earth also. Then you can do as you desire with them. Now you must know this, that all the soldiers and that race will be dead. There will be only five-thousand of them left living on the earth. My friends and relations, this is straight and true.

"Now, we must gather at Pass Creek where the tree is sprouting. There we will go among our dead relations. You must not take any earthly things with you. Then the men must take off *all* their clothing and the women must do the same. No one shall be ashamed of exposing their persons. My father above has told us to do this, and we must do as he says. You must not be afraid of anything. The guns are the only things we are afraid of but they belong to our father in heaven. He will see that they do no harm. Whatever white men may tell you, do not listen to them, my relations. This is all. I will now raise my hand up to my father and close what he has said to you through me."

It was strong medicine. People who talk with God rarely count the cost of their visions.

That stern old war dog, General Miles, now in command of the whole department, felt he had to move quickly against the Ghost Dance cult. He decided to arrest what he thought was the St. Paul of the new religion, Sitting Bull. He then planned to disarm the Indians.

Buffalo Bill was put in charge of the arrest. Cody had hired Sitting Bull for his Wild West Show. The two men were friends. Cody wanted to move up a wagonload of presents for Sitting Bull, and palaver him into coming into the agency at Standing Rock, without the formula of an out-and-out arrest. At Standing Rock reservation, the agent, McLaughlin, panicked. He voted down Buffalo Bill's idea of a peaceful invitation. He had heard rumors that the Messiah was about to visit Pine Ridge and harass the whites.

Chapter 39

THE GREAT CHIEF DIES

Sitting Bull requested a pass to go to Pine Ridge and see the Messiah. If he had been up to trouble, he would surely have slipped away. That day, General Miles ordered his arrest. Was there a plot between the Agent and the General, or between the officers of the Indian Police and the U. S. Army to assassinate Sitting Bull? The New York *Herald,* December 17, 1890, says: "It was decided among those in authority to murder Sitting Bull before he roused the tribes into a holy war." This charge was also made from the floor of the United States Senate. Nothing was ever proven. But the entire action is overcast with murky procedures, accompanied by a nervous sense of guilt.

McLaughlin had a strong Indian Police force at the Agency. Messages went out for all Sioux Indian Police to meet in Sitting Bull's camp on the Grand River. Many rode forty-five miles that miserable December night to be there. It was not a routine arrest. Captain E. G. Fechet, with a hundred soldiers backed by a Hotchkiss gun moved out from Fort Yates and, on the morning of the 15th, was in Sitting Bull's village. At sunrise, Lieutenant Bull Head, Sergeants Red Tomahawk and Shave Head, and a squad of Indian Police, heavily armed, surrounded the old cabin of the chief. They pushed their way inside to find Sitting Bull asleep on the earthen floor. He was nudged awake and told to dress. Like an ordinary sneak-thief he was hustled outside flanked by the Indian officer and two sergeants. The Sioux of the village were by now up protesting this treatment of their leader. The squaws set up a great howling.

Sitting Bull must have sensed that he had to move fast and he feared assassination. He cried out to his captors: "I am not going!" This could have been defiance or a way to save the Indian police from a battle.

Catch-the-Fire shot at the Indian policeman, Bull Head, and brought him down. One version of the story is that as Bull Head fell, he shot Sitting Bull in the body. At that moment or just before, Red Tomahawk, standing behind the chief, shot Sitting Bull in the back. Either of the two wounds on the chief's body could have killed the old man. Indian police on their own had never dared to shoot a great chief before.

At once there was rifle fire from both the police and the outraged Sioux. Shave Head was shot down and so were others of the Indian police.

The police were fighting for their lives and knew it. They retreated to Sitting Bull's cabin and killed the chief's seventeen-year-old son, Crowfoot, with brutal lack of mercy. Captain Fechet came up, dragging his Hotchkiss gun and began firing it with deadly effect into the Sioux, without saying anything or asking what had happened.

The Indian police then proceeded to crush in Sitting Bull's head with their rifle butts. The body was tossed into a wagon and wheeled down to the Agency. There it was quickly coated with quicklime and buried. The method and procedure of his arrest was stupid, his assassination crude and his hasty and secret burial a disgrace to the nation that killed him.

Six Indian police died and two were wounded. The Sioux lost not only Sitting Bull and his son but also the chief's adopted brother, Jumping Bull, and six warriors.

General Miles proposed to disarm the aroused and angry Indians, who smoldered in their rage and remained Agency-tame. At Chief Big Foot's village on the Cheyenne, a remnant of Sitting Bull's followers joined forces. Big Foot saw the fruitlessness of allowing the Indians to feed their fury and began to send his people back to the reservation. Chief Big Foot was arrested. The Indians smelled a new assassination and they took off for the Badlands. Three thousand soldiers were sent to hem them in. On December 28, the 7th Cavalry caught Big Foot's people on Wounded Knee Creek. Chief Big Foot said to Major Whiteside: "We want peace. I am sick and my people—"

Major Whiteside broke in on the chief's plea. "I'm not going to parley with you. Surrender or fight. What is it going to be?"

"Surrender," said the Indian. "We would have surrendered before, if we had known where to find you."

Two hundred and fifty men, women and children moved on to camp by the creek. Colonel J. W. Forsyth hemmed in the Indian camp with four Hotchkiss guns and five hundred troopers. Big Foot lay in his lodge, ill with pneumonia. Forsyth ordered the Indians disarmed. The Indians did not hurry to give up their weapons, and on the colonel's order, the men were searched—lodge by lodge. The 7th Cavalry watched as soldiers tore up bedding and drove men, women and children out into the cold. A shot was fired.

The 7th Cavalry awaited no orders. They fired a murderous volley into the tightly packed Indians. Half the males died or were wounded in the first blast. Unarmed, the Indians fought with knives, sticks, clubs; four-to-one were the odds with the Indians on the short odds, weaponless. Still, they charged the soldiers—squaws, children, old men and women—even the dogs. Captain Wallace was overrun and clubbed to death by the squaws. The Hotchkiss was now turned on the Sioux and rapid fire did its deadly work.

Very few Sioux managed to escape this massacre. Those who did hid in a ravine and were subsequently tracked down by Hotchkiss gunners. The fugitives were shelled to fragments as if at target practice.

The battle ended in a wild chase. The broken bodies of women and children were found two and three miles away from the camp, run down by the killers. Twenty-nine dead soldiers were recorded; thirty-three wounded—a remarkable record for unarmed Indians. No one counted the Indian dead.

A blizzard was added to the horror of the scene. The prisoners and the wounded traveled an icy three days of hell before they reached Pine Ridge. Many more Indians died of their wounds or were frozen stiff in the storm. Three small children were found alive, covered by their dead mothers' bodies. The official burial report lists the soldiers as finding sixty-four adult males and boys; forty-four females and eighteen young children. Big Foot's corpse was found frozen hard as a statue.

Dr. Charles Eastman, who saw the massacre site before the dead were buried, records: "A terrible and horrible sight to see. Women and children lying in groups, dead. Some of the young girls wrapped their heads in their shawls and buried their faces in their hands. I suppose they did that so they would not see the soldiers come up to shoot them. At one place, there were two little children, one about a year old, the other about three, lying on their faces, dead, and about thirty yards away from them a woman lying on her face dead . . ."

General Miles, a good soldier and a just one, brought charges against Forsyth for the murder of the women and children. Forsyth was fully exonerated by the Secretary of War.

An anonymous officer of the 7th is quoted as bragging, after this massacre: "Now we have avenged Custer's death." The officer was reminded that his victims were not all men and none had weapons, while Custer was armed as a soldier.

Indian bands fought on but they numbered less than a thousand against which General Miles threw the largest army ever to take the field against Indians, eight thousand men. Small fights and chases continued as Miles pressed the Sioux into a great huddling mass, moving them toward Pine Ridge. In two days, he moved the Indians thirty miles, pressing them but avoiding any fighting. Miles was never a man for massacre. He could have wiped them all out in half an hour.

A half-mile from the Agency the Indians refused to move on. Guards were set up and the campfires of the Indians flickered in the night. There was Indian rifle fire in the dark camp but no attacks on the soldiers. In the morning some hot-heads among the Indians were observed to have killed their dogs and horses.

On the Plains, the wars were over. General Miles had acted wisely and firmly and avoided an even bigger massacre. The reservations now held twenty-five thousand Sioux in enforced indolence, poverty, and hopelessness.

The Ghost Dance had joined the ghosts. Wovoka died during the Great Depression in a miserable hut, neither honored nor mentioned. No one noticed his death and he was buried in the sands on the shore of Walker Lake. He and his Ghost Dance and the massacres it brought on are linked to our own times by his recent passing. He died on October 4, 1932.

The men who fought Indians were usually the only ones to know his true nature and special virtues. Wrote General Crook:

"In the twenty-seven years of my experience with the Indian question, I have never known a band of Indians to make peace with our government and then break it, or leave the reservation without some grounds for complaint; but, until their complaints are examined and adjusted, they will constantly give annoyance and trouble."

Of the traders and agents who cheated the Indians, the general wrote: "I have never yet seen one [Indian] so demoralized that he was not an example of honor and nobility compared with the wretches who plundered him of the little our government appropriated for him."

General Crook fought for the rights of Indians before the Congress. He died of a heart attack presumably caused by his efforts.

Captain John G. Bourke, one of Crook's officers, pictured the treatment of the starving reservation Indian as follows: "The agent issued supplies by throwing them through the rungs of a ladder—the Indian getting what stuck to the rungs; the agent getting what fell to the ground." Of the Apache he wrote: "No Indian has more virtues and none has been more truly ferocious when aroused."

In the East they were more inclined to go back to the banality of: "The only good Indian is a dead Indian." As late as 1879, the New York *Herald*, on its editorial page, called for the extermination of all Indians. "The continent is getting too crowded." Men, like Theodore Roosevelt, who knew the West more intimately, respected the Indian. Chief Quanah Parker of the Comanches rode in Teddy's Inaugural Parade in Washington in 1905. Even later, Americans in Paris in the 1920's remembered the old guilt. Stephen Vincent Benét wrote:

> I shall not rest quiet in Montparnasse . . .
> I shall not be there, I shall rise and pass
> Bury my heart in Wounded Knee.

Epilogue

Destiny . . . is nothing more than the unforseen coincidence of events, the emergence into action of hidden forces which, in a complex and disordered society . . . no contemporary can be expected to discern.

—FERRERO

Why is it that the Apache wants to die? that they carry their lives in their finger nails?

—CHIEF COCHISE

The frontiers are not east or west, north or south, but wherever a man fronts a fact.

—THOREAU

THE RESIDUE OF VIOLENCE

The ending of the Indian wars left more than a residue of violence on the American scene. The bloody business of annihilation, massacre, lynching, and general lawlessness remains today.

From eyewitness accounts, the thousands of items that can be found in any old newspaper west of the Big Muddy, demonstrates the cult of violence as daily fare, reported with a jolly whoop and holler that show the popularity of uninhibited direct action— long after the Indian was broken or tamed. The stain of violence persisted, and if there were no Indians to fall on, the citizens fell on each other, as this clipping from the *Leadville Democrat* shows:

"Sunday is always an occasion for fast women, rapid men, and all the sporting fraternity to air themselves on the beautiful drive. Toward evening these cheerful souls got hilarious. Presently, some big double-decked rooster opened the ball by jumping at a small courtesan and smashing her nose. The matinee then began. One female armed herself with a beer bottle and created on the head of a well-known gentleman several bumps not down on his phrenological chart. He retaliated by taking a board and damaging her some. Scarcely was this over when another woman drew a revolver and began scattering galena around in a particularly reckless fashion, and was only induced to stop when her solid man seized her by her false hair and mopped up the boulevard with her."

No wonder an uninformed visiting Englishman, Sir Herbert Beerbohm Tree, could write: "America might well be the only nation passing from a primitive society into decadence without ever having known civilization."

EVERYTHING CHANGES, NOTHING CHANGES

The exploitation of the Indian continues on a vast scale. Most Indians today are paupers or neglected wards of a government that makes fine gestures and speaks noble words, but lags beyond

that. Typical is this press story of 1969: INDIANS' TROUBLE DUE TO
FEDERAL LAXITY:

The "excessive" fees and entangled handling of Agua Caliente
Indian estates arose partly because the Bureau of Indian Affairs
did not exercise its full powers.

Also, the Department of Interior, under which the Bureau oper-
ates, delayed launching a full-scale investigation for more than
three years because of bureaucratic delays.

As Mrs. Prieto, chairman of the Tribal Council, puts it: "They
have a little egg on their face, too; they were concurring with all
the accountings."

Critics of the investigation and some close observers feel that
the government's abdication of responsibility toward the Indians
for a number of years, and the delay in starting the investigation,
accounts for the present investigators.

An Interior Department investigation into the handling of Agua
Caliente Indian estates has revealed the concentrated involvement,
as trustees, of two Riverside County Judges and an attorney.

Court records and the findings of the investigation, show an
interweaving of nonjudicial functions involving the two judges.

A preliminary report of the Interior Department investigators
states:

"Our total investigation thus far has revealed a very heavy and
concentrated involvement, but unlike a monopoly, by just a few
individuals . . ." The two judges and the attorney, as well as
a third judge were criticized for "questionable conduct" in the
report, which pointed out the Canons of Judicial Ethics "appear
to touch upon matters sensitive to activities" of the judges.

The Bureau of Indian Affairs, and its parent agency, the Interior
Department, did not exercise their full responsibility toward the
Indians for a number of years.

These federal agencies either failed to seriously question the
"excessive" fees which the report stated were granted to trustees
of the estates, or concurred in decisions concerning these estates
at the Indio Supreme Court. What is involved is this, court records
and the report show:

1. One judge, currently presiding justice of a State Appeals Court,
   was awarded a total of $41,751 from Indian or Indian-related

estates, while he administered these estates at the Indio Court. The fees were awarded by other judges.

2. A second judge was awarded $231,232.59 in fees for serving as a trustee of Indian estates; $61,293.20 while serving on the Municipal Court bench and the remainder while an attorney and Justice Court judge.

3. The third judge, who currently administers the Indian guardian and conservator programs at the Indio court, showed the trustee of an Indian estate some property he wanted to sell his Indian ward.

4. The attorney is the individual who has represented the largest number of Indians and trustees of Indian estates while at the same time representing the first two judges on Indian matters.

The Interior Department estimates that fees levied against the estates were $1,264,000—or about 43% of income. The percentage of trustee and attorney fees to income has steadily decreased from as high as 107% in 1960 to 32% in 1965, the last year for which complete figures are available. The report states the fees were "excessive."

Although a few estates are managed by Indian guardians, most are handled by non-Indians who provide the year-round leadership in civil and business affairs of Palm Springs.

There are brighter notes. While great buffalo herds no longer roam the Plains, conservation now protects the Indian's favorite hunting animal, and there is an overabundance:

TRY A BUFFALO STEAK:
By writing the refuge manager, Wichita Mountain Wildlife Refuge, Cache, Okla., 73527, you can buy a buffalo carcass for $180 or an elk carcass for $90. They won't sell you anything smaller than a half-carcass, but they'll freeze it for you if you'll add $40 for the full carcass, or $20 for a half-carcass."

The last item shows the will to fight may be returning: IDAHO TRIBE THREATENS SURVEYORS:
The tribal council of the Ft. Hall Indian Reservation has instructed tribal police and game-wardens to arrest "anyone who sets foot on the reservation to survey land for the purpose of flooding additiona. Indian lands for American Falls' reservoir." The order is the council's reaction to a proposal of the Idaho

Water Resources Board, which involves construction of dikes on land-adjacent to Ft. Hall bottomlands. Bureau of Reclamation engineers have said the America Falls Dam is weak, and have recommended its replacement.

The Indians oppose any move which would flood more land.

The white man made the frontier, as he saw it, a more equitable world. He created a life of possibility—tough, cruel, but vigorous and purposeful. His victory left the Indian beaten, apathetic, inert. The white culture lived under the assumption that dispossessing the tribes from their lands was part of the nation's manifest destiny. So the war cries and drum beats in time died out, only to be revived much later as tourists' attractions. The Indian was a victim of progress, a progress he neither controlled nor could comprehend.

The white settler found a freedom on the Plains that was without obstruction or limit, if he didn't bust a gut by hard, back-breaking work, or become a pincushion for Indian arrows. Frontier survival called for a package of strength, courage, drive, stamina, and indifference to the rights of the outraged natives. He was aided by the Indian refusal to accept the limitations of the situation as being final. His character was such that, in the end, the Indian retreated to apathy.

The Indian never fully understood white people, just as they never cared to understand him. The tribes did not understand the fierce purposefulness of this society, the irresistible will to power based on a Calvanistic morality translated on the frontier into ruthless and cruel domination of the previous inhabitants.

Not that the white settlers were aware of what they stood for. They were the rind of an expanding, exploding, materialistic new nation. Settlers were either docile, hard-working immigrants or social outlaws. In the cities and settled communities, they had been in rebellion, a rebellion that was sterile and ineffectual. On the Plains, they could fight, strike out, kill to preserve their integrity and their lives.

The frontier was, actually, a testing-ground of a new society— once it had cleared off the Indian; the rulers or grabbers of the nation were designing a future of bold aggression all to produce the powerful nation of the twentieth century. So, facing each other—white and redskin—the conformation of circumstance and tradition on both sides made war the only possibility. The Indian struggled to place himself in a relationship to the past and not in the unknown future. The Indian was vulnerable—take away the structure of ingrained experience, the arbitrary symbols of dreams he based his life on and he was destroyed. He surged with a hunger for absolute freedom unknown to the white world where the history of one culture merged into the next. Indian freedom was based on tribal magic. Physically, this made him strong and determined, but there was no reserve of inner resistance once the magic failed him. White magic appeared so much stronger what with fire power.

The Indian, finally corralled on a reservation, could not think his way back into a world of meaning nor make concessions under the pounding, greedy, indifferent forces of dishonest agents and faithless treaty makers. For the Indian, there was nothing left to communicate to the senses and bring back the old visions. He had no feedback behind reservation fences. Even the brave wars of the past lost their gloss in the retelling. Defeats do not make legends.

Disintegration in the Indian was not reversible against a brisker mass culture with its technology, social changes, status symbols. In the end, the surviving Indians were travelers on their own idiosyncratic road, untouched by modern historic currents. The tribes turned their backs on the determinings of history and sociology, as if aware they had always belonged to nature and not to history.

The Indian was a religionist, never a humanist. He held a joyous, awesome connection, an assertion, with the common flow of his past. His had a fluid yet rooted society that was proud of the elation of its violence. He had an intense spirituality that came directly in dreams and visions from the sky, the animals, the weather, the extreme fervent affirmation in things one could not see, and a dedication to tribal order and a prodigal belief in himself in the scheme of things.

The whites boldly proclaimed: "I am civilization," and in the tragic impermanence of life, destroyed a culture. As Buffalo Bill puts it in one of his dime novels:

"I happened to look up to the moon-lit sky and saw the plumed head of an Indian peeping over the bank. I instantly aimed my gun at his head and fired. The report rang out sharp and loud on the night air, and was immediately followed by an Indian whoop, and the next moment about six feet of dead Indian came tumbling into the river."

Writes the historian Archer Butler Hulbert in one of the strangest tributes ever paid the type of men who destroyed the Indians at the end of his book, *Frontiers:*

What a frontiersman was that Jesus Christ! Who, more than He, was fearless in His "night" because of the undoubted emergence of "hidden forces" which no living man "can hope to discern"? Who so perfect a Witness "of the Dawn"?

FOR FURTHER READING

For those who want to go into greater detail of some of the people and events of this book, the following list contains titles that are mostly available in the original editions or reprints.

Bandel, Eugene, *Frontier Life in the Army*, 1932
Barrett, S. M., *Geronimo's Own Story of His Life*, 1906
Drill, Charles J., *Conquest of the Southern Plain*, 1930
Brimstool, E. A., *A Trooper With Custer*, 1925
Britt, Albert, *Great Indian Chiefs*, 1938
Byrne, P. E., *Soldiers of the Plains*, 1926
Cook, James H., *Fifty Years on the Frontier*, 1923
Cruse, Thomas, *Apache Days and After*, 1941
Custer, Elizabeth Barrett, *Boots and Saddles*, 1885
Custer, General George A., *My Life on the Plains*, 1875
Downey, Fairfax, *Indian-fighting Army*, 1941
Dustin, Fred, *The Custer Tragedy*, 1939
Foreman, Grant, *Advancing the Frontier*, 1933
Garst, Shannon, *Crazy Horse, Great Warrior of the Sioux*, 1950
Grinnell, George Bird, *The Fighting Cheyennes*, 1915
Howard, Helen A., *War Chief Joseph*, 1941
Hyde, George E., *Indians of the High Plains*, 1959
Jackson, Helen Hunt, *A Century of Dishonor*, 1885
King, Captain Charles, *Campaigning with Cook*, 1890
Lowie, Robert H., *Indians of the Plains*, 1954
Miles, General Nelson A., *Personal Recollections*, 1897
Parkman, Francis, *The Oregon Trail*, 1872
Sandoz, Mari, *The Buffalo Hunters*, 1954
Schmitt, Marlin, and Brown, Dee, *Fighting Indians of the West*, 1948
    (a picture history)
Starkley, M. I., *The Cherokee Nation*, 1927
Vestal, Stanley, *Sitting Bull, Champion of the Sioux*, 1932